FEW RETURNED

FEW RETURNED

Twenty-eight Days
on the Russian Front,
Winter 1942–1943

EUGENIO CORTI

Translated by
Peter Edward Levy

Foreword by
Carlo D'Este

UNIVERSITY OF MISSOURI PRESS
COLUMBIA AND LONDON

Copyright © 1997 by
The Curators of the University of Missouri
University of Missouri Press, Columbia, Missouri 65201
Printed and bound in the United States of America
All rights reserved
5   4   3   2   01   00   99   98

Library of Congress Cataloging-in-Publication Data

Corti, Eugenio, 1921–
    [Piu non ritornano. English]
    Few returned : twenty-eight days on the Russian Front, winter
1942–1943 / Eugenio Corti ; translated by Peter Edward Levy ;
foreword by Carlo d'Este.
        p.   cm.
    ISBN 0-8262-1115-1
    1. Corti, Eugenio, 1921—Diaries.   2. Italy. Esercito. Corpo
d'armata, 35—History.   3. Italy. Esercito—Biography.
4. Soldiers—Italy—Diaries.   5. World War, 1939–1945—Personal
narratives, Italian.   6. World War, 1939–1945—Campaigns—Russia
(Federation)—Don River valley.   I. Title.
D764.7.D6C67   1997
940.54'21749'092—dc21
    [b]   97-6121
                                                                   CIP

♾ ™ This paper meets the requirements of the
American National Standard for Permanence of Paper
for Printed Library Materials, Z39.48, 1984.

Text Design: Stephanie Foley
Cover Design: Kristie Lee
Typesetter: BOOKCOMP
Printer and binder: Thomson-Shore, Inc.
Typefaces: Stempel Garamond and Leawood Black

I offer these pages,
through my mother's hands,
to the Madonna of my people,
the Madonna of the Wood.

May they be above all a prayer
for those who shared those days with me,
who fought and suffered with me,
who hoped so desperately with me,
and in the end remained lifeless
on the interminable roads of the steppe.

CONTENTS

FOREWORD

CARLO D'ESTE

World War II was the most oppressive period of Italian history. Italy had been under the authoritarian rule of Benito Mussolini and his Fascist thugs from 1922 until he was arrested and deposed in July 1943. The Italian nation was a study in torment brought about by Fascism and Mussolini's unsavory and ultimately disastrous alliance with Adolf Hitler's Nazi Germany.

Beginning with the 1936 invasion of Ethiopia, Mussolini had attempted to emulate the glory days of the great Roman empires that had dazzled the world with feats of military victory and cultural achievement. Instead, what Il Duce brought to Italy was not glory but anguish through an old form of dictatorship wrapped in new cloth. The failure of Italian-style Fascism was glaringly evident to the great majority of Italians, most of whom longed for an end to the war. Although Italy's new non-Fascist government (headed by Marshal Pietro Badoglio) proclaimed the war would go on as before, within weeks it began secretly negotiating an armistice with the Allies.

The Allied armies had already begun the liberation of Italy when the British Eighth Army invaded Calabria on September 3, 1943. Five days later an armistice was concluded with the Allies. Because Italy's capitulation meant that the Italian government had seceded from the Rome-Berlin Axis and aligned itself with the Allies, an enraged Adolf Hitler called it "pure treachery" and "the greatest impudence in history." Reinforcements were rushed to Italy, and within forty-eight hours nearly 80 percent of the country was occupied by German forces.

With the invasion of Salerno on September 9, 1943, by the U.S. Fifth Army, Italy became a thousand-mile battleground. By December 1943 southern Italy from Cassino to Calabria had been liberated by the Allies, whose campaign against the Germans in vile weather and equally severe fighting conditions soon led to a military impasse.

During the twenty months of the Italian campaign some of the bloodiest fighting of the war in the West occurred in places named Salerno, Cassino, the Rapido River, and Anzio between a veteran German army group led by wily Field Marshal Albert Kesselring and the Allied armies commanded by Field Marshal Sir Harold Alexander. The Allies had intended to liberate Rome in the autumn of 1943 but were thwarted by the Germans until June 5, 1944. The Allied cross-Channel invasion of Normandy on June 6, 1944, relegated the war in Italy to that of a forgotten campaign only one day later.

Hitler installed the deposed Italian dictator at the head of a puppet government wherein Mussolini continued to betray his countrymen, capping his treachery by sanctioning the execution of his own son-in-law, Count Ciano. From September 1943 to May 1945, post-Mussolini Italy was typified by pogroms, enslavement, cowardice, reprisals, betrayal, and mass murder. Even as the battles raged, the Germans became equal-opportunity oppressors elsewhere: persecuting Italy's Jewish population, executing partisans, and even attacking their former ally, the Italian army. Elements of the Royal Italian Army fought side by side with the Allies for the remainder of the war, but Hitler interned 600,000 Italian soldiers in German slave-labor camps, while untold others were slaughtered in the Aegean, in Greece, Albania, and Yugoslavia. More than 7,000 died when British bombers sank German ships transporting Italian soldiers to Greece and eventual internment. Those who did not drown were machine-gunned by the Germans as they attempted to swim to safety. German retribution against Italian soldiers and civilians alike was carried out with ruthless efficiency by the Gestapo and the SS, prompting Mussolini to signal the German garrison commander "thanking him for his kindness to Italian soldiers."

Betrayed by their own government, brutalized by the Germans, Italian soldiers also fought as second-class allies in support of Hitler's legions in the most savage campaign of all on the Eastern Front. In June 1941 Hitler attacked his ally the Soviet Union by launching a massive second-front invasion dubbed "Operation Barbarossa." Hitler deliberately withheld his intentions from Mussolini in the belief the Italians would leak the information to the Russians and destroy the surprise of Barbarossa.

When Mussolini learned of Barbarossa he immediately dispatched on his own initiative an Italian Expeditionary Corps (Corpo di Spedizione Italiano) of three divisions totaling some 60,000 troops to the southern sector of the Eastern Front. The numbers were soon increased to 250,000 when additional units were sent east to form the Italian Eighth Army. Mussolini's motive was not to aid his ally but rather to place Italy in a position to earn an enhanced share of the spoils of an Axis-occupied Soviet Union by contributing militarily to its demise. Mussolini's only concern was that the expeditionary army would arrive in Russia in time to join the fighting.[1]

The Italian fighting units sent to the Eastern Front in the summer of 1941 were held in utter contempt by their German ally. The Italian Eighth Army was deemed fit only for a minor defensive role, and they saw little significant action until late 1942 when the Russians assembled four armies consisting of 1 million troops, nearly 1,000 T-34 tanks, and an equal number of attack aircraft and launched a giant two-pronged winter counteroffensive across a wide front in southern Russia on November 19. Under the overall command of Marshal Georgi Zhukov, the Red Army offensive was designed to break the long German siege of Stalingrad by encircling and trapping the German Sixth Army.

The Thirty-fifth Corps, the first Italian unit to fight in Russia in 1941, was part of the Italian Eighth Army that held a sixty-mile sector of the river Don northwest of Stalingrad. The Don front was not a target of the November offensive, but on December 16, 1942, the Red Army broadened their attacks. During this second-phase offensive the Italians were attacked by three Soviet armies. The Eighth Army was simply no match against this massive Red Army juggernaut and was quickly overwhelmed. Not only were the Italians woefully clothed but they also lacked tanks and antitank guns with which to defend themselves. Within hours the Don front disintegrated.

To avoid death or capture, the Italian and German troops trapped in the Don pocket began retreating in a desperate attempt to break free of encirclement. The flight of the Italians became a horrific odyssey carried out in extreme subzero temperatures, often as low as -30 degrees. Unlike the Germans, who were occasionally resupplied by air, the Italians were left largely to fend for themselves with only whatever each individual soldier could carry on his own

1. Gerhard L. Weinberg, *A World at Arms: "A Global History of World War II"* (Cambridge: Cambridge University Press, 1994), 277.

back or drag on makeshift sleds. The Italians were generally clad in warm-weather shoes that many replaced with straw and blankets torn into strips and wrapped around their feet. Bereft of ammunition resupply or transport, the Italians marched on foot across the bleak, frozen steppe of Russia, virtually without sleep in the dead of winter through some of the most desolate terrain on earth. They left in their wake a trail of corpses and abandoned equipment.

Night and day they were attacked and harassed by the Russians. Thousands died from bombs, rockets, bullets, and from the terrible cold. Only the fittest and the luckiest survived the twenty-eight-day ordeal. Finally, in mid-January 1943, the survivors at last managed to break free of the Russian trap. The Italian Eighth Army had ceased to exist.

In addition to those who died in the fighting and during the retreat from the Don, the official Italian historians later determined that some 50,000–60,000 Italian soldiers were captured by the Russians and sent to POW camps. Only 10,300 were later repatriated. The rest are thought to have died from abuse, starvation, and disease in the unspeakable conditions of captivity.[2]

During the period of the Italian retreat the Red Army not only ended the siege of Stalingrad but also inflicted the greatest German defeat of the war, the annihilation of their Sixth Army. The Red Army victory at Stalingrad in January 1943 not only broke the back of the German invasion of the Soviet Union but also became the most significant turning point of a war that Germany and Italy were now doomed to lose.

The tragedy of the ill-fated Eighth Army was yet another sad chapter in the history of Italy. Gerhard Weinberg notes in *A World at Arms* that Mussolini

> had no sense for the realities of his own country and the situation of his soldiers. They fought hard under difficult conditions with wretched equipment, impossible supply lines reaching all the way back to Italy, and no goal even remotely visible as they quickly lost their initial enthusiasm. The eagerness with which Mussolini squandered the lives

2. John Shaw, *Red Army Resurgent* (Alexandria, Va.: Time-Life Books, 1979), 186. Many in the camps who did not die of starvation perished from pneumonia or tuberculosis.

of his soldiers only contributed to the further weakening of the Fascist regime at home.[3]

Beyond such general descriptions, little has been written about the role and participation of the Italian Expeditionary Corps in Russia. As British historian Richard Lamb notes, "No words are too strong to condemn Mussolini for . . . the despatch of Italian armies to fight in Russia, where they suffered a worse fate than their compatriots in Napoleon's 1812 campaign."[4]

One of the survivors of the retreat was Eugenio Corti, a twenty-one-year-old officer assigned to an artillery battalion of the Pasubio Division, Thirty-fifth Corps. Corti estimates a mere 4,000 men of his corps survived death or capture. During his service in Russia, Corti began jotting down information about his experiences on scraps of paper. While recuperating in an Italian military hospital in 1943, he refined his recollections into the manuscript of *Few Returned.* He did so, he later wrote, mainly to ensure that "I forgot none of those tragic experiences with the passage of time."

However, the war was far from over in 1943, and Corti saw further military action, this time alongside the British against the Axis defense of Italy that lasted until May 1945. To avoid having his manuscript fall into German hands, Corti buried it in waterproof sheeting. Once again he survived, and, after being discharged from the army, he later wrote, "I dug it up; it was in a pitiful condition, much like the state of my spirit. Nevertheless, I managed, with the patient help of one of my sisters, to recopy it."

Italian accounts of World War II that have been translated into English are sparse; accounts of Italy's participation in the Eastern Front are virtually nonexistent, not least because so few Italians survived their ordeal in Russia.

This is not a book about high-level military strategy or the intrigues of politicians and generals. *Few Returned* is an unsparingly honest soldier's story of life at the sharp end of war. An important addition to our knowledge and understanding of the greatest, most tragic event in all of human history, *Few Returned* is reminiscent of Erich Maria Remarque's *All Quiet on the Western Front* and Guy

3. Weinberg, *A World at Arms,* 277.
4. Richard Lamb, *War in Italy, 1943–1945: "A Brutal Story"* (New York: St. Martin's Press, 1994), 3.

Sajer's *The Forgotten Soldier.* Corti writes movingly about the ordeals endured by ordinary soldiers who have little or no idea of—or interest in—the "big picture." Generals are concerned with winning battles, but the front-line soldier's primary motivation is survival. Eugenio Corti was such a survivor.

The end of war rips the fabric of the special bond that men in combat share with one another, a bond so compelling that neither subsequent happiness of marriage, family, nor material success can ever replace it.[5] More often than not, these veterans are racked by guilt and astonishment at having survived and are fiercely determined to honor the memory of their dead comrades.

Corti's moving dedication in *Few Returned* proclaims lost innocence, atonement, and remembrance:

> for those who shared those days with me,
> who fought and suffered with me,
> who hoped so desperately with me,
> and in the end remained lifeless
> on the interminable roads of the steppe.

On a personal note, Corti's account is of special interest. My father, an Italian, born and raised in the disputed city of Trieste, was conscripted into the Austrian army and served in Russia during World War I as a company commander. When Russia capitulated in 1917 his unit was one of many left stranded. He and his men managed to return home alive only because my father was also a paymaster and had in his possession a trunk full of gold he judiciously dispensed as bribes en route. Although a different war, Corti's poignant tale nevertheless has eerie overtones of my father's experiences that were undoubtedly far less brutal but nevertheless sufficiently traumatic such that he would never speak about them.

Since the war, Eugenio Corti has become an increasingly important voice in modern Italian literature. I can think of no better means of introducing him to the English-speaking world than through *Few Returned.*

5. Carlo D'Este, *Patton: A Genius for War* (New York: HarperCollins, 1995), 268.

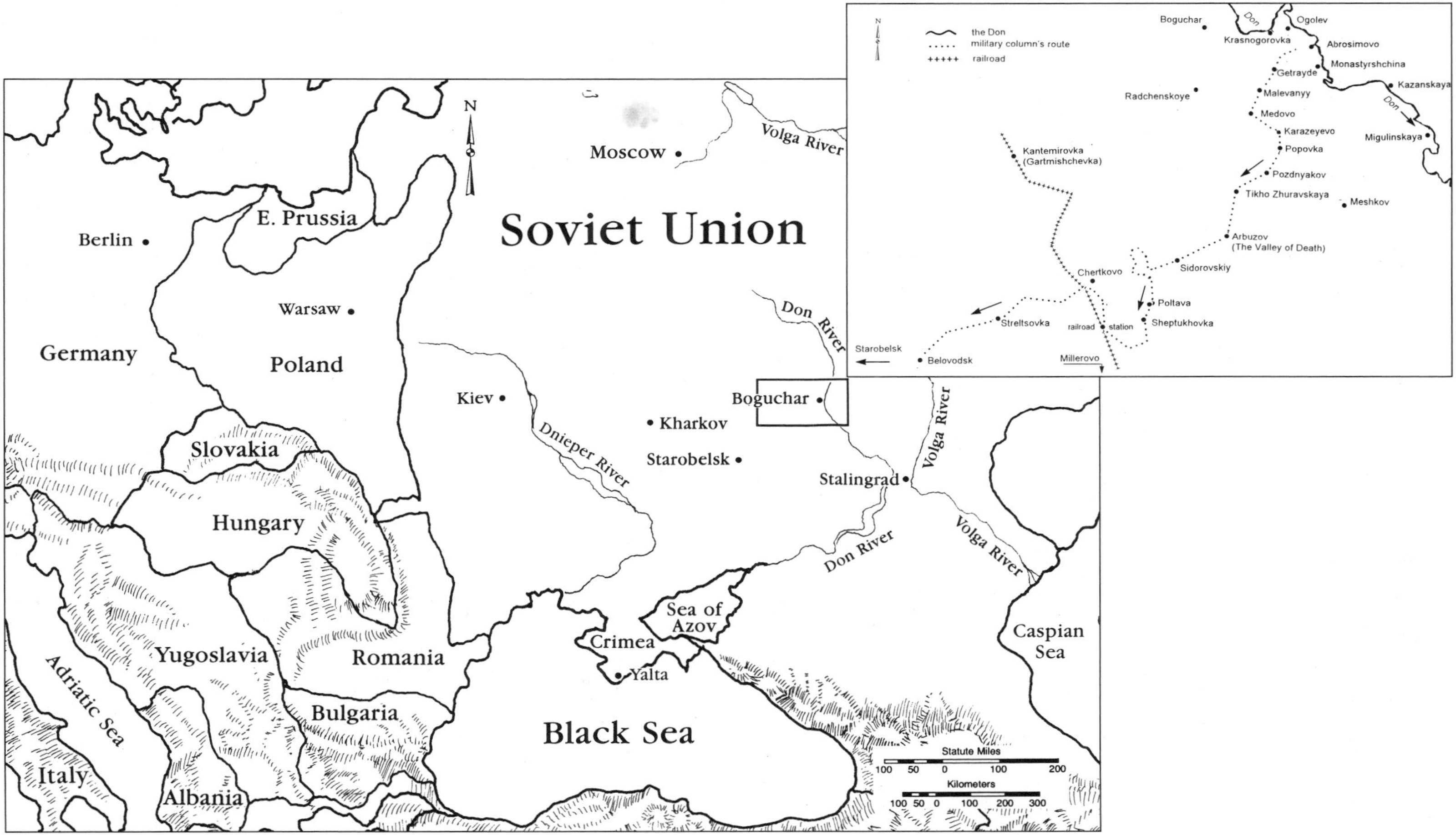
Soviet Union
Moscow
Volga River
Berlin
E. Prussia
Warsaw
Germany
Poland
Kiev
Dnieper River
Kharkov
Starobelsk
Boguchar
Don River
Stalingrad
Volga River
Don River
Volga River
Slovakia
Hungary
Yugoslavia
Romania
Bulgaria
Albania
Italy
Adriatic Sea
Crimea
Yalta
Sea of Azov
Black Sea
Caspian Sea
N
Statute Miles
100 50 0 100 200
Kilometers
100 50 0 100 200 300
N
the Don
military column's route
railroad
Boguchar
Don
Krasnogorovka
Ogolev
Abrosimovo
Monastyrshchina
Getrayde
Radchenskoye
Malevanyy
Kazanskaya
Medovo
Don
Karazeyevo
Migulinskaya
Kantemirovka (Gartmishchevka)
Popovka
Pozdnyakov
Tikho Zhuravskaya
Meshkov
Arbuzov (The Valley of Death)
Sidorovskiy
Chertkovo
Poltava
Streltsovka
railroad station
Sheptukhovka
Starobelsk
Belovodsk
Millerovo

FROM THE DON TO ARBUZOV

"And pray ye that your flight be not in the winter."
(Mark 13:18)

1

This diary recounts the end of the Thirty-fifth Army Corps, one of the three corps of the Italian army that fought in Russia (ARMIR),[†] which until the summer of 1942 was the only Italian corps on the Russian front—the CSIR.[††] The same cycle of operations also saw the destruction of the other two corps: the Second at the same time as the Thirty-fifth, the Alpini a month later. A similar fate befell the few German forces with us there on that sector of the front.

✳

Up to the beginning of December, things had been tolerable on the banks of the Don, even after the "quiet flowing river" had completely frozen over. Exchanges of rifle fire, but nothing too intense, the occasional fire control from the artillery opposite us, and at night the odd surprise attack from one or the other direction.

By mid-December, however, these assaults had gradually intensified, turning at times into small, fierce battles. It was then that we began to suspect, and eventually to realize, that the Russians were preparing an all-out offensive.

The Thirty-fifth Army Corps, drawn up along the river facing north, consisted of the following divisions: the 298th German Division on the left, the Pasubio in the middle, and the Torino on the right.[1] We officers had heard that the sector held by the Pasubio was thirty-three kilometers long; and so the same must have been the case with the other two divisions.

It was to give support to the Pasubio Division that my formation, the Thirtieth Army Artillery Brigade, was deployed in three battalions (the Sixty-second, the Sixty-first, and the Sixtieth) of old 105/32

†Tr. note: *Armata Italiana in Russia* (Italian Army in Russia)
††Tr. note: *Corpo di Spedizione Italiano in Russia* (Italian Expeditionary Corps in Russia)

guns (spoils from the First World War), with the addition of a highly modern army-artillery group (149/40 and 210/22 guns).

I was at the time chief patrol officer[2] of the Sixty-first Artillery Battalion at the Second Battalion headquarters of the Eightieth Pasubio Infantry Regiment, at Abrosimovo on the Don. Our suspicions about enemy intentions were confirmed when, with no warning, the division of Byelorussians ranged opposite us was replaced by fresh divisions of Uzbeks and Tartars, enlisted only a few months earlier. Deserters from these divisions had lost no time in showing up in our trenches, and all of them spoke of the imminent offensive.[3] They were small, slant-eyed men, with yellowish faces, puckered and wrinkled. Descendants of the Mongols of Ghengis Khan's "Golden Horde", they were subjected to the brutal disciplinary methods of the few actual Russians present in the divisions. During an interrogation one of the deserters revealed—with scars to prove it—that his "comrade officer", rather than calling him by name, simply whipped him in the face. They were poorly equipped, possibly because they were regarded as little more than cannon fodder; among other things, they had no tunics and many of them had stuffed hay under the linings of their greatcoats to protect themselves as best they could against the cold. The prospect of falling into hands such as these was hardly appealing.

We had subsequently received warning from headquarters to be on the alert. Despite this, and although enemy numbers were known to be far superior, no reinforcements had been sent to support us, except a few exhausted Blackshirts and the odd German battalion. Evidently the higher commands had no reserves available: by now all had been swallowed up in the furnace of Stalingrad.

At certain points where our line strayed from the river bank, a few enemy companies, by way of further preparation, crossed the Don during the night and positioned themselves below our trenches in various hollows in No Man's Land.

Our 81-mm mortars had pounded them for hours with "high-capacity" projectiles, and no fire had been returned. Once again the way the enemy command used its men seemed appalling to us: one deserter recounted how on the complete annihilation of one of these companies, another had replaced it in the very same position—entrenched in the snow.

These were the conditions we found ourselves in when, at dawn on December 16, 1942, the Soviets launched their giant offensive.

In this diary I don't intend to speak of the ensuing battle, nor of the three days of dreadful hardship following it. But I will say this. On the afternoon of December 19 the Pasubio Division, with the few Blackshirt and German reserves deployed there with us, was still holding out, despite having fallen back a few kilometers on some stretches of the line. It was then that we received orders from the Germans to withdraw to Meshkov,[4] to save whatever was left. This order (the first not to come from our own headquarters) astounded us. The divisions had next to no fuel; so an order of this kind meant that all our equipment would be lost.

2

My battalion, the Sixty-first, began to retreat at around three in the afternoon, as dusk fell (since daylight lasted only eight hours).

All that was left of our fuel was a small residue of diesel oil and gasoline, enough for ten to twenty kilometers' march, that had lain for months in the fuel tanks of the vehicles. Many of the trucks (Fiat 626s and OMs) wouldn't start because they ran on diesel and the temperature of -15 to -20 degrees made it very difficult to get their engines going. The tractors, on the other hand (old Pavesi 4 models), had gasoline engines, and so they all started the first time, with a choral rattling that recalled our dawn departures during the advance.

Not one of the battalion-command vehicles would start; so, after making a vain attempt to charge their batteries, we set off on foot with Major Bellini at our head. Behind our scrap of a column the men from the three batteries who hadn't managed to find room on the few vehicles still in working order fell into regular file, along with their officers. Many of them, irrespective of rank, wore blankets over their shoulders, as a defense against the cold.

We had destroyed nothing. Major Bellini had forbidden me to fire at the wireless chests or at the monobloc engines of the two trucks belonging to my patrols. We had no idea what lay in store for us. We were appalled at the thought that all that material would really be lost, that we would never come back for it . . . Soon enough we'd learn what lay ahead.

The vehicles were the first to leave: those in a condition to get there had orders to await the column of foot soldiers in the village of Meshkov. Immediately after their departure we too set off.

The trees around the gun pits, recent witnesses to some of the most tumultuous hours of our lives, stood bare and dark in the intense frost. On fairer days than this our songs had wafted through their boughs, to be lost in the air beyond. From many of the chimneys sticking out of the ground, there no longer rose the pale blue smoke we knew so well.

Major Bellini put me in charge at the rear of the command unit. This was a sign of trust, but it gave me no pleasure. From my first few steps, I had felt a sort of aching in my left thigh: if it were to worsen (as had happened a few months earlier, on a brief hunting party), within a few hours I would be unable to walk.

In this predicament I had a touching testimony of my soldiers' devotion. Not from those belonging to the two "Observation and Liaison" group patrols, who were all new arrivals from Italy and frightened by the risks the men had run under my command during the battle on the Don, but from the veterans of the Second Battery, my companions in the previous cycle of operations.[5]

It was like this. When I told Corporal Gimondi, a thickset, square-shouldered Bergamask, about the beginnings of this paralysis in my leg, he threw down his heavy pack stuffed with provisions and said: "*Signor tenente,*[†] I won't leave you. If I come out of this, it will be with you; if not, at least we'll still be together." And he stayed at my side for hours, until I was certain I could walk with no difficulty.

Later Corporal Giuseppini also fell into step beside me, and he too stuck by me until I was out of danger—Giuseppini, the fierce gun commander from around Lodi, whose hair was by now completely white, with whom I shared so many memories of this war . . .

In what was now complete darkness, on the road of beaten snow leading to Meshkov through Malevanyy and Medovo, the most formidable column of men I have ever encountered was gathering.

There were thousands and thousands of us, dark figures moving along the white road that twisted and turned across the endless wastes of untouched snow.

Mingled with the men were numerous sleighs drawn by Russian cart horses (generally two horses to a sleigh), the odd cart, and a lot of motor vehicles.

At a crossroads the major ordered the group to turn off to the right, making for the line of the Sixty-second Battalion, and

---

[†]Tr. note: The form generally used by lower-ranking Italian soldiers to address first and second lieutenants alike. The author was a second lieutenant.

possibly joining up with them. But the Sixty-second had already gone, abandoning their twelve guns in the pits. This was the first case of panic I had come across during the retreat.

Some of the breech blocks of the twelve remaining guns had their striking hammers still in position: puzzled by this, we set about removing them, flinging them far off into the snow.

Back on the road again, a short time later, we came across one of our Second Battery guns that had skidded downhill and off the road. A man had been crushed under the wheels of the gun carriage: he lay on the ground, an oblong heap of dark rags against the white. Together we pulled the gun back up onto the road, and it set off again swinging this way and that behind its tractor.

We resumed our march in the flood of men and vehicles, heading south.

*

Little more than an hour after our departure we went through Getrayde, a small village on the supply lines, its stores and headquarters all abandoned. A tall brick building, solitary among the thatched shacks, was on fire, staining the sky red. Every so often a burst of light flashed forth out of its flames, accompanied by devastatingly loud explosions. It was an arms depot that our men had set fire to. In several of those explosions heavy grenade bases flew out, whistling loudly off into the red sky. Some of these skimmed our heads, then smacked fearsomely down onto the snow.

At Getrayde we began to get the impression that this was not so much a retreat as a flight. Abandoned in total disarray were trucks, motorized carts, sleighs, and materials of every kind. The snow was mottled with innumerable dark stains, objects discarded by those who had been there before us: articles of clothing, blankets, instruments, ammunition boxes, and, to our dismay, machine guns as well—first the weapon, then the tripod—and tubes or plates from 81-mm mortars, and then again clothes, and articles of all kinds. This disheartening sight was to accompany us for several kilometers.

Other roads and tracks converged at Getrayde, so that the road south out of the village was literally choked between its two banks of snow with men on the march.

Here, for the first time, our hitherto orderly company of marchers —the men in triple file, with the commanding officers in front and the three batteries at the rear (how we officers shouted at them to keep in line!), was thrown into disarray by bands of infantrymen and Blackshirts slipping into our midst. Among these were men from divisions who in the battle on the Don had lost their comrades, down to the last officer.

We walked on, keeping file as best we could. This was to last until about two in the morning. Then, beyond Medovo, the group was broken up in the stream of men coming back in the opposite direction. The road ahead had been closed by the enemy . . .

But one thing at a time. Now that perfect formation had been broken, Major Bellini no longer stopped every half-kilometer to check that the soldiers were still keeping exactly to "threes", and I and the battery officers walked behind him at the head of the column. Gimondi and Giuseppini still followed faithfully at my heels.

As I walked on I was beset with anxiety. "Will we manage to slip the enemy's grip in time, or be trapped in the pocket?" The other officers, and the major above all, seemed to dismiss the possibility of there being any danger of this. The soldiers didn't realize what the situation was, and their mood ranged from the blindest trust to uncertainty to the beginnings of panic. I personally was pessimistic— but was still a long way from imagining the full reality of the situation.

Only much later was I able to reconstruct things. For the past three days the Russians had been flooding out over a wide expanse of country about forty kilometers west of the Pasubio, across the front of the Second Army Corps' Ravenna and Cosseria Divisions. They were being joined from the east by other Russian forces who had broken through the front of the Third Romanian Army one hundred or so kilometers from us,[6] the aim being to close the pocket. Beyond the broken Romanian line lay Stalingrad, encircled since November 23 by massive enemy forces, and beyond that still the German armies of the Caucasus, who were by now in a completely untenable position.

This, then, was not just a difficult situation limited to one sector. The entire southern front was going to pieces.

We walked on.

Several times at a crossroads we caught sight of a small, makeshift wooden arrow, one of many with the word *Bellini* pointing the way to our abandoned positions. The stake supporting it could only just be seen sticking out of the snow.

Endless wastes of low hills, stretching interminably into the night. Wherever we looked, snow.

In the small valleys, bare trees with frost-covered branches, rigid in the grievous cold.

Behind and on either side of us, the glare of distant fires.

I prayed. God is at man's side, especially in times of trial. I asked for His aid, humbly, fervidly, simply.

*

We had now been walking for hours, and by now Malevanyy was well behind us. The cold was intense (around -20 degrees, I reckoned), but we were relatively fresh and managed to bear it.

Occasionally I exchanged a few words with Major Bellini, and also with Second Lieutenant Zanotti, the group adjutant, a chemistry student from Milan University, twenty-one years old like me. Zanotti, a cultivated fellow from a well-to-do family, carried his sleeping bag as if it were a suitcase and with Milanese affability declared himself confident that we would soon be out of danger.

The map-reading officer Palasciano also took part in these fitful conversations, as did the medical officer Lieutenant Candela, Second Lieutenants Lugaresi and Carletti of the Second Battery, and Mario Bellini, one of the group commanders. The major, who had spent eight years in Somalia, and found the Russian cold particularly unbearable, tried to keep morale up by joking and playing down the danger. Who knows how much effort this must have cost him! We all knew that on the line he had never ventured out of his shelter, unable to endure the temperature.

Meanwhile, as fuel ran out, more and more of our brigade's vehicles, particularly the tractors complete with their loads, were being abandoned along the road. The Sixtieth Battalion, and ours too, had literally strewn the road with them. No less numerous were the light guns of the Eighth Pasubio Artillery—the huge 149/40s and 210/22s, the very latest models, hooked onto their obsolete Breda tractors, immobile and ignored by all.

It broke my heart to see them. How much effort and expense that equipment must have cost Italy! And all it had taken for everything to be lost in this fashion was the order we had received a few hours earlier.

Every so often we overtook an infantry wagon, its horses exhausted or on their knees in the snow, unable to take another step. In the gentle, snow-sullied eyes of those animals, looking now this way, now that in supplication, there was an expression of almost human anxiety.

I learned that Corporal Tamburini had been abandoned on one of the Second Battery trucks. I knew Tamburini well. A few hours earlier he had had his legs crushed when a piece of artillery slipped position. Finding himself alone on the fuelless truck, the luckless fellow had watched the men streaming past him in flight. At the thought of those yellow-skinned Uzbeks who would be advancing from the Don possessed by the frenzy of victory, he began wailing, begging the men not to leave him there, saying he would sooner have a bullet through his head. Instead, he was abandoned to his wailing. This I was told, a few days later, by the very men who had abandoned him.

We walked on into the night, the snow's reflection making the surroundings gradually clearer to our now accustomed eyes. Every hour or so the column halted for about ten minutes (the *alt orario*, or routine halt), as prescribed by regulations. Many of us then sat down in the snow.

During one of these pauses Zanotti fell asleep: at -20 degrees and in the snow! But he had had no sleep the night before and was exhausted with that overwhelming exhaustion known only to those who have been on the front.

*

Just before Medovo, some German columns converged with ours from a side road; and before long the stream of men had divided into two parallel files: on the right the dark Italian uniforms, on the left the Germans in their bulky white outfits. The latter all wore felt-padded boots.

At once, the difference between us became all too clear. Above all, the Germans possessed fuel and a very large number of mobile trucks; every machine gun even had its own (possibly Russian) tractor with plenty of fuel. They were also equipped with an incredible quantity of Russian sleighs and carts, drawn by two or three horses. There was one for every eight or ten soldiers. This enabled the soldiers to take turns resting on the sleighs; they carried nothing, not even arms, and had all their equipment and provisions as well. If, from sheer exhaustion, one of the Italians attempted to climb onto their vehicles, he was driven off with yells and curses.

This was just a foretaste of what was to come.

Meanwhile, the number of our own trucks continued to diminish. Those still in motion were clustered with men, and amid the dark uniforms there was the odd white German uniform, evidence of Italian kindness.

The monumental Bredas, proceeding up the road with their colossal 149s and 210s in tow, looked like human honeycombs: men on the engines, on the cabs, on the tarpaulins, on the guns themselves, seated or clinging wherever they could. Incredible struggles occurred to secure a place or what seemed like one, since there were a great many exhausted men from the three days' combat in the snow.

I caught sight of one of them, a tiny figure writhing on the ground in convulsions. At that particular moment the column had halted, so I got a few soldiers to pick him up, and when we got to an uncovered truck, asked the Germans to take him on board. They raised no objection. At the time, before I knew them better, this seemed altogether natural.

About an hour later I saw a soldier in a state of delirium: the first of many I was to come across. He was a wretched infantryman, sitting in the snow on the edge of the road, babbling of green fields and murmurous waters, and declaiming sentences out of novels such as those of Salgari.†† I tried to stop what may have amounted to forty German trucks; but one after another our allies greeted my signals by either ignoring them completely or just yelling. Thus, I improved my acquaintance with them.

At last an Italian vehicle appeared: a Breda with a 210-gun carriage. I waved it down and got them to lift the poor fellow onto it, resist as he did. Before moving on the driver warned me that he only had enough gasoline for another seven or eight kilometers. So the man's fate was sealed.

We walked on.

The beginnings of the paralysis in my leg had not yet left me. More than once I pondered this predicament. Why did Providence permit it? If the paralysis had developed, I would have been doomed from the very first day. Was it that Providence wished to demonstrate through direct experience that a man's life literally hangs on a thread?

††Tr. note: Emilio Salgari (1863–1911), Italian author of adventure novels.

Hearing I was in difficulty, the major suggested I get onto the first available vehicle. By now it must have been past midnight, and we had left Medovo behind us, passing above it to the right.

Just beyond the village, on a great expanse of snow, the Blackshirts of one of the M Battalion legions,[†††] the Tagliamento, I think, were bivouacking. Nearby stood a bewilderingly large heap of abandoned Italian vehicles of every sort. Among them were the last of my brigade's Pavesi tractors, guns and all.

Some time after that, when the column halted, I walked up to a German crawler tractor that was towing a trailer of gasoline drums with an antitank gun in tow. It was under the command of a little, aquiline-nosed second lieutenant. We spoke in French. I played the "gentleman", the only language, apart from violence, that Germans understand. I got a place on the trailer for myself and a soldier from the group who was also not well.

Before we moved off, another Italian second lieutenant climbed up beside us. The German protested. Other Italians thronged around, wanting to join us too. We left, stopping every so often.

Sitting motionless made the cold still more intense, almost unendurable. So the soldier, and then the second lieutenant, got off.

Others got on.

The German second lieutenant shouted in protest.

Halt, forward, halt.

At a village after Medovo (Karazeyevo possibly), we made another stop. Gasoline was unloaded from the trailer to fill up some of the trucks. I took the opportunity of drawing close to a huge bonfire surrounded by a sea of men: they were burning a store of provisions. I was finally able to warm myself for a few minutes. Finally!

I returned to the trailer, and we set off again.

And here the first sights of soldiers dead from exhaustion or the cold met my reluctant eyes. At first I refused to believe what I saw, desperately hoping I was mistaken: small oblong heaps of rags on the beaten snow of the roadway, revealing themselves as infantrymen reduced to blocks of ice, their torment expressed in fences of bared teeth.

We moved on.

The wide road was still occupied by the two great marching columns.

[†††]Tr. note: The M Battalions were highly trained Fascist assault troops. The letter *M* stood for *Mussolini*.

Suddenly we began to encounter isolated men coming in the opposite direction. These too soon became columns and took up so much of the road that we who were advancing were compelled to stop. Jumping down from the trailer, I questioned some of the officers who were streaming back. Confusedly, they told me that the pocket had been closed ahead of us—for some hours now they reckoned. It was about two in the morning of December 20.

I took leave of the German second lieutenant and walked back to the village. Careful to keep out of earshot of the soldiers, I told Major Bellini the grim news. Then I entered an isba†††† crammed with people, to warm up a bit.

To our knowledge, no Russian had ever escaped from the German pockets.

††††Tr. note: An isba is a Russian peasant house with a thatched roof and walls made either of wood or, as in this case and almost exclusively throughout this diary, of mud and straw bricks.

3

After only a few minutes, orders came for the Thirtieth Artillery Brigade to form up. Disbanded soldiers from the Sixtieth as well as the Sixty-second had joined the Sixty-first; many from the Sixty-first itself, however, had lost contact with their battalion.

Besides Major Bellini, outside the isba, I could hear the voice of Captain Rossitto, commander of the First Battery.

I took my time before going out because, apart from sheer fatigue, I was appalled at the thought of plunging back—and after so short a time—into the atrocious cold.

When I finally emerged the battalion had vanished: on the road of ice all that remained were a few haggard stragglers, mingled with the crowd of men from every division.

In the freezing, clear night, I called out loudly, again and again. Nobody heard me.

The endless solitude was speechless, speechless too the gray men thronging it.

How insignificant those men seemed! Our surroundings seemed deserted, indifferent to their presence.

I had to catch the battalion up as soon as possible!

I joined the huge column that, leaving the Meshkov road on the left, was heading south out of the village, on the road to Popovka, where the Germans were reported to have attempted a breakthrough.

Suddenly some tractors belonging to the Eighth Pasubio Artillery came by, their guns bedecked with men in tow. I sprung up onto the running board of one of these tractors; and it was hoisted up like this that I covered the six or seven kilometers separating me from Popovka.

Day was breaking.
All around us, endlessly, stretched earth and sky.

*

When I got to the village, I came across a few acquaintances from the Eightieth Infantry Regiment. Lieutenant Correale (a philosophy teacher in civilian life) was exhausted and unnerved after the fighting of the last few days; he had difficulty getting words out, and his voice was hoarse. He told me that if he were forced to walk just one more day, he would die.

That was the last I saw of him.

And now the conversations Correale and I used to have with Major Pacini during some of those evenings in the Second Battalion mess at Abrosimovo on the Don come back to mind. With boyish enthusiasm, the two of us, who had precious little experience of soldiers from other countries, sang the praises of the Italian fighting man. The major, an elderly Piedmontese, with an exceedingly wrinkled face, told us we were wrong.

Sitting apart at a small table, Second Lieutenant Bernabè would cast angry glances across at us since it was late: all the other officers had turned in, whereas we showed no sign of leaving the mess. Bernabè, a very recent arrival from Italy, slept in that room. He had been a second lieutenant for no more than two months.

Then came the days of heavy combat. One moonlit evening Bernabè set off on a sleigh to join a company (pleased, despite everything, finally to be taking command of a platoon)—and died. Major Pacini died too. So many men from that battalion died.

When the worst was over, I had bumped into Correale, limping about in search of soldiers (mainly Sicilian recruits, new arrivals from Italy), who were trying to sneak off from the line. This convinced us that the major had been right after all.

Some things are best forgotten.

Of the Second Battalion, Captain Lanciai and Second Lieutenant Fabbrocini, a Neapolitan, were also there. Like Correale, Captain Lanciai had some difficulty walking.

We halted.

It was broad daylight when the Germans, with their powerful armored cars (eight or nine heavy ones) headed westward out of the village to make the breakthrough. This at least is what everybody said they intended to do.

They were followed by their baggage wagons, and behind these marched most of the Italians, in two enormous, tightly packed streams, black against the snow.

The whole immense valley around Popovka was now swarming with men, and many more were still pouring in from the direction of Medovo to the north of us.

I had fallen in beside Fabbrocini, the commanding officer of the half-destroyed platoon of scouts from Abrosimovo. We had been through so much together and got along well.

We halted on the crest of a very long hill. There the Germans were conducting a number of maneuvers to gull the enemy, as we later concluded. But of an attempt at a breakthrough there was not the slightest sign.

Fabbrocini and I waited with others in the terrible cold, sitting on the snow among tall, dry grass. We were joined by a few of Fabbrocini's scouts, who had not yet lost their confidence.

Behind us, nesting between the folds of land, and covered with straw and snow, were the isbas of Popovka. Ahead—to the south and west, we reckoned—stretched the immense snowy wastes, hidden by icy fog, without a sign of life.

Suddenly I had to get back on my feet because I was half-frozen.

I started wandering about on my own again, and finally, in the midst of a crowd, bumped into my commander, Major Bellini, who had several officers from the brigade with him.

It was getting witheringly cold: it was hard to believe that we were still alive, after so many hours of suffering. It was absolutely essential, while waiting for the breakthrough, to find some kind of shelter . . .

Captain Rossitto—a thickset, red-faced man—made it his business to find shelter for us all in a particular haystack he had in mind. We waited, but he showed no sign of returning, so the major eventually moved on. We trudged slowly back to the village.

We never saw Captain Rossitto again. I subsequently heard that he had found a bottle of cognac on an abandoned German wagon and that, out of his wits with the cold, had virtually downed the lot. This may well explain why later he didn't realize we were leaving Popovka.

We entered an isba, which was only partially occupied by Black-shirts.

Suddenly, a number of mortar shells exploded among the huts and along their snow-clad dry stone walls. This was the first enemy fire to fall on the column.

If the Russians were firing mortars, they were obviously very close at hand.

But where they were exactly remained a mystery.

We didn't ask ourselves: in the condition we were in, a little warmth was simply too precious a thing for anything else to interest us.

My sojourn in the isba was short-lived, however: the major ordered me to go in search of (if I remember correctly) Colonel Casassa, the commander of the Eightieth Infantry Regiment, to ask him for instructions.

I steeled myself and went outside.

*

I wandered about for hours before learning that the colonel was up on the broad hill to the west, where we had already been, among the swarming myriads of soldiers from every division.

It was past noon. I noticed that a good many men were leaving the village again, since the breakthrough appeared to be imminent. I was told this by a few senior Blackshirt officers.

While trying to make my way back to the isba where Major Bellini was, at about two hundred meters from it I spied a Russian tank that had not been there before.

I made inquiries. Apparently, it had come hurtling into the village a couple of hours earlier. A German antitank gun was positioned there and, when the tank was at a range of some hundred meters, had knocked it out. Three or four men—one no more than a boy—had been flung out of its turret, then shot by bystanders as they attempted to fight it out from under the tank.

Corporal Giuseppini later told me that this tank had suddenly appeared along the Medovo road, followed by two or three others, which kept some distance away. Between its banks of snow the road was still crammed with men on the march. The tank had wreaked appalling havoc as it came along this road, firing its machine guns incessantly and crushing men, sleighs, and horses beneath it. Giuseppini reckoned the number of dead at as many as five hundred.

The perpetrators of this huge massacre were themselves doomed to die immediately after their victims.

I couldn't help admiring the really perfect organization of the Germans, who, in all that confusion, had still ensured that the village was defended against enemy tanks.

I told the major what had happened, and he at once decided to move to an improvised "garrison command" that I had found. I was to follow him. This wiped out my hope of being able to rest in the warmth.

As on the previous evening, my socks were drenched because the snow seeped through the instep of my shoes. I had switched from boots to shoes a few days before the retreat but hadn't found the time to get ahold of long socks with antisnow gaiters or at least troop bandages: this made me particularly exposed to the danger of frostbite.

We never reached the so-called garrison. Before getting there we encountered several senior officers, acquaintances of the major's who were on the move with groups of soldiers. Before long we too were back on the hill with many of our own men, all those we had been able to muster.

Soon it would be dark.

We hadn't eaten the previous evening, and all we had managed to swallow that day was snow and a little freezing-cold, dense water.

Here and there in the last light, between the hill and the village, numerous fires were sending up heavy billows of smoke, for the Germans were burning everything they couldn't take away with them. Between one fire and another the carcasses of countless horses lay on the grubby snow: these exhausted animals had been slaughtered to prevent their falling alive into the hands of the Russians.

To my surprise, I saw 2nd Lt. Zoilo Zorzi coming toward me. He was from Verona and was the dearest friend I had made in all my months on the Russian front. Chief patrol officer of the Sixtieth Battalion, Zorzi had been with me on my officers' training course at Moncalieri and together with Mario Bellini, Antonini, and myself had come to Russia in June.

When we had begun the retreat the previous evening he had been on the Don in the village of Monastyrshshina, in the valley of Abrosimovo, surrounded, in a deconsecrated monastery, with his patrol and what remained of the First Battery of the Eightieth Infantry.

He told me they had managed to slip away only at the last minute. They had heard that along the roads leading to Medovo hordes of Uzbeks were giving them chase: swarms of them had been seen in more than one place.

Since the beginning of the battle four days earlier, I had lost all contact with Zorzi. We were both enormously relieved to find one another again. Although the cold made speaking a dire business, we conversed at length, and warmly. Meanwhile, all about us on the beaten snow, the hordes of soldiers were gathering into columns. Many of the units were reforming.

✻

Total darkness fell. It got still colder; you just had to keep moving.

Like many others, Zorzi and I paced back and forth along the column of the Thirtieth, then started jumping up and down and clapping our hands together or against our arms to get warm, exhausted but unremitting. By this time we all wore masks of ice and frost on our faces, particularly on our balaclavas in front of our nostrils.

Major Bellini was, I could see, suffering unspeakably. He was a little sharp with me, almost as if, by discovering the "garrison headquarters", I had made him go outside too soon . . .

The temperature continued to drop.

Who knows what degree it reached that night! Not that we thought of the cold in those terms: it was something murderous besieging us from every side, causing us immense suffering, busying itself with tearing and sucking the life out of our limbs. It was as unhurried as it was untiring, as if it knew it could take all the time it wanted and that as time went by we would be more and more exhausted.

How often, then and later, I was to have this sensation!

A short way from the column of the Thirtieth there was a low, dry stone wall on which Zorzi and I occasionally sat for a few minutes. But then we got up and again started jumping up and down insistently to save our feet from frostbite. One hour followed another.

A general's car was parked near the wall, and our major continually walked over to it, nervously, to exchange a few words through the window and receive instructions.

Around us, column after column had formed, facing in every direction. Farther off, on the brow of the hill, the official column, headed by the Germans, could be seen winding away into the darkness.

At around nine in the evening we noticed a massive arrival of trucks, guns, carts, and foot soldiers. This was the Torino Division, an impressive array of men and vehicles.

They fell in behind us. They had, I heard, tried taking a different road, southeast, but had found it blocked. The idea now was that we should try heading southwest in a single body.

By way of a contribution to the tank support they would be given, the Germans asked the Torino Division for one thousand liters of gasoline. This amounted to all the small reserves they had available. The Germans' request was met; the gasoline was handed over to them immediately.

This was how the various divisions had converged: the Pasubio (lacking its command), the Torino, units from the Ravenna, the odd units from the Celere, as well as the 298th German Division (incomplete and commandless) with eight or nine tanks. Of all these divisions the Pasubio had seen the worst of the fighting on the Don. There were also two Blackshirt legions ("M" assault battalions)—the Tagliamento and the Montebello—which were by now in a state of semidestruction.

How many of us Italians were there when the pocket closed around us?

About thirty thousand, we reckoned, though this was obviously a very rough estimate.

A glassy, black scrap of steel stood out against the white snow of the road. Every so often one of us stepped out of the column and sprung onto it, hoping that there, at a palm's distance from the snow, our feet might find some respite from the pitiless torment of the cold.

But no, not the slightest benefit was to be had. So we started jumping up and down insistently on the sheet. This still didn't do a bit of good, so we returned to the column.

After a while hope revived once more, so back we went to that scrap of metal.

4

It was almost midnight when the Thirtieth Brigade was able to get on its way.

The immense column, kilometers long, proceeded in orderly fashion: the men on the left; the vehicles some eighty meters to the right; in the middle one or two files of sleighs, carts, and horses. The Germans led the way.

It was a job keeping the soldiers in order and preventing them from overtaking each other and making hurriedly for the head of the column, where they would enjoy the direct protection of the Germans. This piteous frame of mind was in fact taking root; above all because of the disorder in their ranks, the Italians were beginning to lose confidence in themselves. There was also the fact that we no longer possessed any automatic weapons: we were equipped with very few machine guns, while the submachine guns (no doubt excellent, but too heavy in those conditions to carry on our backs) and the light machine guns (lamentably poor weapons, which worked badly at low temperatures) had all been abandoned. So the only arms we had were rifles and muskets. The officers, and some of the experts, had pistols. In addition to my pistol, I had a semiautomatic Russian rifle equipped with a telescopic sight.

As usual, I kept myself busy. And it was now that for the first time a subordinate refused to obey an order of mine. A sergeant in my battalion whom I didn't know refused to keep in file. Hardheaded beneath my mask of ice, I was still determined not to give in to general disorder, fearing that this might also lead to an incalculable loss of lives. So I was about to shoot at him, as prescribed by regulations. I refrained from doing so mainly because I had the impression that he was delirious. I asked him to give me his name: once we were out of the pocket I would make sure he paid for this act of insubordination before a military tribunal. But he never returned from the pocket.

We walked on.

My fervid dialogue with God, which had been frequently interrupted since the beginning of the march and then resumed, kept pace with our steps.

The night was very dark.

The road descended gently, endlessly, toward an invisible valley bottom: here and there on the opposite slope we could make out the faint luminous signalings of the Germans.

At the very steep start of that ascent an appalling quantity of gun carriages and vehicles were lost, mostly Italian. Thanks to their numerous Caterpillar tractors, the Germans saved most of their material. They studiously avoided helping us. Not that this made much difference: we were now almost completely out of gasoline.

The ascent lasted hours, as the descent had.

So long as we kept walking, the cold seemed less of a torment.

Curiously, from rumors we had heard, we were practically convinced that we would be out of the pocket by dawn.

✻

Dawn came, spreading a first light across the endless wastes of snow.

After completing the interminable climb, we had entered a village of scattered isbas: Pozdnyakov. Around it the Germans had placed a considerable number of their long antitank guns on the snow; the tanks were positioned at the crossroads in the village.

Word had already gotten around that we were free, but now we heard the following news: "We are still in enemy-invaded territory, in a more dangerous zone, in fact, than the one we have just come out of, because it is more infested by enemy tanks."

We gritted our teeth to stave off despair.

It was about six in the morning on December 21.

We had stopped, and the Italian column still continuing its ascent was pressing on us from behind.

The previous day's shouting began again, together with the orders yelled repeatedly by the officers, which as usual were met by the troops' idle pretence that they hadn't heard. Little by little the men, shoved by those coming up behind them, ended up flooding in all directions and above all toward the main cluster of isbas.

Most of the men were convinced that the Russian line, facing that of the Germans, was not far off.

What we didn't know was that there were no permanent lines as such. Ahead of us there were only frenetically advancing enemy infantry divisions and armored brigades, lords of all the negotiable roads. We were moving in their rear.

Groups of soldiers started flocking out of the village, heading this way and that in search of friendly lines.

Some of them drew farther and farther away.

There was a serious danger of their losing contact, which would be disastrous if the Russian tanks arrived . . .

How was it possible that nobody took things in hand, that so many human beings were being allowed to go toward their destruction?

We were oppressed by the sense of the inhuman immensity of the landscape. Against it our every effort seemed so paltry. Into our souls there crept the same sense of fatalism, of the pointlessness of struggling against one's destiny that belongs to the inhabitants of those lands.

I took a grip on myself: such monstrous disorganization was inadmissible! So I tried to see what I could do: like a tiny stubborn ant, I attempted to muster as many as six regiments on a huge space of open ground. I was helped by Lieutenant Maccario of the Second Battalion of the Eightieth Pasubio Infantry Regiment and by a few other officers.

We partly succeeded. All the men were in such a state of bewilderment that they now obeyed anyone who gave them precise orders.

In front of us large, ever swelling contingents of men were gathering.

I was well aware how paradoxical my situation was. If only there had been an energetic senior officer in my place! But the senior officers seemed to have become dull witted: later experience taught me that if the cold diminished the initiative of young men like myself, in the older men any initiative was paralyzed or at least semiparalyzed.

Luckily, the disorderly swarming petered out, and little by little most of the men made their way back to the village.

I was informed that on the other side of a mound, among the wretched houses, a general was mustering as many men as he could. So I led my six scraps of column behind the mound, where they joined the troops assembled before him.

Other Italians were joining the column from every direction.

Finally, the general ordered us to move out of Pozdnyakov, about one kilometer southeast, and there "get ready for the breakthrough."

From what we could gather, there were four generals with us at the time: X, Rossi of the Torino Division, Capizzi of the Ravenna, and possibly another, whom some mistakenly claimed was Boselli, commander in chief of the Pasubio. After a few days, Boselli's name was no longer mentioned, nor anyone else's name in his place.

I can't remember who commanded that maneuver.

The organization—or attempted organization, as we were waiting to move off again—took place on a very wide expanse of apparently flat ground sloping down into a valley.

Down in the valley we could now see the Germans: orderly as ever, they were already on the march again. Their column was flanked by a tank patrol.

I did what I could to reorganize the troops. But how can you expect people who are unused to being well ordered in normal civilian life to become orderly, as if by the wave of a wand, simply because they find themselves in uniform?

The carabinieri (of whom there were a few dozen) attempted to help us officers by forming cordons, but to no effect. No sooner had the mass of men begun to break the files of four that ran through the valley (and all had become more impatient to follow suit) than some enemy bullets, fired from who knows where, fell on the main body and head of the column.

The soldiers responded raggedly, firing at random.

Enemy fire became more accurate; a bullet even grazed my head: possibly my gesturing to keep order had caught someone's attention and I'd been recognized as an officer.

In the end, the rabble doubled back onto the column, spilling into the valley in a bevy of streams. Some of the men were wounded.

I now witnessed one of the most wretched scenes of the whole retreat: Italians killing Italians.

Our patrols, which on the initiative of individual officers had been sent up onto the surrounding ridges, were suddenly showered with bullets from the column. And in the chaotic shooting that ensued, members of the same column killed one another.

My throat was sore from shouting.

I had lost my small service cap, which had fallen and immediately disappeared in the tide of men as I was doing all I could to check their advance with my arms outspread.

It was pointless to make any further effort: we had ceased to be an army; I was no longer with soldiers but with creatures incapable of controlling themselves, obedient by now to a single animal instinct: self-preservation.

A last attempt to restore order. I remembered having seen, abandoned in the vicinity of the village, two or three Eighth Artillery 75/27 guns in perfect working order.

I stopped a tractor that had nothing in tow. We just had to go back and salvage at least one of those guns.

There were several wounded on that tractor: with desperation in their eyes, they begged me not to insist, to let them go on.

I let them go on.

Capless now, wearing only the balaclava on my head, I made my way downhill, through that huge confusion.

On reaching the track made in the snow by the Germans, I came across Adalberto Pellecchia, a Neapolitan second lieutenant from the 201st Artillery Regiment. He was standing there with a tractor and an antitank gun on the track's edge and seemed calm. I was pleased to see him: we had been fellow recruits in Piacenza and hadn't seen one another for a year; we greeted each other enthusiastically.

From what I could gather, he had already been there for a few days with several Italian and German squads. And he explained the situation as he saw it. The Russian line was only twenty kilometers off, possibly less. Beyond it was the German line, "and behind that, freedom." The Germans had forced a corridor for us with their tanks and were managing to keep it open in the teeth of pressure from the Russians. Conclusion: Only a few hours marching, and our tragedy would be at an end.

With hope revived, though somewhat puzzled, I took leave of Pellecchia.

A little farther back several officers were vainly attempting, once again, to get the troops back in order.

*

Every so often, as I walked slowly and alone along that track of beaten snow, I was overtaken by Italian trucks bursting with men.

Suddenly a Guzzi truck appeared, with only the driver and one soldier. I jumped on. The two men took me aboard: they raised no objection and were even respectful.

Little did I imagine the unbridled, incredible race I was letting myself in for when I jumped on that truck.

The driver was possessed by a craving to flee at all costs: as soon as the way was clear, off he tore at breakneck speed: any second he might overturn the vehicle or run someone down. Before this happened I managed, by dint of sarcastic remarks, and raising my voice, to put some kind of brake on his folly.

But not for long. Mortar blasts, coming from some unidentifiable spot on the surrounding heights, began plummeting down on the column. Judging by its low frequency, the firing was probably coming from a solitary weapon: it was trying to strike the points where the rivulets of troops converged, switching from one to the other according to the number of men moving along them.

This time there was no holding our driver back: although the track now ran slightly uphill, the truck careened along it desperately.

We got through the mortar fire unscathed.

Farther on the vehicle had to stop once, twice, or three times because the powdery snow on the track prevented it from getting over a number of uneven patches. So we had to get off and push. My two chance companions seemed in the throes of heavy fever.

The track steepened; a trickier halt; a truck rattled past us. Without a word our driver abandoned his vehicle and after a short run succeeded in catching up with the other one.

We saw him retreating into the distance, clinging onto the rear tarpaulin, bumping this way and that.

Neither I nor the remaining soldier knew how to drive the truck; so all we could do was abandon it. We took to the road again—on foot.

5

From what Pellecchia had told me, I reckoned that within a few hours I would be out of the pocket.

Every so often I found myself passing men prostrate in the snow along the roadside, in a state of total exhaustion. They looked desperately at us who were still able to walk and passing them inexorably.

I tried to persuade some to resume the journey, to instill energy into them: we were so close to safety!

Endless snowy plateaus.

Undulating land.

The various rivulets of men and vehicles had converged into just the one river, and this coiled away into the silence as far as the eye could see, like an interminable column of ants.

A sleigh had gotten stuck at a difficult point on a slope.

It was carrying wounded men who were staring anxiously at the driver as he did his utmost, in vain, to get it moving again. The horses were utterly exhausted: one was on its feet in agony, benumbed, completely encrusted with ice, spectral. Its eyes, in that poor exhausted head, bespoke unspeakable apprehension. The other horse, which was nearly at the end of its strength too, seemed, by contrast, to heed the imploring tone in the driver's voice and was making desperate, ineffectual efforts to get moving again.

I went my way. I shuddered at the thought that before long those wretched creatures on the sleigh would be left there, abandoned on the roadside in the vast silence.

I continued on my own way, alone, with my blanket over my shoulders.

By now the column had thinned out considerably.

Around midday I reached Tikho Zhuravskaya, an attractive village with a beautiful church (though it had no doubt been transformed into a depot, like all the churches I visited in Russia). It lay at the foot of a long, gentle slope.

As I entered the village I saw a truck loaded with wounded men that had smashed through a wooden parapet running along the roadside and sunk through the ice of the brook beneath it— apparently as a result of a mine exploding.

A short distance away, in a large square, abandoned likewise, I could see two or three other truckloads of wounded soldiers.

One of these men came dragging himself arduously toward the column, stretching out his arms to us, shouting. The wounded men on the truck down in the river kept silent.

I gritted my teeth and walked on, between the houses.

I stopped briefly to quench my thirst at one of the usual Russian wells near ground level, with a lever made from tree trunks. A German, who got there after me, told me to clear off, to make way for his horse.

I started making my way uphill, among the last houses.

A little later, a German lieutenant I was passing shouted at me in Italian: "Only the wounded on the sleighs, no baggage!" "I like that!" I thought. "A fine thing for the Germans to be telling us that!"

But as soon as I was out of the village, what I saw explained his words: there was a sleigh loaded with crates and bundles, led by two soldiers from the south of Italy (I could see at a glance that in civilian life they were two penniless wretches of the most piteous kind, at long last the proud possessors of something).

Every so often on the sides of the road there were exhausted men, unable to walk any longer and awaiting death.

I got the driver to stop the sleigh and gave him a severe scolding; he replied haughtily that I was to mind my own business. So I walked up to the load, took hold of a full sack and flung it down into the snow.

The driver nearly assailed me. He angrily threw the sack back on the sleigh and drove off again.

I kept at his heels for a few dozen meters, my hand on my pistol, uncertain whether or not to execute him. Regulations and the voice of duty told me I ought to shoot him; but I'd already seen too many dead Italians and had no wish to add to the number. And then again, to kill a poor wretch who had never had anything in life . . . Convinced as I was that we were near our line, I finally decided that when we got there I would wait at the end of the column and, if the sleigh arrived without any wounded, turn the two men over to the authorities.

I left them in no doubt as to what I intended to do—they looked at me in a state of extreme agitation, knowing, however, that they would never manage to fire their rifles before I fired—and continued my journey.

It wasn't true, though, that our line was a few hours away: it was days away, weeks away. I never saw that sleigh again. Later, I greatly regretted not having shot that man, even if it would have meant loading him onto the sleigh as the first of the wounded: I kept telling myself that countless instances of weakness like mine accounted for the confusion in which we found ourselves . . .

An exhausted German lay practically dying in the snow: German sleighs and wagons went by, and no one paid him the slightest notice.

We walked on.

I stared at the horizon, where the column was disappearing over the rise of a gentle slope, convinced that on the other side there was the much longed-for line; but when we reached that point, there was just another endless descent, and opposite it another interminable ascent: switchbacks—that day we went up and down six or seven of them.

In the early afternoon I began to feel the effects of the endless march. Thankfully, I was able to cover a stretch of the road on a truck: balancing on the front bumper, chest-high with the windshield. We were almost in the plain and were moving along fast.

After a while the truck had to fall in behind a long file of other vehicles that were stationary on the road. Beyond them the road appeared deserted.

I jumped down and continued on foot.

At the head of the vehicles there was a silent crowd. Two German antitank guns were placed at the sides of the otherwise deserted road.

Not a sign of movement above that desolate solitude: the endless whiteness of the road stretched away as far as the eye could see, between expanses of dead grass.

The rumble of distant cannon fire could be heard, but only for a short time, for it was immediately absorbed by the solitary wilderness.

The Germans explained why we were forbidden to walk on ahead: a tank battle was being fought. It appeared that the enemy tanks had broken the flow of the column and that the German tanks were trying to reestablish it by giving battle.

After about half an hour, silence reigned again.

We were allowed to go forward.

Rumor had it that not far away there was a small village in our hands, and this filled us with hope.

We skirted a very extensive wood. For no apparent reason, several soldiers fired one or two musket shots; the shots increased, and there was an all-out shooting contest: yet we knew very well that there was no one in the wood.

I yelled vainly to put a stop to the firing, above all because it might attract the enemy's attention.

A German soldier, finding himself in our midst, and beside himself with contempt, had started bawling at us.

I had to admit he was right. By now we weren't dealing with soldiers but with undisciplined, bewildered men. Not one of them had the slightest will to dominate instinct any longer. All had but one longing: to get to friendly territory, without wasting time heeding the dictates of reason—to get beyond the deathly limbo separating us from our world.

Certainly, to do this it would have been very useful to reestablish order and reorganize the divisions. This was a task for us officers . . . and in fact, how many of us, in other circumstances, had not risked our lives to prevent disorder? But now what could we do? How could we forbid men who hadn't eaten for days to search for food? Or to search at night for a less mortally cold corner to sleep in? How, when the column halted, could we forbid them to walk to and fro to avoid frostbite, even if this occurred in any case?

We greatly blamed the Germans, who at the time had not supplied us with the fuel we were entitled to. They themselves were not only well supplied with fuel but also had food; they had clothing and blankets to keep them warm.

Our innate dislike of them was steadily increasing.

Beyond the great wood there were endless stretches of snow-covered country.

The road suddenly widened into an expanse of beaten snow, scored in every direction with tank tracks.

Here to our surprise we saw that a large number of antitank guns had been positioned. Next to the huge German guns there were a few small Italian pieces. Keeping guard, these guns were awaiting the enemy tanks from a slightly different direction than the one we had come from and from which the column was still streaming . . .

We continued our journey.

It was getting dark.

*

Again, all the wagons were stationary.

They were waiting for darkness before covering a stretch of road on which the Russians—who were completely invisible—were firing sporadically with mortars and automatic weapons. For the time being, the Germans seemed to have no intention of responding.

I sat down on the mudguard of the truck that was in file with the others, bearing its tragic cargo of wounded.

Tiredness is not the word for how I felt. By now all of us were living on nerves tensed against the agony so as to avoid being overwhelmed by exhaustion.

We still had no idea (only days later did I learn, and even then received no details) that behind us, near the village of Pozdnyakov where we had halted at dawn, the last section of the Torino Division had been attacked by enemy tanks and infantry, which had wrought havoc.

As visibility decreased somewhat, while the trucks remained stationary, the men on foot began to pass: they walked down into a hollow and climbed the slope facing it toward an unseen village that was said to be in our hands, outside the pocket.

On both sides, someone was keeping the enemy at bay: both to right and to left of us we could hear the insistent volleys of automatic arms.

Tracer shells flew up in quick succession into the gelid, violet sky.

I remained seated on the mudguard.

An extremely young infantryman from southern Italy, no more than a boy, slowly came limping up to me. Both his feet were frostbitten and were wrapped in scraps of blanket tied up with string; he was, I seem to remember, leaning on a small stick.

He was crying; he wanted a place on the truck. The lieutenant commanding it replied that no place was to be had. The infantryman seemed to be at the end of his strength; he now wanted to sit where I was sitting. I and the others who were sitting there tried to explain to him that it was useless my giving up my seat to him: when the truck got going, he would have had to keep balance, and he wasn't up to doing that.

With ferocious selfishness I resisted his insistent entreaties; the truth of the matter was that within me a coldness was forming that was no less merciless than the cold surrounding me. My eyes followed the poor young wretch as he limped away again; in my soul I felt a useless torment.

By remaining stationary we were finding the cold increasingly unbearable. My soaking feet had become like ice. Suddenly and deliberately I leaped down from the truck, which had not yet moved off, and started walking again.

I was joined by a soldier who had gotten down from the other mudguard. He said his name was Carnaghi. He seemed to know all about the place. He said he had been sent there several times by his command and gave me his version of things, the gist of which was that we would see safety before dawn.

I won't repeat our conversation, if that's what it can be called. The night that was beginning was the third I had spent without getting a wink of sleep; I hadn't eaten for two and a half days; I had walked for hours on end; and most of all, there was that cold.

I had difficulty keeping the reins on my mind.

At the bottom of the valley two soldiers were lying on the snow, practically dead.

The column of men passed them in the dark, like a sluggish, indifferent river. I managed to get one man loaded onto an Italian sleigh.

Suddenly my friend Mario Bellini caught up with and overtook us, in breathless search of Second Lieutenant Treves. The latter had arrived from Italy a few days earlier and had been entrusted to Bellini, who was to train him in patrol life. They had lost sight of each other about an hour earlier. They were never, alas, to find each other again.

Together with Carnaghi I continued the slow climb.

33

Here was the beginning of a village. There were a few large sheds, probably stables, set well apart from each other. The Germans at the head of the column had halted here.

I went up to one of their officers, introduced myself, and asked him what the situation was. He replied lazily (from then on I never again spoke to German officers, unless it was absolutely necessary). Around the village were the Russians: we had to break out, either by following the direction we had marched in or by veering right. We could in any case count on enemy resistance being minimal.

When would we pass the line? He couldn't say but thought it would be soon.

I sat down with Carnaghi a few steps away from a hut in the company of other soldiers.

We waited there motionless.

A minute-by-minute struggle against frostbite. Not a minute's peace for our nerves.

We exchanged words, possibly in an attempt to cope with that nervous tension.

Words also flowed between the other dark silhouettes sitting or squatting in the snow nearby.

Rosaries of assorted automatic weapon fire: our soldiers' hearts instinctively sought those belonging to weapons that were now so familiar to us.

There opposite us, from a small, steep ridge, a Russian machine gunner began intermittently firing off strings of tracer bullets.

We watched them as they came over hard on the heels of each other, riddling the sky in one direction, then in the other, resembling large drops of incandescent matter.

The Germans, and the Russians even more, made extensive use of tracer bullets.

From one of the German tanks, all of which were lined up on the edge of the road, a sudden volley of fire started from the direction of the submachine gun.

Silence, then again the rattle of the submachine gun. Another volley and the same reply. Another volley, then another.

After each shot the machine gunner paused, then started firing again.

The tank had to suspend fire to avoid wasting ammunition.

It had, I thought, armor-piercing shells that, by exploding well into the ground, could do no harm to the tenacious, courageous machine gunner.

Suddenly behind us, on a slope descending toward the valley we had come from, and up which men were still trudging, we saw the flashes of white light illuminating men running toward each other across the snow. The light was coming from hand grenade explosions. The sound of shouting also reached our ears: "*Urrà, Urrà . . .*" "*Savoia . . .*"† Before long this shouting ceased.

In the wide spaces between the shacks, Russian mortar shells began exploding sporadically. We were less bothered by these: mortar shots were old acquaintances by now . . .

Finally, Carnaghi and I got up from the snow. The cold was tormenting us unbearably: masks of ice again covered the mouths and noses of our balaclavas. We had to find a place to sleep: indoors if possible, but failing that, out in the open, in the hay.

But all the large sheds and the other shelters were occupied by the Germans, who drove the Italians off with harsh shouts, ready, should they meet with resistance, to use their weapons.

I lost sight of Carnaghi.

As I wandered on alone amid the sluggish crowd and the fitful bursts of mortar fire, I met three unknown fellow officers who filled me in on a piece of news that I believed immediately, since it was what I myself feared: "The Germans are preparing to break out, leaving the Italians behind them."

So I decided not to sleep, to keep watch.

As I continued in the same direction, the buildings, though still very rustic, became less like stables, and there were more of them.

Some had been hit by mortars and were on fire.

In the dim glow of those fires, I walked past a wide, shallow hole. A lot of Italians were lying packed and squeezed together, attempting to

---

†Tr. note: *Urrà* and *Savoia* were the respective Russian and Italian battle cries. The Russian troops shouted *Urrà*, a Turkish word meaning "Kill!" In their battle cry, the Italians invoked the Royal House of Savoy.

defend themselves from the cold by hugging each other, like wretched naked snakes in their winter holes.

On the side of the hole there was a soldier from my patrols. He pointed to a dark patch of men who were forming up at the foot of a small hill: "It's one of the two Blackshirt legions," he said. "They're getting ready to make the breakthrough with the Germans."

So he too had the idea that a breakthrough was being planned without the Italians being told! I urged him to keep on the lookout and did likewise with others I came across in my wanderings, people I didn't know and who had asked me nothing. Finally, I approached an isba that had collapsed among the flames and sat down as close as I could to the fire.

It was the very early hours of December 22.

*

From the pyre of flaming, smoking rubble: the characteristic, greasy stench of blazing houses.

The ashes I was sitting on scorched me with a vengeance. But at least I felt a bit of heat, after so much cold.

Never so much as in those terrible days was I so aware of the strong link that exists between warmth and life.

Having taken off my shoes and socks, I was able to dry the latter somewhat.

A heavy tiredness was invading me: but, with nerves tensed, I continued to keep an eye on the Germans in case they decided to abandon us.

Meanwhile, I had a moment's respite. In my benumbed mind the woeful events of those days began parading before me, my soldiers and friends, who were dead or had been taken prisoner (to be dealt what fate?) or had scattered in the retreating stream of men; the faces of many I might never see again; our old, abandoned guns.

Up to that moment, I had been secretly pleased that I had recently been transferred from the Second Battery to the patrols, with men who sought only to shirk my authority: I felt that if I had stayed with my old soldiers, I would never have allowed them to scatter or allowed those who could still walk to abandon those who couldn't. I would also have insisted that they carry all their individual weapons. The men would certainly have obeyed me. Yet how much more difficult it would have been to proceed through that chaos . . .

36

Now that shameful thought had vanished. Emotion magnified everything; suddenly I found myself weeping.

It was the only time I wept.

After what may have been an hour of salutary warmth, I put on my shoes and got up. It was still dark.

I was convinced by now that the Germans had abandoned us.

So I made my way resolutely to the foot of the low hill, where previously the Blackshirts had been mustering, and myself set about mustering men.

And men from every force and division were congregating there from every direction. I intended to get them organized and then follow the Germans, who had certainly broken out of the pocket.

Possibly five hundred men assembled; to get them in order I was helped by Second Lieutenant Fabbrocini, formerly in command of the Abrosimovo scout platoon, and a few NCOs, who had also come in response to my calls. Our idea was to take the same route that the German officer had indicated the previous evening.

I have a rather confused recollection of ordering an NCO to parade the troop, almost as if we were in barracks. His "Attention!" had a paradoxical ring to it in the black torment in which we found ourselves; but I steeled myself to ignore the paradox. I gave a short, vehement harangue (which, I saw, had its full effect on the minds of those men) and then turned about to start advancing. We were all firmly determined to fight our way through, should the enemy have already closed the passage.

Little did I know that no German division had broken through, that I was simply about to lead that whole company of men into the enemy's midst.

But Providence interceded, proving (as she was to prove on later occasions) that, however firm our determination, we men cannot evade her designs. ("We are nothing more than small, docile instruments in her hands"; I kept repeating this to myself in the days that followed.)

Fabbrocini started arguing with me more and more stubbornly over which direction to take. I realized that, if they saw us arguing, the soldiers would lose confidence in us. But Fabbrocini was adamant: according to him, we should have been attacking in quite a different direction.

This saved the day: the soldiers no longer followed us.

In this predicament a major appeared and asked me to put the company "at the general's disposal", since "company commands" had been set up. What that meant exactly I couldn't say; but I complied with his request nevertheless.

The upshot of this was that all these men got mixed up with the crowd again.

With a few other officers, who had turned up in the meantime, I tried to join a company.

One thing followed another.

In order to decide what to do, we entered a semiruined hut, left vacant by the Germans, I learned, so that we could use it as an infirmary.

I was soon convinced that all these initiatives were mere castles in the air; so I abandoned everything and left the hut.

It was still dark.

The major now spread word that we were to hide, to conceal ourselves from the enemy, who had us surrounded by now.

I spent all my time before daybreak getting groups of men stowed away into hiding places.

ARBUZOV ("THE VALLEY OF DEATH")

6

Day broke, and my mind cleared once again, my surroundings appearing curiously different. I was to continue to see them like this in the three days that followed—the worst days of my life.

For we were at the entrance to the village called Arbuzov, the terrible place that will live on in the memories of the survivors of the Thirty-fifth Army Corps as "the Valley of Death."

Few people in Italy have heard of it. Yet it was here that we came to know the full horror of war, a horror unmatched perhaps by other more sadly famed places of the last war.

Only we survivors have spoken about it, but initially, as long as Fascism lasted, we did so almost covertly and cursorily; then, as Italy began to fall to pieces, we did so to deaf ears. This is the way men are: circumstances conspire to make things of scant importance become talking points and thereby acquire fame, while other things of enormous objective importance remain practically unknown.

This is one of the reasons I am writing today: so that everyone may know about your sacrifice, my brothers, my thousands of brothers, who perished in that terrifying misery. But what chance do I have of receiving a more than ephemeral hearing if my voice is parched, after such torment, and within me there is a desert?

Noon came, afternoon came.

Still without a bite to eat.

Meanwhile, men in the thousands were continuing to pour into the village from the road until, extensive though it seemed, it was crammed with them.

All the isbas, however, with the exception of the infirmary, were reserved for the Germans: even our generals were compelled to remain in their freezing automobiles.

Arbuzov lies in a large, oval-shaped shallow valley.

It consists mainly of an agglomeration of isbas lying slightly above the foot of one of the two main slopes: the northern one, if I remember rightly.

Set apart, on the slope, to the east of this agglomeration, there are numerous sparse shacks fairly close to each other at first, then increasingly far apart as if someone had deliberately scattered them.

On the opposite side, to the west, a very long row of isbas leads off from the agglomeration; flanked by a road, it climbs the slope obliquely then widens out, higher up, into a smaller agglomeration.

Finally, from this very long line another line of dwellings, spaced some distance apart from one another, branches southward, tracing a sort of wide, backward parabola across the hollow and along the foot of the opposite slope, in the direction of the larger agglomeration. It stops short of it, because at the bottom of the valley there's a swamp.

At the time this marshland formed an amorphous expanse of snow-powdered ice, with massive banks of dry marsh reeds, incessantly shaken by the wind, giving one an extraordinary sense of desolation.

Things were like this: the larger agglomeration and part of the main line of isbas, with the overhanging slope, were in our hands; all the rest belonged to the enemy, whose favorite nesting place was among the reeds at the bottom of the valley, while their heavy armaments were behind them, positioned beyond the summit of their slope.

Luckily, there couldn't have been many enemy troops that first day. Gradually, however, their numbers seemed to grow, and on the thousands of Italians massed in enormous dark patches in and around the main agglomeration of houses, an increasing number of mortar shells fell, killing a good many men. Moreover, many of those who were wandering from house to house were also hit by the automatic weapons.

All around, the Germans had extended the embryo of a line.

What were we waiting for? Why didn't we go forward toward the free zone?

By now that zone was beginning to appear indefinitely far away.

Some of the Germans explained things as follows: "Soon the panzers, our armored columns, will be arriving and will open the road . . . ."

After busying myself so much in the course of the morning to get the men safely hidden from enemy sight and attack, I decided after midday to look for a place to sleep. I hadn't slept for three nights now, and even at the time I left the front on the Don, I already had more than my fair share of sleep to catch up on.

Slowly I did the rounds of most of the village, in search of some corner in some dwelling, but it was no use: the Germans had occupied every house, every nook and cranny.

This was without doubt one of the consequences, but also one of the most serious causes, of our disorganization.

Retracing my steps, I got to where the long row of isbas broke off from the village.

*

Here there was the hut that had been allocated to us as the infirmary. It consisted of only two rooms. At the back it had a small stable with bog-grass walls, which was, by some miracle, empty.

I entered the stable. Five or six soldiers followed me in there, including some from the command division of my brigade: I remember Nane, a Neapolitan volunteer, as being one of them.

I lay down on the straw opposite the door. I propped my inseparable semiautomatic Russian rifle against the wall at arm's length and, stretching out on my blanket that was stiff with frost, made ready to sleep.

I had taken off my shoes and socks because, as usual, the latter were soaking wet. The men had lain down likewise here and there, in the rigid semidarkness.

Seven or eight minutes went by.

We were still awake when the door suddenly flew open.

There in the doorway was a soldier with a rifle leveled at us; from his short fur-lined overcoat he was easily recognizable as an Italian. He shouted something like: "Cowards, surrender immediately . . ." and hurled insults at us; he had a southern accent. I couldn't make out what kind of individual we were dealing with but suddenly saw the burst of gunfire, followed by a cry from the soldier on my immediate left: "Mamma mia! Mamma mia!" He had been hit in the head.

The door slammed shut. I reckoned that the traitor, or madman—whichever he might be—was reloading his gun to fire again. I leaped up, grabbed my rifle, threw myself to the ground against a jamb of the door, hiding as best I could behind a drawer that happened to be there, and brandished my rifle.

Among other sensations, there was the particularly unpleasant one of the freezing straw against my naked feet.

All the soldiers in the stable had thrown themselves to the ground behind me, terror stricken. I could hear them trembling.

One mumbled: "All right, all right, we surrender . . . ." I snapped at him to shut up. And now the door opened once again, but not completely, and only for a few seconds. To let a rifle barrel through? I can't remember clearly; I know that I pressed the trigger, but my rifle didn't fire, a hitch that had already occurred with that war trophy. This time it couldn't have happened at a worse moment. I immediately changed cartridges and waited.

We had sounded the alarm, and there was some movement outside. Suddenly the door opened once more and was about to slam shut again. This time my gun went off. I intended to fire behind the man's back to put him at my mercy and sound a greater alarm. I was convinced that it was the same man who had fired at us a few seconds earlier.

But as he was hurled back, the bullet got him. It passed slightly under the skin of his back, some twenty or thirty centimeters, from his left side to his right side.

He fell to the ground.

From his face I got the impression that he was one of the host of delirious or demented, of whom there were all too many in the column.

I picked him up and with the help of the soldiers carried him to the infirmary, where for the time being there were only a few Italians and some Germans who were in no way wounded. Behind us came the soldier who had been wounded in the head, holding himself strangely stiff as he walked, his face a sea of blood.

The man who had been wounded in the back clutched my forearm and shouted again and again: "Don't leave me, *signor tenente*, don't leave me . . . ." He had a southern accent. I asked him repeatedly if he had been the one to shoot in the stable. He never replied; all he did was repeat the same words.

I had sent for a medical officer, but none could be found.

So I had the man with the back wound lifted up again, and we took him off to a nearby German infirmary. After much explaining and arguing, which neither I nor the German doctor could make much sense of, the wounded man was bandaged without being disinfected. The German claimed that he had no disinfectant. When I then tried to get him to treat the man with the head wound, the doctor said it was out of the question.

I had no choice but to leave without having achieved anything else.

It was dark by now.

I was dropping with exhaustion.

But that tragic day wasn't over yet.

In the only small heated room in the Italian infirmary there was just the one bed, and it was on this that I intended to put the wounded man. But there were now two or three German soldiers lying on it. I asked them politely to leave, but to no avail.

I thought shouting might do the trick: again, nothing.

So with both hands I grabbed one of them by the wrist, pulled him to his feet, and pushed him against the wall, where, scowl at me as he might, he stood motionless. Then I tried to do likewise with another of them, but once he had been dragged to his feet, this one was not so submissive as his companion; he pulled out of his belt a hand grenade complete with handle and raised it above my head like a club. I made for my pistol. The other Germans in the room felt for their guns.

For a moment we stayed in that position. The men who were with me tried to sneak off. Only one of them stayed at my side, whispering to me to come away: "*Signor tenente,* you have no idea how terrible the Germans are!" By a sheer miracle I managed to resolve the situation without getting us killed. I exclaimed haughtily, in my stilted Russian: "I am an officer, a 'gentleman': I will not sully my hands with you. I will go and speak to your officers."

Once again, though barely this time, the English word *gentleman* seemed to make some impression on the Germans.

But try as I might with several of their officers, I had no success.

Eventually I settled the man with the back wound on a bench in the second room of the small house: a cheerless enough place, for instead of doors and windows it had huge breaches in the wall.

In a moment of lucidity he gave me his wallet, insisting that I let his family have it, if I should chance to survive this inferno, and reassure them that he had died with his thoughts directed at them and at God.

I tried to cheer him. But when I asked him once again if he had been the one to fire at us in the stable, he didn't reply. So I still didn't know, and in the days that followed shuttled between one conviction and another, until I determined to torment myself no longer.

We settled the other wounded man in the room as best we could, having in some manner covered the hole in his skull with a huge sock, the only bandage we had.

We went outside again.

I was dying of tiredness.

Bright tracer bullets were chasing each other across the sky, which was almost dark by now.

God was in that sky: I stood mutely and grayly before Him, in the immense cold.

Alongside me was my misery, and my wish, come what may, to continue being a man and a man commanding men.

I returned to the freezing cold stable.

Before long I was deep in slumber, huddled under the blanket that the cold had stiffened to sheet metal.

7

After a few hours I was awakened by a soldier, shaking me insistently and saying: *"Signor tenente,* Germans and Italians are getting ready to leave. They're already forming up."

It must have been close to midnight.

I sat up extremely reluctantly.

To go out again, into that murderous cold! True, the temperature in the stable was below zero, but at least it was possible to be there without having to struggle minute by minute against freezing to death.

My socks and shoes were frozen; it was torture getting them on. By a supreme effort of will I got to my feet. I woke up the others who were there with me.

Some of them followed me outside, but most remained: many, by now, had given up the struggle.

Outside we could see people lying everywhere on the beaten snow. Near the infirmary a major was organizing a unit consisting of half a company in which we were soon included.

But it wasn't true that the unit was about to leave.

A short way off, on the edge of the village, we could see a sort of natural trench (possibly the bed of a stream) running parallel down the valley: the major ordered us to enter it and take up position.

On the right the Germans continued the line, with numerous automatic arms, and far off on the left, too.

All we had on our stretch of trench were ordinary rifles and muskets and my Russian semiautomatic.

Night hung heavy over us.

From the sides of our trench a few bare trees stretched lean arms, petrified by the frost, into the sky.

We did not, however, regard them as our companions in suffering. That night every living being had too much of his own suffering to worry about that of others.

For a while I stayed still where I was, trying to take in the situation of the sector.

There, ahead of us, among the reeds at the valley end, the enemy must have been nestling in considerable numbers: numerous machine gunners were in fact firing insistently from that direction.

I had the impression that they were getting steadily closer. Their tracer bullets scored the sky continually above our heads. Way off to the left, German tracers crisscrossed with them.

Finally I made a move to inspect our stretch of the line and to check the condition of the men. And I made a bitter discovery: apart from those closest to me, all the others, officers and soldiers, had gone.

I gave orders as best I could to the remainder, assigning each of them a good position, and checked out their ammunition: only very few had a fully loaded charger: six bullets.

Six bullets!

I went up and down along that sliver of trench, telling everyone to be on the alert and not to fire unless they were absolutely sure. Then I returned to my position and sat down in the snow with my blanket pulled over my shoulders.

The cold was appalling. Every so often, though sitting like that, I stamped my feet insistently on the snow to prevent them from freezing.

(How many frozen men there were by now! Many had replaced one or both of their shoes with pieces of blanket or fur tied around their feet with string. We had already seen a fair number of these the day before.)

For a while I was sorely tempted to make off like the others; tight lipped, I fought this temptation and finally freed myself of it.

Actually those few hours of sleep in the freezing stable, which I still regarded as a paradise, had, without my yet realizing it, marvelously restored my strength.

With ears cocked in case the enemy made a move, I silently began to pray.

Now and then I broke off my conversation with God to reflect.

How trivial were many of the things to which I had hitherto attached such importance! Studying, for instance—what a ridiculous waste of time!

What was true, on the other hand, was God; what was true was my mother's love for me.

Thus, beneath my mask of ice, in the darkness of those hours preceding what I believed would be the enemy attack and with every likelihood of dying, more than at any other time I had a clear vision of reality.

Meanwhile, time passed slowly.

Every now and then I stopped praying or reflecting to stamp my feet insistently again on the snow and to clap my hands together or against my arms to keep them from freezing. As at other times, I had the feeling that I wouldn't manage to survive another hour in that cold. Half an hour? But half an hour is a long time . . .

And the hours went by.

Occasionally, in my mind's eye, I could see the sun-drenched gardens of the Riviera. What warmth there! Warmth! What an infinitely alluring, inexpressible thing: "O Lord, let me return there one day!"

Not a shot from our side.

Disoriented by that silence, the enemy was approaching very slowly, but approaching nonetheless.

In front of our natural trench there was a small gorge, a fold in the land, into which the major leading us had sent a few men by way of a vanguard. These men suddenly came running back toward the trench, telling us that the Russians were extremely close.

I looked right, toward the German line: they were all calm and passionless, as usual. With heavy white hoods pulled over their helmets, they had taken up position behind their rapid-fire machine guns.

Likewise when I looked left. People eating, sleeping in the warmth of the isbas, taking over for each other every two or three hours; well armed. Their discipline and organization were as admirable as they were odious.

First light.

The Russians always attack at dawn; they are as monotonous as their land. We knew from experience that they never changed routine.

The cold was at its peak.

The enemy seemed to be approaching the stretch of line held by us; it seemed to me all too clear that they were about to launch their attack.

I did the rounds of the men again, in order to exhort them and cheer them. Some had fled. Getting wind of this the Germans suddenly sent two soldiers armed with submachine guns to take up position behind us at appropriate distances from each other. Woe betide anyone who now tried to abandon position!

I smiled wryly to myself at the thought of our propaganda about Soviet commissars holding their men at gunpoint . . .

Time seemed never to pass; ever more intensely we felt in our blood the imminence of the attack. The soldiers were wan and mute in their positions, some of them sitting with their backs to the enemy. Bullets hissed over the trench, but no one seemed to care anymore.

No one sought shelter; and even I, as I walked back and forth, felt them pass at a hair's breadth without giving them a moment's thought.

Only six bullets per head! What difference did it make if you died a few minutes earlier or later?

Meanwhile, behind us in the uncertain twilight, we could see men collecting here and there among the isbas and forming up as best they could. Many others were milling about in a growing swarm; a short distance away I caught sight of several I knew: among them Colonel Matiotti, commander of the Thirtieth. What was afoot? But what did it matter to us? We were about to be assailed by the enemy, so we could scarcely be expected to be interested in what was happening behind us. I tried out my rifle: the empty cartridge case got jammed in the barrel. There seemed to be no way of getting it out.

So, ramming that weapon down against the ground, I smashed it up, since it was more dangerous for me than the enemy, and pressed the pieces down into the snow. I would fight with my pistol and nothing else.

The time had also come to destroy my diaries. Along with the camera (which was then in the hands of my orderly, wherever he might be), they were the only thing from my baggage that I had bothered to take away with me.

Their pages contained numerous critical remarks about the Germans. I didn't like the idea of their being used for enemy propaganda. So from the pocket of my greatcoat I removed, and tore to shreds, the three notebooks in which from the day of my arrival at the front I had painstakingly recorded my war experiences.

Those shreds too I buried in the snow.

Then, suddenly, I decided to remove my officer's stars. Considerations and memories became entangled in my weary mind: of infantry officers whom I had often seen going into attack without their stars, but most of all the stories I had heard of atrocious torture meted out to Italian officers by their Bolshevik captors.

If by chance I were to fall into enemy hands, I would pretend to be an ordinary soldier.

I should have known how vain it was my making that wretched resolution: unlike all my fellow compatriots, I was still wearing my long officer's greatcoat (when they had distributed the short round-collared, fur-lined overcoats to the battalion, I was out on patrol on the Don, and I hadn't since found the time to procure one). I also had on my holster belt: I would have been recognized as an officer immediately, even at a distance.

I performed that sad operation slowly, barely able to use my numb fingers.

In the days of normal warfare, when there was no less a danger of dying, I would never have dreamed of making such an aberrant decision. Now, so that the memory would remain to taunt me, I made it.

This was one of the cases—and alas there were to be others—in which my hand was guided by the incredible force, unknown to me at other times, of the survival instinct.

True, I later repented, deciding that if I were to fall into enemy hands, I would immediately declare my rank: Mario Bellini can vouch for that. But that's cold comfort. The memory persists and always will.

To complete my harebrained plan, I also tore up my identity documents; finally, I destroyed the sacred pictures I had in my wallet and buried several small relics that my mother had given me on my departure: I didn't want the Bolsheviks to destroy them if they found them.

Then, after checking my pistol—sitting in the snow, half-frozen, calm—I waited for the enemy to spring on us. Once again I didn't seem to be bothered by the idea of dying.

Yet this was not the case. The fact of the matter was that, deep down in my soul, something was rebelling dully and tenaciously against the prospect of the end. I couldn't imagine myself as a corpse in the snow, as, try as one might, one cannot hold one's hand over too hot a stove.

It is incredible how attached man is to life! Several times it had seemed to me, in more distant days, that the idea of dying didn't bother me. But when I found myself actually face-to-face with death—even when I was there of my own will—it was a different story. I had observed others and knew for certain that all men, even those most contemptuous of death, those who court it, those who perform the most reckless and crackbrained actions, always hope not to die. Something within them, something stronger than them, keeps this hope alive.

And this was what I once again felt within myself.

And if I tried not to think about it, to shut myself off in simple indifference, I failed.

In the heat of the moment, your will can thrust you toward death, as if you were engaging in a great game with her. But if death approaches slowly, no will in the world can completely master a living heart.

Occasionally a different thought crossed my mind, giving me a flash of comfort and even, for an instant or so, a sense of security: it is impossible for God not to listen to my mother's prayers.

It was getting steadily lighter.

Suddenly I was seized by a blind rage against the Germans, who treated us as slaves, and against my compatriots: for seven hours now we had been keeping watch in the trench at that temperature, and not one of the others had thought to relieve us. I sprang up and, heedless of the two German submachine gunners, climbed out of the ditch and bounded off in search of my colonel. Did we all want to freeze to death?

I found him immediately. He promised to take matters in hand at once. But when, still running, I got back to the trench, the other Italians were no longer there. They had been relieved by German soldiers, who were standing there motionless behind their submachine guns, which they had already positioned. I couldn't have been away for more than three or four minutes.

8

Meanwhile, in the village the Italians were continuing to gather into increasingly large formations. I thought they were planning to attack in a specific sector in order to force a passage; but they were getting ready for bayonet attacks in every direction, aimed at widening the enemy circle, which was fiercely squeezing us into a restricted space where all too many fell victim to the fire that came their way.

And soon these attacks were launched fanlike in all directions, beneath the somber sky.

As I made my way between the isbas amid men from every division, I came across a small group of "old" artillerymen—*vecchi*, from the Second Battery.

One of these was the tractor driver Guido Rivolta from Paina (a village near mine: Rivolta regarded himself as my *paesano*, the sort of tie that runs deep with Italian soldiers). As soon as he saw me he announced, with his customary queer smile, which seemed forced even when it wasn't, that he had a loaf of biscuit, a whole loaf, and intended to share it with me. Still smiling in that strange way of his, he added: "In any case, I've already had my fill." The truth of the matter was that he was probably starving like everyone else.

I accepted gratefully.

But before he had time to take the biscuit out of his pocket, a band of men came past, heading back up the slope toward a sort of natural canal, destined for action to the northeast, above the area of scattered isbas. Without more ado, I instantly banished every memory of my recent nervous tension and joined those men.

That's our Italian temperament for you.

I was still determined to fight, as befits a soldier. This didn't last long . . .

My old comrades—my *vecchi*—followed me. I picked up a musket on the way: there were a fairly large number of abandoned Italian weapons and, sad to relate, they belonged not just to the dead.

We came out of the canal and immediately came across some corpses: they still looked like human beings, so their deaths must have been recent.

Meanwhile, throughout the valley the din of combat was increasing both in volume and in intensity. We too thrust forward.

We were greeted on all sides by enemy fire.

Yelling and laughing, we thrust still farther forward.

Some fell.

Was it a sniper—a *cecchino*—who had spotted my long officer's greatcoat? Or a machine-gun volley fired at our whole group?

I suddenly felt a small blow between the nape of my neck and my neck itself; I bowed my head as if someone had given me a cuffing but continued to run forward.

Our band of men, which included other officers as well, had joined up with others.

On reaching a hollow in the land, I stopped and, squatting down, slipped off my balaclava to take a look: a bullet had gone clean through me, leaving two small holes a few centimeters apart just below the nape of my neck. I probed the skin: not so much as a scratch.

So I bowed my head and simply and fervently thanked the Madonna.

Guido Rivolta had followed me; he was half lying on the snow beside me and was smiling in sympathy. Then he took the biscuit out of his pocket and placed it in my hand; I split it in two by banging it against my knee and gave half of it back to him; each of us ate his respective half, while the bullets wailed around us.

Meanwhile, we looked at each other and smiled.

Bayonet attacks!

I shall never forget that day.

Not everyone took part in the attacks. On the contrary, most stayed behind in the village—dark, constantly moving masses, scattering continually under Russian mortar and gunfire.

In spite of this, that day the enemy front was routed everywhere, and by the afternoon our postings encircled the whole valley where Arbuzov lay.

It was the last great display of Italian heroism.

In those attacks almost all the best men fell (this is not rhetoric; it's the simple truth).

Together with Rivolta I again thrust forward with enthusiasm. There was more disorder than ever, and before long I somehow lost sight of my "fellow villager". I was never to see him again: very possibly—though only later did this come home to me—what he had so fraternally shared with me was his last biscuit, his last piece of bread.

As I proceeded through the uproar, I was particularly troubled by the incessant "ta-pum, ta-pum" of the enemy snipers, which meant a victim at practically every shot. Everywhere, the ground was strewn with dead bodies.

Being a good shot (in Italy I had won some junior shooting contests), I decided to turn myself into an Italian sniper—a *cecchino*.

Stretched out on the snow behind a rise in the ground, I tried to discern the enemy (every now and then I could see them, usually a long way off and on the move), and when I succeeded in getting one in my sights, fired at him with my musket. I shifted position continually, moving forward all the time. How handy my Russian semiautomatic rifle with its telescopic sight would have come in now. (It was in fact the same model that the enemy snipers used . . .)

I had come down from the top of the ridge into the eastern outskirts of Arbuzov; a scattering of isbas. These small, very rustic houses followed, at irregular intervals, the two sides of the road, or rather track, which twisted away into the distance.

Everywhere, everywhere, there were dead bodies: Italians, Russians, then Italians, and again Italians.

Here and there, collapsed or seated on the snow, a wounded man at death's door was invoking his mother or screaming in agony.

Other wounded men were carried hastily to the rear by one or two fellow soldiers: more so than by physical suffering, their faces were scored by anxiety at what would now befall them. They had in fact been maimed fighting for everybody, but nobody could help them now.

Forward. The bullets whistled everywhere.

I passed a German mortar that was firing from the cover of a ruined shack; around it were its gunners dressed in their dirty white garb.

Nearby, some isbas were burning; the flames were not abundant, though; they seemed to be proving a poor match for the immense cold.

I lay down behind a snow-clad rise, among a group of dead men, and took to sniping again.

A good many bullets came whistling very close to my head, furiously.

So I grabbed a helmet that was lying on the snow: a brown one, because, unlike the German helmets, ours had not been stained white. I noticed that it had a bullet hole smack in the middle of its visor, so I put it on back to front, then flung it away.

Every so often I managed to spy the enemy moving down there among the houses: I took quick and careful aim, then fired. Did I hit anyone? They vanished.

Forward again. A number of times I crossed from one to the other side of the meager road, amid the bullets that had gone berserk.

Just off the road, behind a large, very low pile of snow-covered straw, four or five men were positioned; around them, in a semicircle, lay an array of dead men.

Bent double, I bounded off the road toward those men and was thankful to reach them. They looked at me in dismay. One of them said, "Providence is on your side, *signor tenente!* In front of us, forty meters off, there's a Russian machine gun. No one can get here; I don't know how you managed it . . . ," and gesturing with his hand, and his chin, he indicated the surrounding corpses, whom I had just made my way through.

I turned back to those men lying facedown in the snow or looking up into the sky—those half-closed eyes, in which the liquid was fast becoming ice; some of the corpses were stiffening into the strangest postures.

Something had to be done about that machine gun; what we needed was a mortar!

I thought of the German mortar positioned farther back. It was no good sending a soldier: the Germans wouldn't have listened to him. And, in any case, how would they feel about becoming potential targets for the machine gun?

I had to decide: back bent, swift as lightning, I leaped over the dead bodies and dashed to the shelter of the first isba, which was not far away.

I thanked Providence: this time, too, I'd made it.

✳

I hurried back to the German mortar. But at the very moment I reached it, the mortar men were explaining to other Italians that they no longer had any shells: the ash-colored ones scattered on the snow weren't German, but Russian (obviously abandoned by retreating enemy mortar men).

Other bombs had to be found, and at once. The mortar men looked at me mutely.

I decided to go in person to the German command in the village; I set off at a brisk pace.

Among the scattered isbas there were many men—Germans, mainly—calmly waiting for the attacks to end.

Along the road, on the snow between isba and isba, and to the side of the isbas, more corpses.

In the village, near the isba housing German headquarters, I found an Italian colonel and drew his attention to the business of the mortar ammunition. Not long afterward, a sleigh with the ammunition I had asked for left in the direction I had come from.

Around German headquarters there was a particularly dense throng of Italians; from some of our trucks, which were crammed with wounded, moaning could be heard.

I saw men collecting ammunition in a blanket, from whoever wasn't fighting, to take to the scene of action.

Having put a few chargers in my pocket, I took to the meager road again and headed back to the zone where I had joined in the combat.

But it wasn't only in that sector that battle was raging. Stopping in the shelter of a small house, I was able to observe an extraordinary scene being enacted on the opposite side of the valley. There, too, there were men—Italians and Germans—who, having gotten beyond the valley, were keeping up the attack. And there in front of them, from the whiteness of the snow, Russians were coming out with their hands up.

It was a tragically priceless spectacle.

Some of the Germans observing it near me made no disguise of their enthusiasm.

I continued on my way.

In a bottleneck between two isbas, a German 20-mm machine gun was placed, giving support to the bayonet attacks on the other side of the valley where the Russians were giving themselves up. Someone realized that the Germans were shooting at the Italians: he immediately shouted at them to cease fire; someone ran up to me and asked me to order them to stop firing. When I got there, the Germans had already suspended fire: they looked at me uncomfortably. I walked on.

Every so often a Russian prisoner, escorted by some of our soldiers, was conducted to German headquarters.

More of our wounded, being accompanied pitifully to what, for the record, were called "dressing stations".

I passed one who was being helped along by a friend, leaving in his wake a steady trail of red blood, which shone out against the snow. I stopped him. A bullet, possibly from a machine gun, slitting his veins and arteries, had penetrated both wrist and arm at the level of his biceps. Some attempt had been made to stanch the arm wound with a cloth; the wrist wound hadn't even been looked at. Reprimanding the man's escort, I quickly took my filthy handkerchief out of my pocket and tied it as tightly as I could around the wounded man's wrist, then sent the two men on their way and washed my blood-drenched hands with snow.

From then on I had to do without my handkerchief. I was to replace it as best I could with shreds of lining that I tore from my greatcoat whenever necessary.

A short time later, out of the blue, I bumped into a former companion from the officers' course: Sandro Negrini, a tall, gangling Pavese, always ready for a laugh. He was sitting all alone in the doorway of an isba.

He explained to me that he had only been in Russia for a few days, "and I've already landed in a pocket!" I said to him, "Do you want to come to the attack?" "For the love of Mike," he replied, "I'm only just back from it. I haven't even a single bullet left in my pistol!"

In his hand he was holding a beehive's frame full of wax and honey: "Not bad as a mouse catcher," he declared, and asked me: "Want a bit?" I stayed with him a few minutes, ate the honey, and we chatted a bit longer. He was the same old joker as ever.

Finally I said good-bye to him and set off again. I was never to see him again either.

At the height of the German mortar the hissing of the bullets had again intensified greatly. The bayonet attacks had, however, reached maximum pitch, or perhaps even exceeded it, since everywhere the enemy, though still fighting, was in retreat and flight.

I walked on.

Throughout the valley, wherever the attack had come through, the ground was littered with corpses, mainly ours. Men who had had to fling themselves forward with bayonets raised against submachine guns and machine guns. Since there was almost nowhere that the attack hadn't passed, wherever we looked the snow around us appeared to be strewn with the dead.

As I have said, it was mainly the Italians who conducted the attacks; the Germans backed them up with the artillery positioned in the village, posting the odd contingent here and there among us, and giving tank support to the attacks at the key points.

Our command no longer existed by now.

There were, as I have said, three or four generals in the pocket. But they stayed, with other senior officers, in small groups at German headquarters, just looking on. To all intents and purposes, we were under the command of the lieutenant colonel commanding the German troops—all of us.

I was only a subaltern, but my officer's spirit suffered from this state of affairs: what I found most intolerable was our disorganization. When I was back on the firing line, I realized that, rather than resuming fire, my time would be much better spent making some attempt to coordinate the various bands of men in my sector. Several officers and soldiers were in fact asking themselves (and some had asked me too) how far forward we should take the attack. They were worried because the attack was assuming a highly irregular character.

This was because in some places the Russians, whom we hadn't managed to put to flight, were still to be found at the center of an island we had created around them; at other points, however, our isolated groups had pressed forward, quickly driving the enemy way, way back.

I could see them moving around down there and dodging between other isbas that appeared in the distance. Like many Russian villages, the outskirts of Arbuzov consisted of dwellings set wide apart from each other.

I resumed my musket fire. Then, since I was increasingly nagged by the problem, I got up and returned to German headquarters to ask how far forward the attack should be taken.

On the road that I hurried along, isbas were burning.

I entered one that had been ripped apart by a shell. There I found some sunflower seeds. I thrust a few ravenous fistfuls into my pocket. There was nothing else to eat—away!

A colonel (if memory serves me, Lieutenant Colonel Rossi of the Eighth Pasubio Artillery) took up my suggestion and went in to ask the Germans what we were to do. Their reply was: "The attacks are to be taken as far forward as possible, as far, that is, as communications will reach."

In my sector, our spearheads were now tracing a sort of long contour running from top to toe of the slope. On that contour I decided with Colonel Rossi to stop the new line.

Meanwhile, just outside the village, a few hundred meters from German headquarters, I had noticed some Italian soldiers crouching in a ditch: I couldn't figure out what they were up to. Before returning to the combat zone, I joined them and squatted down on the snow at their side.

They described the scene for me: In front of them was the marshiest and most densely wooded part of the valley bottom; no attack had been launched there, and the Russians were still there, hiding among the marsh reeds and firing around them in more or less every direction. To the right, our men (those whom I had seen taking so many prisoners) had by now reascended the far valley slope and were almost at its top. Far off, to the left, the attacks I had taken part in were still going on.

With my head just above the ditch, I was trying to make out the enemy troops nestling among the reeds, when a spray of snow rose three or four meters away from me: a few centimeters higher and the shot would have killed me because the direction was right.

I had been lucky again and again thanked the Madonna for my luck. I fired a few musket shots into the maze of reeds (vainly, since I couldn't see the enemy), then beat it back to my combat sector.

When I got there I informed officers and men alike, as best I could, how far the new line was to go.

In fact, the new line stopped there.

It was midday; almost everywhere the real attacks were over. Yet almost everywhere there was still the rattle of rifle fire. I went back to the village again.

✳

The whole valley, I repeat, seemed to be strewn with the dead. There were also a vast number of wounded. With anguish we felt that we wouldn't be able to take care of them: all of them, or nearly all, were doomed to die within a matter of hours.

Some "dressing stations" had been created: I particularly remember the one in Arbuzov by the infirmary hut.

The two rooms forming the hut and the stable were now so crammed with men that it was utterly impossible to walk around in them.

The wounded were even lying on top of one another. Even from outside, their groaning and screaming could be heard—it sounded so small in the terrible cold.

When one of the few soldiers who had devoted himself to looking after them came in with a little water to ease their plight, the groaning was joined by the shouts and oaths of those he inadvertently trod over.

But the most wretched spectacle of all wasn't what we found inside the house, but outside on the ground around it.

Here the snow had been leveled a bit by straw, and on this straw several hundred wounded men were lying.

They had been left in every kind of position by those who had hurriedly brought them there—but they weren't touching each other, so that one could walk among them.

Most of these men kept silent. It must have been between -15 and -20 degrees. Most of them were huddled under wretched blankets that were encrusted with snow and, as usual, as stiff as sheet metal; some had no blankets, and all they had to protect them were their overcoats. Dead men already intermingled with the wounded: their wounds, some of which were monstrous, had been just barely bandaged, and they had been unable to resist the terrible struggle against a conspiracy of loss of blood, hunger, and cold.

It was hard to distinguish them from the wounded; both were equally motionless.

One, just one, doctor went the rounds of this vale of tears, exhausted, trying as best he could to treat the men.

Somewhere or other I heard—I can't recall whether it was that day or in the days that followed—that he had been wounded no less than twice by enemy shell splinters while performing amputations with a cutthroat razor.

Another much larger dressing station had been fitted out in an isolated spot on the slope above Arbuzov. Here, in front of a haystack, which was some eighty meters long and four or five meters wide, a lot of straw had been laid, and on it, in neat triple file, lay innumerable wounded men. They also lay at the two shorter sides of the haystack. On the other larger side, by contrast—facing the top of the slope— only very few were to be seen, because this side was fully exposed to the icy breeze that, in these higher spots, only increased our torment. These wounded men were slightly better protected than those down in the village, since they had straw over them by way of blankets.

When I got to the center of Arbuzov it was past midday.

A thin wintry sun had risen, grimly illuminating that spectacle of infinite misery.

9

I was increasingly tormented by hunger.

I noticed that a few people were moving around the sparse isbas lying beyond the valley bottom. I decided to go there in search of food.

I crossed the flat valley bottom, covered with marsh reeds.

In the middle, in a sort of natural trench, lay a great many enemy corpses, almost all Europeans, in their heavy gray-khaki uniforms.

I don't know why, but I had the impression that those dead men emanated the tragic sense of the ineluctability of the destiny of the Russian soul. Each and every one of them must have fallen, I thought, feeling that their hour had irremediably come and that it would be utterly pointless to rebel against it.

Other enemy corpses lay only a short way back from the road I was walking along; in the pale winter sun, the snow gleamed dimly around them.

One I remember in particular: thickset, with a bundle tied to his back. I stopped for a moment to observe him and to inspect his immobility. In the snow in front of his mouth a small hole had formed; into it a lot of blood must have trickled.

For all I knew, at that very moment, in some far-distant thatched isba, somebody was thinking anxiously about him.

I walked on.

More sparse Russian corpses, most of them behind screens of snow among the reeds, reduced likewise to statues of ice, many of them with bare, yellowish feet, because the Italians who had been there before me had removed their high felt, snow-powdered boots.

As I walked on, a soldier mounted bareback on a Russian cart-horse rode past me; he stopped briefly and said: "German headquarters have announced that the panzer divisions are due to arrive in half an hour." I couldn't believe my ears and asked him to repeat what he had said: the soldier had in fact just come from German headquarters.

I felt a great surge of joy, though the repeated disappointments of the preceding days gave me every reason to take what I heard with a grain of salt.

I believed in the arrival of the panzers simply because I wanted to believe in it.

I had now crossed almost the entire valley bottom and was quite near one of the isbas I was bound for when I spied an Italian second lieutenant sitting all alone on the snow on the edge of the road. When I came up to him, he gave me the hint of a salute with his hand.

He had a melancholy smile on his face. I returned his salute and said: "Don't I know you? Who are you?" He told me his name, and said he belonged to the same formation as mine, the Sixtieth Battalion. It was then that I remembered that we had met not very many days before.

"You know," he said, still smiling in that rueful way, "they got me."

"Where?"

"In the belly."

"Has the bullet come out?"

"No."

I fell silent for a moment; in a few hours he'd be dead.

"Cheer up, a belly wound isn't that serious after all," I said inanely, hoping to rally him.

"I know," he said.

"In any case," I added, "you know that the panzers are on their way?"

"I know, I heard it. Let's hope they get here quickly, because if they don't, for me . . . ," and he shook his head, and that smile widened.

At a loss for words, I took my leave of him: "Well, bye, then," and walked on.

There he remained sitting silently on the roadside, looking around every so often.

Near the first isba there was a red-haired, freckled soldier, hollering like a man possessed and pointing a pistol at the few other soldiers who were trickling by, telling them to head up the slope he was pointing to: "An officer left me here; he gave me his pistol. He told me I was to send them all up there, where the line is forming."

Then he begged me to relieve him for a bit: he was keen to find something to eat.

I agreed to relieve him.

I remember seeing Italian ammunition and Russian arms on the ground, against a wall. I stopped a few men, got them to load material, and dispatched it all up to where the line was forming. But it was quite pointless ordering the men to go to the line: they would have beaten it back the moment they were out of sight.

I don't remember whether the red-haired soldier reappeared.

I do remember that I eventually entered the isba, pistol in hand, looking for food.

I was greeted by a wretched spectacle: on the floor of a room, the corpse of a gigantic old man with a long whitish beard was lying in a vast pool of blood.

In the small corridor connecting the dead man's room with the rustic hallway I had just come from, cowering against a wall, terror stricken, were three or four women and five or six children. Russian children: thin, delicate, waxen faced.

Standing in front of them, at a table on which there were some rustic containers, a soldier was calmly eating cooked potatoes.

He greeted me: "Come, *signor tenente*, there's something to eat." I put my pistol back in its holster and tried to reassure those poor creatures: "*Nema bajuscia*,[†] don't be afraid, I've only come in for a bite to eat." I put my hand to my mouth, to make myself understood.

Then I sat down with the soldier and started to eat as well.

Only one of the containers, a small cauldron, contained boiled potatoes. I wolfed down five or six of them, one after the other. Petrified, the children and the women watched me all the while with wide eyes.

I stopped eating.

But in any case how warm it was in that house! I lingered a few minutes, then, having done all I could to urge the women and their children to eat something too before the soldiers came and devoured the lot, went out again into the terrible cold.

---

†Tr. note: When addressing both Russians and Germans, the Italians used a somewhat corrupt, makeshift form of Russian that they had picked up on the front. In order to conserve the flavor of this, the author's Italian transcriptions have been kept throughout the text whenever an Italian speaks or hears Russian.

I would have given my eyetooth to sleep in that isba, even on the floor, but it was too far from the main body of our men; the panzers might be arriving that night, or the enemy might attack, and if I stayed there I'd be cut off.

Around the scattered isbas small groups of white German uniforms were gathering. Heaven help anyone who approached them.
So I headed back to the village.

*

Meanwhile, the Russians, who, after being driven out of all their positions, had temporarily suspended their heavy gunfire, resumed it from more distant positions.

In and around Arbuzov there was still a massive concentration of soldiers, somewhat resembling the overflowing crowds who packed the squares of our cities during the political speeches preceding the war.

In the middle of this crowd mortar shells, cannon, and *katyushas* began exploding again. That afternoon too the slaughter was appalling; many men died.

We began to become acquainted with the full horror of the *katyusha*. Its sixteen 130-mm shells plummeted in a more or less straight line, one after the other, rapid as hail: from one end of the crowd to the other there was generally a distance of some two hundred meters. On hearing the hissing and tremors of the approaching shells, everyone in the area under fire immediately flung himself to the ground. The violent smoke of the explosions was followed by a terrible rumbling; the *katyushas* chose their victims at random among the defenseless men.

When the whistling of the large shell splinters had stopped, each man sprang to his feet and made off somewhere else, eager to find somewhere free from enemy fire.

On the beaten white snow, there remained the black stains of the clusters of dead men, as many as four, five, or more for every shell fired.

That afternoon I too was among those who flung themselves to the ground, or else fled, harried by enemy fire.

I had joined the main body of the troops who were awaiting the panzers, but the panzers showed no sign of arriving.

More than once, I had occasion to observe how loud hand grenade explosions are, if heard at close quarters—so loud that, try as you might to rebuild them in your brain, you never quite manage to.

Early evening finally brought a novelty that wrung cries of joy from us. In the sky above us a number of German triple-engine planes flew over, parachuting ammunition and gasoline. They then described a few circles over the valley, as if to hail us and assure us of their aid; then they flew off again.

So we were not abandoned after all. So German headquarters was in fact in radio communication with higher command. So, sooner or later, the panzers too would arrive.

Night fell fast.

In the last few hours I had come across some of my friends and colleagues: Zorzi, Antonini, Bellini, and a few others. They told me that our much beloved Major Bellini,[††] commander of the Sixty-first Battalion, hadn't managed to make it here. Was he dead? Had he been taken prisoner? No one knew. He had last been seen the morning of December 21 at Pozdnyakov shortly before the fiasco in which members of the same column had fired at each other.

Poor dear major! During the summer, without so much as a word to me, he had deftly taken my defense against a dangerous report by the postal censorship that dubbed me as "anti-German". He had then sent for me and taken me vehemently to task for being so imprudent, urging me in no uncertain terms to use at least a shred of common sense when writing home.

I can see him now, in my mind's eye, as he was at the beginning of the retreat: in his smart beaver greatcoat, a blanket over his shoulders, his pale gray balaclava, and his cane in his hand. I remember his fatherly voice: *"Oh, ragazzo . . . ,"* the two words with which he habitually addressed me.

If only he could return one day!

Second Lieutenant Silvi, a Tuscan who belonged to the Third Battery, was also missing, as was Captain Rossitto, commander of the First, and several other officers.

[††]Tr. note: In this account the author refers to two men bearing the same first and surname: his fellow second lieutenant Mario Bellini (also see Author's Notes 19 and 23) and his commanding officer.

We exchanged this news with hardly a word of comment. "Where can they be now?" we thought, and then: "Sooner or later it will be our turn . . . ."

I had set about looking for a place near some house where I could lie down and sleep. I was exhausted. I hadn't given myself a moment's rest that day either.

Near a stable that was being used as an infirmary (another little "infirmary", in the precincts of German headquarters), I saw some men around me fling themselves to the ground; this was immediately followed by the hissing of *katyusha* shells.

I too flung myself to the ground. For the first time I found myself within the strip of the explosions. As I've said, sixteen shells in about two hundred meters: I heard a longer explosion, then a shorter one, another, then another again—all of them incredibly powerful. The earth trembled; it was like an earthquake. It seemed the explosions would never end; I desperately commended my soul to God.

I rose unscathed.

In the darkness, the exploding *katyusha* shells were scattering innumerable small golden spheres about them, like huge drops of incandescent matter. This distinguished them easily from every other kind of projectile.

10

Eventually, I lay down on the beaten snow by the isba that housed German headquarters, among a host of other Italians, and tried to sleep in the insane cold.

Zorzi and Antonini, also in search of a place, joined me: the former, solid and cheerful; the latter, tall and lean.

Antonini lay down beside me. But staying still like that only made the cold more and more unbearable. The thin, appallingly freezing breeze continued to grow in intensity, and when a wind is coupled with low temperatures, the torment is double.

Suddenly I could stand it no longer. I got back on my feet and wandered off in search of a place that offered some kind of shelter.

I was walking amid an expanse of dead men.

There was reason to envy them: rigid as they were, like blocks of ice, they no longer felt the devastating struggle against the cold. I remembered the haystack with its innumerable wounded, standing above the village, and made my way toward it; there, possibly, I would find somewhere to bed down.

In a smaller stack, in deep niches hollowed out of the straw, there were some sleeping Germans. There was still some room there . . . But just try disturbing them.

Nearby, on the road, a German was bickering with some Italians over a large horse, insisting that it was a German breed. At first our soldiers succeeded in not giving it away to him, but then the German returned with some comrades, and they led it away. I didn't know what to say: it did in fact belong to a breed (which we called *normanno*) that was far more common in northern Europe than in Italy. I didn't as yet know how the Germans conducted themselves with stuff of ours that had somehow or other landed up in their hands.

In the big haystack I found a place of refuge from the wind, on the edge of the expanse of wounded men.

I laid a little straw on the snow, sat down, took off my shoes and socks, stuffed the socks into my shoes and, to make sure they weren't stolen, put the latter under the straw by way of a cushion; then lay down and pulled the blanket up over me. On top of the blanket I put more straw: this made the cold a bit more bearable.

I tried to doze off.

The sky overhead was smothered in darkness; the glares and noises of our war, still rising here and there, scarcely licked it.

A few meters away, harnessed to empty sleighs, there were some horses, resembling statues of flesh immersed in the suffering of the cold.

Suddenly one of them came up to me and started laboriously munching the straw that was covering me.

To drive it off, I gave its dark muzzle, with its snow-blotched nostrils, a violent punch, then tried to rearrange the straw over me.

The muzzle returned, and I dealt it another punch.

Back it came; more punches.

Any pain it may have felt from my blows obviously counted for little beside hunger and starvation.

Eventually I dragged its creaking sleigh a few paces farther off, and fell asleep.

This was short-lived enough; I woke with my teeth chattering violently. I was shaking with cold, like a twig: the horse had consumed my entire blanket of straw.

Enraged, I was about to kill the animal, which, by waking me, had sent me back into that torment. The only thing that stopped me was the thought that it was to be used to transport the wounded.

Meanwhile, other men were turning up there to sleep. Some soldiers had scaled the haystack and were throwing the straw down on the ground. The surface area of prostrate bodies was fast growing.

Quite near me, between two men in a long row of wounded, there seemed to be a vacant space: hidden there under the straw lay another wounded man—by the looks of it in the direst condition. Some of the newcomers noticed this apparently empty place and made a dash for it, leaping onto the wounded man, who screamed in agony and cursed them. This happened several times that night.

Once or twice, one of the sleighless horses standing beside the others tried to get near the straw in order to eat it, and, scared by the tossing and wailing bodies beneath its hooves, bolted forward over the heap of wounded men.

The freezing wind gathered force again. You could now hear it whistling. Then the snow began falling in cross-gusts. Some people claim that when it rains it isn't cold; but this cold was of a monstrous intensity.

Some must have been dying of it.

I kept picturing the wounded down there in the village clustered around the infirmary hut. Most of them were utterly exposed to that devastating wind. And they had practically no straw to cover themselves: what little they had was all under them, to keep their bodies out of contact with the snow.

I felt duty-bound to make at least three or four journeys down there, with men carrying straw, to give them some kind of covering.

But the idea of getting up, putting on those shoes, and those socks, which were now reduced to small blocks of ice, was more than I could bear.

I was still in this state of indecision when Zorzi, Antonini, and several others from the Thirtieth Brigade turned up. They too were seeking a place of shelter against the wind.

I suggested to Zorzi that we take the straw to the wounded. He replied wearily that he was mortally tired and simply didn't feel up to it.

We tried to sleep again.

But I was unable to sleep. Thoughts and reflections, quite different from, if not the opposite of, my earlier ones, suddenly began to well up and gain ground in my mind, making me radically rethink my previous approach to things. Enough with busying yourself helping others . . . this retreat of ours was no longer a retreat: it was a series of desperate attempts to flee the slaughter that had already claimed most of us . . .

Eventually, after careful reflection, I decided that I would spare myself as much as possible and at least save my own skin.

I still ruefully recalled the ardor that had inspired me before we began that horrible retreat. Twice I had been recommended for gold medals in the field.[7] Had the retreat begun two weeks later, those medals would have been mine. How certain of myself I felt at the time (and that was just a few days earlier!): "mathematically" certain. Since the beginning of the campaign, the determination to do my duty at any cost had seemed unshakable. It was with this determination that I had risked my neck several times and in several circumstances.

And now here I was having to recognize that there is something stronger than death: there are many dead men, one after the other . . . there are ten, one hundred dead men in succession.

A man can die once, even more than once; but he cannot continue to die, endlessly. If he is a man.

I've no desire to justify myself. Certainly, selfishness got the upper hand that night, and the memory is still here with me. But I also found it harder to pray, after making that decision.

Nevertheless, I probably owe my survival at Arbuzov to that decision. And by surviving, I was able, when we were away from there, to save many lives.

For everything follows the law of Providence, which, in times of greatest trial, leads men by the hand as if they were children.

Finally, I fell asleep.

After a few hours I woke up again. My teeth were still chattering, and I was shivering impossibly with cold. Others around me, tired though they were, couldn't get to sleep either. I began talking to a man lying beside me: quite an educated lad, from the stores back on the supply lines. He thought I was a simple soldier, and we conversed for a while as equals.

This too helped keep me going.

The breeze was hissing, driving incessant spirals of horribly cold darkness in that seemingly endless night.

I fell asleep again.

It must have been close to dawn when I was awakened by the sudden din of men shouting: "The Russians are coming . . . They're practically at the haystack."

All the unwounded (hundreds by now) were getting furiously to their feet. Many were already hurriedly leaving that mantrap.

I put on my shoes as fast as I could, catching my breath at the imminent prospect of possible death.

I couldn't find one of my four socks (when I later had the chance to inspect the three I had put on, I found that none of them matched: this still baffles me; not only that, but the heels were missing from all of them, so that the heels of my feet touched the leather of the shoe, which was like metal).

I grabbed my musket and sprang up to see what was happening. I had two hand grenades in my pocket: I checked that they were still there.

Finally, I realized that it was a false alarm.

It was still dark. Like a few other gray figures, I went down into the village and wandered among the houses, the sleepers, and the dead, waiting for dawn.

Dawn lost no time in coming.

So I hastened to the infirmary hut surrounded by wounded men.

*

Over the wounded, over their rigid blankets, their overcoats and furs, a light layer of powdery snow had formed.

Some of them, by tossing and turning, had partly broken it up.

But the snow that was intact, and the absolute immobility of the others, confirmed what I had feared: in the course of the night many of them had been transformed into pieces of ice.

I lifted some of them from the blankets and overcoats that also covered their heads: their faces appeared petrified into the yellowness of frozen human flesh.

I remember one of those dead men. Wounded in the belly, he had been bandaged up as well as possible. He probably hadn't been able to move, and whoever had bandaged him hadn't bothered to readjust his clothes, so the middle of his body had been left naked. He must have started freezing from the belly.

I removed—and got others to remove—the blankets and overcoats of the dead, to distribute to the living who were themselves awaiting death.

The soldiers were loath to perform such an operation; I was forced to threaten them with my pistol to get them to obey me.

I myself set about stripping some of the corpses that were lying among the most nearby houses in the village. This was an arduous business, because their arms had become rigid as ice: beneath my insistent tugging the corpses rocked stiffly.

Those fur coats greatly attracted me, for I still lacked one, but I managed to refrain from keeping even one for myself: I took them all to those poor wretches who, seeing them in my hands, cried out for them and, unable to move, haggled over them, shouting through clenched teeth.

I then thought it necessary to better organize the distribution of drinking water. Some of the soldiers were already distributing it on their own initiative, carrying canvas buckets back and forth from the trucks to a nearby well. I got things organized, and before long everyone had as much drinking water as he wanted.

I walked among the wounded, distributing the water myself with a small mess tin. It was so cold that the metal stuck to the men's lips, and it was agony tearing it free.

Many, possibly delirious from fever, were shouting at me to give them the thick brown water. I gave each as much as he wanted.

As I bent over them, I told them that the armored columns would soon be arriving, together with columns of trucks that would carry all of them away.

How they longed for those panzers to arrive! How they hoped! How many of them died with that last hope in their hearts! But the panzers never arrived.

I tried covering some of the wounded with a little straw (what I found lying on the snow between the men); then I left the infirmary hut and once again took to wandering around the village.

11

With the light the enemy shells had returned with a vengeance; their heavy arms had once again started to slaughter us.

I have a hazier memory of that morning than of the others. I spent it wandering back and forth between the houses and in the environs of the village, one moment vainly seeking something to eat, the next fleeing an area under particularly heavy fire.

Many of our trucks that had made it this far, and were by now all earmarked for the wounded, eventually used up all their gasoline by continually switching positions in this way.

Above us, on the slope above Arbuzov, I found General X's abandoned Alfa Romeo. I rummaged ravenously through it and found to my surprise, in the empty trunk, a small can of meat in a state of almost complete conservation. I shared that meat with someone; I don't remember whom.

Several times the Germans formed into columns; but these broke up after a while. What on earth was going on?

When I asked one of them whether the panzers were about to arrive, he replied with a glum expression: "Malo banzin!" ("There's little gasoline!").

That day saw one of the *katyusha's* most successful massacres. Every twenty or thirty minutes I heard the characteristic hissing of the shells coming our way, and one after the other we saw, swift as lightning, the smoky cinders of the explosions. They pounded away particularly at the row of isbas connecting the larger agglomeration of houses in Arbuzov with the smaller one.

Some of these isbas caught fire.

In the afternoon the enemy was forced to give us a bit of respite because several times in the sky above us the German triple-engined planes appeared, parachuting material down to us.

Each aircraft dropped six large, shell-shaped bundles; the planes circled over the valley a few times, then departed.

We watched those aircraft avidly: we found their form and color repugnant and alien, like the uniforms of the German soldiers. But they did at least hold out some hope for us: so each time they appeared we greeted them joyously, eager to see others.

The Germans fired flares into the air with their signaling pistols, but more, I think, as an expression of joy than out of need.

The planes dropped gasoline as well.

If only the familiar outline of some Italian plane had come into sight! If only the slightest thing had been dropped for us! But nothing. Not until we got to Chertkovo were we to see a single aircraft of ours.

That afternoon a fairly numerous succession of German planes flew over. Unfortunately, some parachutes failed to open, so a number of the dummy bombs full of ammunition exploded and plummeted to earth.

This happened in one place where there was a particularly large number of Italians. There was a fearsome cloud of smoke. Word had it that a general and a number of colonels had been killed; from what I was to learn later, a colonel and three or four other senior officers had been killed.

All hell broke loose again among the mass of men.

✼

I again ran into Mario Bellini, my friend from Assisi.

From the beginning of the retreat he had been wearing a dark green balaclava, sporting a tassel of the same color. That tassel made me think of carefree skiing races back in our distant homeland: it was hard to believe that such happy moments had ever existed.

Bellini's face, with its strong Roman profile, was severe; he was tall and robust. We had attended the same officers' training course at Moncalieri, after which we had been posted to the same depot, then sent together to Russia. On our way to the front we had fallen out with each other, and this antagonism had persisted until the days of the great battle on the Don. In that battle Bellini had been recommended for a silver field medal.

On meeting again, at the time my battalion was being drawn up, after months of not seeing each other, we had exchanged no more than a cold handshake. That day, however, both his observation post and the battalion to which I was attached were routed by the enemy: suddenly, grief at what had happened had thrown us into one another's arms. And that had mended our friendship.

Now we walked side by side and, our hands in our pockets, our blankets over our shoulders, began walking through the village, speaking slowly to each other. The cold, intense though it was, seemed disposed to concede us a bit of respite.

Eventually we took the road trampled by countless feet across the snow, which skirted the long string of isbas—which I have mentioned several times—and connected the main agglomeration of houses in Arbuzov with the smaller one.

The road was very wide and went slightly uphill. In front of us a pale specter of sun was now setting, just at the top of the slope.

Occasionally we passed some burning isbas that had been hit by the *katyushas*. In the surrounding snow, but mainly on the road, dead men were lying. They had been dead for two days, for one day, not long anyway. Those who had died less recently were encrusted with frozen snow; small heaps of gray rags, robbed of all human form; at times you needed to take a close look at them to realize that they had once been men. Then you could make out their faces, blackish and rigid, with a strange rigidity produced by an amalgam of death and ice.

The bayonet attack had passed this way too: in several places Russian corpses lay mingled with Italian ones, but how the Italians outnumbered them! The odd Russian Maxim machine gun still stood in the middle of the road, its dead gunners still manning it. Behind it were groups of Italians who had been mowed down as they threw themselves into attack. Some had their bayonets fixed in position.

There was, I remember, a Blackshirt lying on the ground on top of his musket that had its bayonet fixed, face down in the snow, but at such an angle as to be visible. In the unspeakable inhumanity of that sunset on the immense stretch of snow and corpses, that soldier, fearsome though he must have been in the attack, had lost every semblance of fearsomeness. I bent over to take a look at him, then drew back a little.

So small in that limitless setting, he seemed to express a timid, immense lament.

I spoke to Bellini about these dead men. Just how many of them were there by now? We were both deeply upset. And back there in the distant *patria*, nobody knew of their sacrifice. We of the army in Russia lived out our tragedy while the radio and newspapers went

77

on about something else altogether. It was as if the entire nation had forgotten us.

During the morning word went around that all the Russian prisoners had been shot by the Germans. The Italians alone had taken more than two hundred prisoners in the bayonet attacks of the previous day.

I later heard that these rumors were true and was given the details. The prisoners were lined up in rows of ten by the Germans, then a soldier shot them with a machine pistol, more often than not in the head.

To my knowledge, not a single Russian prisoner captured during the tragic retreat was spared.

The favorite spot for those massacres was a little ravine just outside the village, though many were killed in other places as well.

We came across some of them during our sad march.

I remember a Russian boy in a soldier's uniform who couldn't have been more than about fifteen or sixteen years old, lying by one of the isbas on the edge of the road. He had been reduced by now to a piece of ice: supine, legs and arms raised and splayed out, his round face turned skyward, his eyes open and crystallized by the cold. A thread of congealed blood near his temple showed where the bullet that had killed him had penetrated.

I stopped to look at him: he too, like the Blackshirt I had come across shortly before—indeed, more so—seemed to emit a terrible cry of protest against the monstrousness of war. In him I seemed to see the entire Russian people, who for so many years had groaned and suffered pain unimaginable to us. That poor little Russian soldier!

Others too, no older than the Russian boy, had been taken prisoner. Those who witnessed their murder by the Germans told me that they too, like their older companions-in-arms, stood there with heads held high and faces fierce beneath their fur helmets. Yet their eyes betrayed fear and a desperate regret.

In the depth of my heart my dislike of the Germans grew; it was fast becoming a dumb, persistent rage. I had difficulty in obeying God's commandments and not giving way to hatred.

It must be said, however, that during those days the Russians of the Red Army treated their prisoners in the same way—not a single German was spared by them, and Italians too at times met the same fate.

It was extremely painful for us—for we were, when all is said and done, civilized men—to be caught up in that savage clash between barbarians.

If only here at least, at Arbuzov, the Germans had spared the prisoners! By now we were almost convinced we would fall into enemy hands and that by conducting ourselves like that we were digging our own graves . . .

Bellini and I walked on as far as the highest part of the village, then made our way slowly back.

The day was dying above the mauve-colored snow of that vale of tears.

Once again the cold began to torment us.

We passed the dead Russian boy again, and again I seemed to hear his cry of protest.

When we got to the main agglomeration of houses in the village, we went in search of a corner to sleep in because darkness had fallen.

12

I don't know where it was that I first lay down. I know that after a short time, driven by the cold, I resumed my wandering. I met Bellini again, and he told me about a fairly well-sheltered place on a patch of open ground in the village, which he had just come from. We went back there together, lay down again, and were gray, immobile figures in the dark, on the snow, among so many others.

We were soon on our feet again, because the torment of the snow prevented us from falling asleep.

We began to think, and to tell each other, that in the smaller agglomeration of Arbuzov, which we had left shortly before, it might be possible to find a place in one of the isbas. Besides, there were large haystacks into which we might be able to stow ourselves.

This thought took root in us, becoming, with the mounting cold, an obsession.

We joined the road again near the higher part of Arbuzov.

Night had fallen. Nevertheless, the reddish-blue fires of the still-blazing houses lit our way.

Their glare also played on the dead stretched out on the snow; but we no longer looked at them, absorbed as we were with the struggle to keep ourselves alive.

We arrived. Italians lying all over the place, out in the open. Around the haystacks, a lot of Germans.

We wandered in the darkness from one isba to another, attempting to enter them. In vain. They were all crowded.

We were falling to pieces from fatigue.

From a hut, we could hear the monotonous moaning of a Russian child, wounded for all we knew: *"Papi, troski vodì . . ."* ("Daddy, a little water . . . Daddy, a little water . . . Daddy, a little water . . .").

Through a slit in the door a small sliver of warm, faint light filtered; but it was impossible to open the door, since it was blocked by too many bodies of our compatriots lying on the floor, enveloped in a dreadful sleep.

After repeated, useless attempts, we remained where we were in the snow with our feet near that semblance of warmth, eyes closed, heads bowed.

And still there was that interminable moaning.

It wouldn't stop.

It wouldn't stop.

I kept pressing my frozen, creaking blanket over my head and over my shoulders.

Several meters farther on, we took refuge in a hole in the ground, under something that was, I seem to remember, the roof of a small henhouse.

I have a very hazy memory of what subsequently happened—part of it I don't remember at all. I moved off after a few hours, leaving my blanket behind me on the ground: I was in the grips of fever. Mario told me that I suddenly broke into a run; I was heading unwittingly toward the Russians, and Mario was barely able to catch up with me and restrain me.

I was trying to argue with him and raving like a madman.

Then, for some reason, we lost sight of each other.

I remember wanting at all costs to sleep with a bit of straw over me to protect me in some manner from the cold.

On a wagon I found a blanket, which I picked up to replace the one I had lost, then wandered off into the dark between the houses and the haystacks.

I lost all sense of direction.

I was joined by a soldier who claimed to know these places; before long he too had lost his bearings.

Finally, we found some straw on the ground, near some slumbering Germans. We lay down; I took off my shoes and socks and, huddling under the blanket and a bit of straw, managed to fall asleep.

It was fearfully cold that night, worse even than the preceding nights, and our resistance was much diminished.

*

When I got up in the morning, it was still pitch-dark. Every trace of delirium had vanished, though, and my mind had cleared again.

By my calculations, it was Christmas Day; so I took it as such, even though I knew that most of the others were of the opinion that Christmas was the following day. We had lost track of the days.

In the hours before first light, as I walked on to keep myself from freezing, I prayed with extreme fervor.

Way off in the valley, tracer bullets quivered through the darkness in quick succession.

Every so often I thought of my house and of the familiar color of winter on its walls early in the morning.

Yes—my little brothers would soon be crying with joy at finding their presents around the Crib. And even my father would have lost his patriarchal sternness: I could see him laughing together with them. Then off they would all go to Mass and then gather in the warmth of our large living room. How warm it always was in our large living room, in winter.

Would I ever see my house again?

Little by little I began to be troubled more than anything else by the thought of how grief stricken my mother would be should I fail to return. And I made this the subject of my prayer to the Madonna, the Madonna of the Wood, who is the Madonna of my people: Let no such sorrow be inflicted on my mother.

And so, as I strode over the beaten snow, I prayed and struggled all the while against the cold.

I wasn't the least bit worried about the previous night's fever, since I felt that my mind was still in one piece.

In any case we men are mere trifles in the hands of Providence.

The memory of Italy returned to my mind. You need to have been far away from it to realize just how beautiful it is and, above all, how fit it is for living in. Memories and reflections came and went (the Riviera, its heat . . .). Then, as usual, I succeeded in banishing such thoughts.

Somewhere or other a soldier from the Thirtieth, whom I didn't know, had found half a Parmesan cheese. He came up to me as light broke, with a throng of men in tow, and asked me to divide that precious piece of food.

I immediately began distributing it. The cheese had hardened in the cold, so I placed it on the beaten snow and started knifing off pieces with a bayonet. At any other time I would have found its smell unbearable, but now . . .

82

Suddenly some men came by, telling us that there were orders for everyone to parade down in the village.

I stopped distributing the cheese.

I started once again halfway down the long, corpse-strewn sloping road because there were just too many eyes gazing longingly at the food.

I did my best to respect the soldier's wish, by giving it only to members of the Thirtieth.

At a certain point the soldier wanted what was left, to take away with his friends. So I broke off a piece for myself and a bigger one for the colonel and the other officers; this I gave to an artillery man from my patrols who had been following me for some ten minutes: he was a taciturn lad, with large dark eyes, who had proved invaluable to me at Abrosimovo on the Don during the battle. He was the bravest of my new soldiers—an Emilian. I think his name was Clementi.

As I walked on, I ate the portion I had saved for myself; meanwhile, I thanked God the Father for having sent me the daily bread I had asked for shortly before.

Down in the village we found everything in a state of movement; rumor had it that we were about to depart.

I shuddered at the thought of having to abandon so many hundreds of wounded men on the snow to the mercy of the ruthless enemy.

I went to the "dressing station" located near German headquarters to see whether any of my old companions, my *vecchi*, officers or men, were there.

As I wandered among the wounded and the dead, I asked loudly: "Is there anyone from the Thirtieth Artillery?" No one replied.

I was on my way out when I heard someone call my name: "*Signor tenente!*"

I turned around and saw, outside the shack, among the other wounded men, a small fair-haired soldier whose face was vaguely familiar: "*Signor tenente*, I've been hit! Lucky you, always up there in the line among the firing, and still in one piece!"

His voice too was familiar, even though I couldn't identify him. "But who are you?" "I'm the *Caporalino*, the new wireless operator from the Second Battery," and he told me his name, which I can't remember now. At this point I recognized him; I had, in fact, been the one to dub him with that hardly very original nickname of *Caporalino*.

My first thought was that I must somehow find a way to save him.

83

So I went searching among the sleighs, which, in the turmoil following news of our imminent departure, were moving all over the place. I chanced upon an empty one.

I no longer remember who or what the driver declared that it was intended for. Politely, but with a touch of menace in my voice, I got him to take the *Caporalino* on board; Clementi helped him to the sleigh, while I made sure it stayed where it was.

I ordered Clementi to follow that sleigh "always," and to give the wounded man part of the "officers'" cheese. The *Caporalino* thanked me; he was so moved he could barely get a word out.

From the sleigh he made every effort to smile at me in gratitude, despite the anxiety he must have been in the grip of.

My eyes followed the vehicle as it merged with the others then vanished from sight. Clementi disappeared with the sleigh as well, and I never saw him again.

Needless to say, the colonel and the officers never got their piece of cheese.

Several days later I met up with the *Caporalino* again at Chertkovo. He told me that the sleigh had gotten him as far as a few kilometers from the town; there the mule, or horse, whichever it was, had collapsed in the snow from exhaustion. So with great effort he had done the rest of the journey to the town on foot.

As I recall, he told me that Clementi had stuck admirably to his charge: he hadn't let that sleigh out of his sight for a second.

I left that "dressing station" and went on to the other one near the so-called village infirmary: a small house and stable with a straw-covered earthen floor on which many wounded men were lying in the freezing semidarkness.

Here, and particularly in the stable, great agitation reigned, because these wounded men had gotten wind of the departure preparations. Many were shouting.

We were still under the impression that we would indeed be leaving, but only after the panzers arrived; a column of vehicles were on their way with the panzers to collect the wounded. I repeated this to those desperate men who, tossing about on the straw, were shouting at me not to abandon them but to take them away.

In the ensuing silence, one of them at the back of the stable said: "Let's just hope that's true. Because we know that the Germans have

84

killed all the Russian prisoners. God help us if the Russians take us here, among their dead!"

The infantryman I had wounded in the back on our first day in Arbuzov was also there.

When I called out his name, he recognized me and immediately took to repeating the very same words I had heard three days before: "*Signor tenente*, don't abandon me . . . *Signor tenente*, don't abandon me . . . ."

He was as pop-eyed as ever, possibly more so. And again it occurred to me that, in the throes of delirium, he had been our assailant in the stable.

But had it really been him?

I'll never be able to answer that question: during those days an increasing number of men were going delirious, and many, besides, were going temporarily out of their wits, then reverting to their normal selves. So it was impossible for me to form an opinion based even approximately on that man's psychological state.

Poor fellow! I did all I could to find him a place on a truck or sleigh; but no second miracle occurred: not even a mouse would have found room on the handful of Italian trucks, and the sleighs too were full to overflowing.

Vainly I tried to persuade the Germans to take him onto one of their half-empty sleighs.

In the end I wearily gave up, consoled somewhat by a new order we had received: "Everyone is to move down to the valley bottom among the rushes; do not worry about the wounded; all of them will be picked up."

As soon as we finally left Arbuzov, Providence was to entrust me with an awesome task: to lead hundreds of human lives to safety, that and that alone.

So I didn't keep my promise and abandoned the infantryman.

Since then, occasionally, I can still hear his voice: "*Signor tenente*, don't abandon me!" And then my voice, with its customary self-assurance: "Don't worry, I won't abandon you. When I give somebody my word, I keep it."

✳

I walked heavyheartedly toward the valley bottom. What was afoot?

Crossing an irregular patch of wasteland between the last houses of the village, where the German tanks were assembled, I saw one of those low, gigantic ones (the best)[8] with its gun knocked out by an explosion in the muzzle. The flamethrower, one of its distinguishing features, had disappeared, and the muzzle was splayed open like a lily.

Unfortunately, the number of tanks, on which most of our hopes were pitched, was also diminishing with every day that passed.

When we left the Valley of Death there can only have been five or six left because, from what I gathered, lacking gasoline, some had had their track-supporting hubs cut to make them unoperational and had then been abandoned.

There I was now with numerous other soldiers and officers, among the rushes and on the frozen ponds at the bottom of the valley.

Trucks packed with wounded men followed us across the ice or went to and fro along the road crossing the valley bottom. It was all too clear that their chief drivers had no idea what to do.

Meanwhile, the Russians had started firing again at the village from every direction.

That day too took its toll of dead and wounded.

Katyusha shells exploded among those poor wretches lying on the ground at the dressing posts, ripping apart their already mangled bodies.

The number of frostbite casualties was growing fearfully.

Some men, utterly exhausted by their ceaseless efforts, lack of food, and more still by the murderous cold, were abandoning themselves on the snow to die there in silence.

Hope in the arrival of the panzers had again become faint.

Shots close at hand, too close for comfort.

Billows of smoke from the firing rose violently here and there among the marsh rushes. We saw stripped branches, severed by the shell splinters, falling sadly to the ground.

Inside our skulls, the lacerating blows of the explosions. Again!

We tried to dodge the blows as best we could, shielding ourselves where the land jutted up.

At long last, orders came through loud and clear: "All Italians are to assemble in the wooded *balka* dividing the side of the valley facing Arbuzov."

13

Before long (it was now midmorning) we were there: four or five thousand Italians mustered and lined up as well as could be expected.

This meant that an enormous number, the majority in fact, were still scattered about the main valley.

The mouth of the *balka* (a natural rift in the land) was about one hundred meters wide, around four or five meters deep, and flat-bottomed. Since it twisted and turned we had no way of telling how long it was.

The bayonet attack had passed this way too. There to bear witness to this was a Maxim machine gun abandoned on one of the edges, a black shape against the pallid background of sky. Around it, I seem to remember, lay its dead Russian gunners.

General X summoned all the officers present, division by division. There were about one hundred of us in all.

We hoped he would have some positive news to give us.

Instead, he told us that we had to reorder the regiments and fight until our strength gave out. Maybe the armored columns would show up; maybe they wouldn't show up at all, in which case we were to die fighting.

While the general spoke, some of us, bent more or less double in the grip of the cold, brooded over his words: so we were to die!

When he dismissed us, the various regiments mustered here and there but kept within the *balka,* or gully, between the sparse, bare trees growing there.

There was a coming and going of officers, shouting orders to form up. Then word ran around that we were not to shout, because the enemy was close at hand.

The Thirtieth formed up as well, and I too went back and forth, shouting at first, calling the men to order.

I found myself among people I knew.

All of us, officers and men alike, seemed altered in some manner, crumpled, as it were, by so much strain and suffering. We recognized one another not so much from our appearance as from the mute exchange of looks.

There was Colonel Matiotti, commander of the unit, distinguished as ever, his pale face stubbled white. Major Y was there, the only one of our three battalion commanders.

I was overjoyed to see my Veronese friend Zoilo Zorzi: as always, it was a real comfort being able to exchange a word or two with him.

And there too I again ran into that other friend of mine, Mario Bellini, who teasingly inquired where I had "sleepwalked" off to during the night.

And there were Second Lieutenants and Lieutenants Antonini, Candela, Bona, Zinzi, Maestri, Zavattaro, Bosin, and Trivulzi and Captains Pontoriero, Varenna, and Barcellona.

But how many were not there!

Our major, for one, whose fatherly smile now seemed a distant memory. Missing too was the commander of the Sixty-second Battalion, who had abandoned everybody on December 19 and managed to give the enemy the slip. I was to meet him again only when we were out of the pocket.

Of the second lieutenants of the Sixty-first Battalion the youngest was now missing as well: Palasciano, from Taranto, whose dead body had been seen by several of the men. In a week's time he would have been twenty.

Captain Varenna, from Como, commander of the "ammunition and provisions" unit, had gotten ahold of a large cow with a red and white hide, which one of the soldiers kept tied by the horns. The beast exhaled dense showers of steam from its nostrils; Varenna planned to cook it and ration it out as soon as possible.

The men had no sooner mustered than Colonel Matiotti split them into two classes: armed and unarmed. The numbers more or less balanced.

The armed men were subdivided into four or five platoons of about twenty soldiers each.

The colonel then picked those officers in the fittest condition, putting them in command of the single platoons.

Surviving patrol officers such as Zoilo Zorzi, Mario Bellini, and myself were left in peace.

The patrols made ready to go to the line. The beast in me, which had the upper hand at that moment, was already rejoicing at having been spared along with my friends, when Zorzi suddenly stepped forward and asked the colonel in a low voice if he too could be attached to a platoon.

His rustic Veneto face wore its customary expression—candid as always, modest as always—the same expression, I remembered, with which he put up with the odd gibes of his colleagues because, being a member of *Azione Cattolica*,[†] he disapproved of certain conversations they had.

The colonel granted his request. The platoons left immediately for Arbuzov.

Bellini and I silently watched Zorzi's retreating figure; we never saw him again.

I should like these few, inadequate words to be a *canto* to the memory of Zorzi, the best of the many men I met during those cruel years of war. He was simple in spirit and profound in thought, and he was very much loved by his soldiers. He was also extremely courageous, as befits a man.

For a long time, Zorzi, I kept hoping you might still be alive and your voice re-echo in some remote corner of those endless lands, and I awaited you in silence.

Meanwhile, the snow will have thawed, your clothes lost some of their icy stiffness, and you'll be lying in the mud in these sweet spring days. Sunk too in the mud and decay, your forehead and eyes, which were ever turned heavenward.

I made a vow for your return. We would have gone together to fulfill that vow.[††]

But you didn't return!

Still, I'm convinced that I shall find myself speaking to you on countless occasions in this wretched life. How thin a veil separates this life of mine from yours! We'll walk together again, as we walked together side by side along the pathways of the steppe on those summer days of 1942.

†Tr. note: "Catholic Action".

††Tr. note: The author is referring to a Roman Catholic practice, now largely in disuse, of vowing to impose a specific act of penance on oneself. In fulfillment of his vow, the author would have performed such an act if Zorzi had returned—together with Zorzi himself.

Do you remember how the never-ending, never-changing song of the quail hung in the sun—the voice of the unknown surrounding us?

Today, perhaps, your white bones mingled with the earth and the grass can still hear that rural song, which bewitched us so at the time—and it will seem like someone weeping.

*

When the armed units had left, we received orders to stay in the gully until further notice.

We were not to light fires, nor raise our voices.

As he was on his way with Captain Varenna in search of a suitable place to slaughter the cow, Captain Barcellona, a Sicilian, was stopped by an unknown senior officer and put in charge of a training company.

He departed with that company; we never saw him again.

The ferocious cold wouldn't let up: and though we kept it at bay for a while by shaking ourselves and stamping our feet on the snow, it stubbornly returned to beleaguer us, and we couldn't go on jumping up and down forever.

So, with oppressive sluggishness, what I believed to be Christmas Day dragged by.

The men who had been given the task of slaughtering and cooking the cow came back after a while empty-handed, declaring that they had been robbed of the animal, which they had already cut up into pieces, by Germans and fellow Italians. The former had been high-handed, the latter simply famished.

So there were no rations that day either.

Among the sparse isbas situated only just outside the entrance to the valley, enemy *katyusha* and cannon shells started exploding, making an almighty din. We could hear other shells exploding in more or less every other part of the main valley.

We had congregated into a small group of officers: Pontoriero, Varenna, Bona, Sanmartino, Antonini, Bellini, Candela (the medical officer), and a few others.

Occasionally one of us, overcome by fatigue, sat down in the snow but very quickly got up again. Sometimes we would talk, though the cold made the very act of thinking painful. Since the cold prevented us from taking off our gloves, even the heaviest smokers thought twice before lighting up.

Once again our main concern was: will the panzers come? But we tried not to talk about it.

We were so hungry that we kept imagining things to eat. The most appetizing dishes trooped through our minds: among other things I remembered chocolate, honey, the *torrone*, and the remaining mouthwatering items in the parcels I had received from home, which I had set aside for today—Christmas Day. The Uzbeks had fallen on those. Possibly, together with the sweet stuffs, they had gobbled down the antifreeze fat and even the shoe polish, though this was no cause for merriment.

We then stopped thinking about food and began jumping up and down again. What tormented me most of all were my feet inside their soaking socks.

Meanwhile, the hours dragged by.

On the frozen surface—near the scene of the "great summons", where we still found ourselves—there was a small group of five or six dead Italians next to a mule, which was also dead. They must have been hit by a shell shortly before we got there, for their blood was still fresh: it formed a large pool in the middle of which lay the mule, partly weighting down one of the corpses.

How red that mixture was of human and animal blood! It was the only bright patch of color in the dismal grayness of the surrounding landscape.

Suddenly I came to a decision. I walked up to that tragic company: one of the dead men (a Blackshirt) wore around his neck as a scarf the regulation sash body belt: I slipped it off him, cut it into two equal strips, then returned to my small group of comrades.

Here Lieutenant Sanmartino (who was at the time commanding the Second Battery—a man short in stature) was sitting in the snow pathetically rubbing his feet with antifreeze cream.

I asked him for a little and, taking off my shoes and socks, greased my feet too, then wrapped them in the two strips of sash, and put my shoes back on.

This brought immediate relief.

On the other hand, the bridge of my foot was now aching since, without the sock, it was completely exposed above the shoe. Soon I had no option but to put my soaking socks back on, after strenuously wringing them out.

We tried to focus our conversation on Christmas. I was eventually convinced that I was wrong: Christmas must be the following day.

Every now and then I left my colleagues and walked up and down the gully, then retraced my steps.

At times all hell broke loose among the troops in one or other of the musters because someone thought he had spied the Russians on the edges of the *balka* only to find that they were just other Italians.

The enemy started pounding away at the main valley very close to us, above all with mortar and *katyusha* shells. More often than not these flew just over our heads, exploding only a short way beyond one of the edges of the *balka.*

Meanwhile, more and more men were gazing at the mule with famished eyes. Some went up to it and tore off bits of meat from its ribs with a bayonet.

Since we were still forbidden to light fires, they ate the meat raw; they found it disgusting but still managed to get it down.

I myself drew near, asked to borrow the bayonet, and set about tearing off a small scrap of meat. Gola, the loader of the third Second Battery gun, gave me a hand, smiling in sympathy as he did so. His crew-cut hair (like a toothbrush, pushed down under his balaclava) was hidden, so that his face, which had once been sprightly, now looked tiny and wizened. But he wasn't aware of this and tried to behave as normal—canny-eyed and with his usual composed peasant's gestures.

I carefully beat the meat against the snow, and the result was a sort of frozen, ice-encrusted steak. I started eating it.

"Here," I thought, "are your just deserts for all your overeating at lunches in times like these . . ." When death is at hand, one's sins, even the most venal ones that normally seem altogether insignificant, loom large.

I was increasingly troubled by that dead man's body under the mule's carcass: many had set about tearing off pieces of meat, and its entrails fell on the corpse in clusters, and some of the men, albeit unintentionally, trod on it.

No one would agree to lug it away. So I drew my pistol and compelled two soldiers at gunpoint to give me a hand. As we were doing this, a *katyusha* shell whizzed heavily over our heads, bursting, with an almighty bang, against the edge of the gully no more than a few dozen meters from us.

We all hurled ourselves to the ground: when I got up, after the whistling of the huge fragments had ceased, the two soldiers were nowhere to be seen; they were so repelled by the job I had gotten them to do that they'd scuttled off.

So I forced two others to do it, and, eventually, the dead man was dragged some distance away across the snow. As best we could, we laid the other corpses alongside him.

The most intense cannon and *katyusha* fire was on the land to the side of the gully only a few hundred meters away from us by now.

However, these onrushes of smoke were, we could see, getting closer and closer—so the slaughter was about to begin—then they moved off again.

Just one mortar shell landed in the *balka*, killing several men.

Afternoon.

As I walked back and forth over the snow with the other officers (we were all exhausted and had practically lost all hope; the soldiers likewise) news came that made us almost jump with joy: an NCO, just back from German headquarters, announced that he had been informed that the panzers were only two hours away along the road.

On the innumerable gray forms standing there, one beside the other, waiting (but how many were really waiting?), the hours however continued to pass, and no further news arrived.

No distant sound that might possibly have been the panzers.

At sunset the cold intensified. And right through the day it had been so cold that we'd constantly felt we wouldn't be able to resist for many more minutes.

Darkness fell.

*

In the sole company of Mario Bellini, I again began walking through the *balka*.

Mario suddenly found that he had a few pieces of biscuit in the bottom of his pocket. He took them out one by one and shared halves with me. How grateful I was!

We ate them slowly, but they were soon finished.

93

Tracer bullets began scoring the darkness of the sky. Some entered the gully too, skimming one of its banks, passing among the bare trees, and finishing up in the snow on the opposite slope.

There were some men there, particularly next to a wretched, useless framework of a few dry branches built for a senior officer. That utterly useless structure had the semblance of a house, which possibly explained why it was continually attracting men around it.

Suddenly we heard a cry coming from that direction: someone had been hit in the stomach. There was no hope for him. He groaned loudly for some time, calling his mother's name, then was heard no more.

Again we needed to find somewhere to sleep.

I had in mind an isba with a haystack next to it, which stood just outside the gully. Next to it there was an underground storeroom (a common feature of Ukrainian houses), where I knew there was a family. What if the two of us bedded down there as well?

How wonderfully warm it must be down there!

But . . . what if the panzers were to arrive in the meantime?

We eventually decided to abandon the idea of the storeroom and to content ourselves with fetching some straw from the haystack.

Providence again came to our aid: for that night, in fact, the column was to silently form up again and depart.

As we were setting off, all hell broke loose among a group of men.

I went over to see what was going on. A tall soldier, whose arms were being held by the others, was loudly protesting his innocence. In front of him a corporal, who claimed to have escaped from Russian hands, was excitedly declaring that he had seen the soldier mixing with the enemy on friendly terms: so he must be a spy.

The soldier (who, judging by the way he spoke, was from Varese) suddenly shouted that he belonged to such and such a battalion of the Thirtieth Artillery. So I questioned him. What he had to say was so astounding that I sent for Major Y, commander of that battalion.

The soldier repeated to the major that it was true he had been a prisoner of the Russians. He was one of an enormous column of captured Italians (five thousand, if I remember correctly), who had been told by the Russians that they were to be taken to Millerovo, loaded onto trains, and sent to work on the supply lines.

(Millerovo in Russian hands? Mario Bellini and I exchanged glances: if the Russians had gotten that far, then we were done for. We didn't believe him. Yet what he said was true: the enemy had gotten as far as Millerovo and was about to surround and besiege it. It was a good thing we didn't know this.)

The soldier continued his tale. Suddenly the guards had opened fire on the Italians. "There were thousands of them, *signor maggiore*," the soldier cried to Y, "and they were all killed. Do you know, I saw Captain . . ." (his name escapes me, but he was from the Sixtieth Battalion) "drop dead, with a bullet, here, in his head."

He claimed that he had managed to save himself only because there was a friend of his with the Russians, from the same battalion, whom he had grabbed ahold of and used as a shield against the Bolshevik who wanted to kill him. They had let him go on the understanding that, when he got back to us, he would become a spy. There were other traitors from his battalion with the Russians. But now, he said, he intended to remain loyally with the Italians.

As he was telling us all this, the other soldiers around us shouted that they wanted to lynch him. He was terrified of the other soldiers.

Was he delirious? Or was he telling the truth?

Bellini and I didn't know what to think. Today, now that I've learned from survivors of Russian imprisonment that a good many Italian prisoners met this fate, it seems likely that he was telling the truth.

I took Y to one side and reported the episode that had befallen me three days before, when the soldier had fired at us in the stable.

The major said to me: "I really don't know what to think. One thing is certain, though: before long we'll end up in Russian hands, and we'll all be killed. I'll keep an eye on this man; at the last minute I'll 'give' him a bullet through the head. After all, even if he isn't a spy, he'll be killed in any case."

And, for that evening at any rate, the episode was over.

Many days later Bellini told me how things had ended. Y had had second thoughts and had taken the soldier along to General X. Since the column was full of delirious men with a mania for being spies, the general, hearing that he had been a normal enough lad before the retreat, had ordered his release. The soldier had then asked Y for a written declaration certifying his good conduct and the impossibility of his being a spy. If he wasn't given that declaration, he had said, he would return to the Russians.

Y refused. So he went off and was never seen again.[9]

❊

After this small to-do, silence had returned to the gully among the frozen, black tree trunks. Men lay here and there on the snow in the hundreds. Others, just as many, were still on their feet.

In some of the groups men were murmuring to each other. I heard someone say: "Ah! If instead of these barbarous beasts we had the English around us! Who would think twice about giving himself up? . . ."

The odd gray figure wandered about in the dark, seeking a less turbulent corner to sleep in.

With Bellini, I reached a haystack situated just outside the mouth of the *balka*.

We had words with the Germans, who didn't want us to take the straw: for all they cared, we might just as well die, so long as they were not disturbed.

We returned to the gully with our two blankets full of straw.

Part of it we laid on the glassy ice of the stream. Then we too lay down, pulling our blankets over us, and on top of the blankets the rest of the straw. I had learned to place my wet socks next to my body, under my tunic, to avoid waking up and finding them reduced to small blocks of ice.

We fell asleep huddled against each other.

This, for the record, was Christmas Eve—the real one.

14

It wasn't long before we woke up. It was bitterly cold.

While we were sleeping, someone had stolen the straw that was on top of our blankets.

We tried to settle down again and, still huddled against each other, managed to get back to sleep.

A short time later we woke up again because the monstrous cold was making us shiver from head to toe.

With the blankets over our shoulders, we walked back and forth in the darkness for a while, bearing our painful exhaustion, limbering up in order to recover some warmth.

I made a promise to the Madonna (not in the form of a vow, though, for I no longer trusted myself) that, if she allowed me to return home, she would inspire the whole of my future life.

And it is partly to keep that promise that I am writing now.

The hissing of *katyushas*.

We flung ourselves face down in the snow. Some of the shells burst with a furious roar in the gully around us: the darkness was filled with those small incandescent spheres racing through the sky. "Lord help me!" But my mouth was gagged.

One shell burst almost directly on us, so near that we were showered, particularly on our heads, by a mixture of snow and topsoil.

At last we got up again; we tried to smile at each other.

When we got back to where we had left it, all the straw was gone.

We managed to fall asleep seated on the large shrubs that had been arranged in some manner on the snow.

At about nine we woke up again. The cold was so bitter that I felt I was going mad.

Again we got to our feet. And it was then that an officer, with a strange air about him, approached us, saying he had a "grave suspicion" to communicate. Then and there I thought he must be delirious. Hadn't another approached us a few hours ago with the same queer expression, to ask us if he was an officer or a simple soldier? He complained of having a ring around his head that robbed him of his memory. Like many infantry subalterns he wore no stars, but the identity card we found on him said he was a lieutenant.

"If you want my opinion," he said, "the Germans have gone, abandoning the Italians!"

I was sorely tempted to give him a rough answer.

Since we were on our feet in any case, and had to keep moving to warm up, Bellini and I decided to check this out. We headed out of the gully, toward the haystack where we knew that a German squad was sleeping.

Here, to our consternation, we found that the officer's suspicions were justified: the Germans were gone.

Only it wasn't fair to say they had abandoned us, because most of our compatriots had gone with them.

But this we were to learn only a few hours later.

*

Abandoned!

About fifteen hundred men were left in our gully, but all or almost all were either weaponless or without ammunition.

What a massacre we were in for in a while . . .

In front of the valley mouth, whiter than the snow around it, ran a track of beaten snow.

Every so often some stray soldier passed along it: he didn't speak, but the light, regular sound of his hurried steps lingered mysteriously in the air behind him.

Two Germans in their white uniforms appeared; one was limping.

I stopped them and demanded: "Where are your comrades?" whereupon one of them burst into tears and replied: *"Camarad cicai . . . camarad cicai . . ."* ("Our comrades have gone").

Down there, in front of us, an impenetrable silence hung over the village of Arbuzov.

We tried to penetrate the darkness with our eyes, but all we could make out was the red glow of some isolated burning hut and its sober halo reflecting on the snow.

Bellini and I resolved without more ado to wake all the officers who were in the gully and work out a plan of action with them.

Soon, when word had gotten around, we had formed a group of seven or eight officers. Only one of these was a senior officer: an infantry major, a thin, lean, old fellow whom the cold seemed to have reduced to a state of complete dotage.

The only other officer from the Thirtieth Brigade, besides Bellini, was Candela, the medical officer from my battalion. Of Y and the others, who had been there at nightfall, there was not a sign.

The old fellow refused to believe what we told him. He asked Bellini and me to accompany him to "divisional headquarters", which meant a house in the village where, he claimed, General X resided.

We set off, leaving the gully once again; but as we were joining the road at the valley end, we suddenly heard, coming from the village, directly ahead of us, the deafening rattle of rifle and machine-gun fire: "*Urrà . . . Savoia . . . Urrà.*"

Then silence.

Then, once again, shouting and firing from other parts of the village.

The Russians were overrunning Arbuzov, and there at least some of the Italians were trying to fight it out to the bitter end.

Possibly Zorzi was there.

The major finally realized that our proceeding was pointless.

On the road there was a German truck that had been abandoned shortly before: some soldiers, who had followed us, jumped onto it to rummage for food. We too managed to procure a long half-loaf of bread, which Mario and I shared between us, and to fish some preserved meat out of big cans. We spread a thick layer of meat on the bread and avidly tucked into it.

Our ruined eyes gleamed with satisfaction.

The major, himself intent on eating out of one of the cans, was in no state to concern himself with anything else for the time being. Poor old fellow!

We went back into the gully where the other officers were awaiting us. No one knew what to do. Many terrified soldiers came thronging around us. Time was running out; a decision had to be made. So I put the major on the spot: "You can choose: Either we all move to the edges of the gully, or we fight it out; or else we too try to force a passage southwest."

All the major could think about was his stomach.

A very young captain snapped: "Cut it out! It's obvious by now that we must all die. At least let's die fighting!" And he started shouting: "Those who don't want to die without defending themselves, come with me."

He set off for the mouth of the gully, and there took up position with some two hundred men and possibly some NCOs as well.

*

Those of us officers remaining began discussing a plan of action. As we did this, we slowly made our way back up the valley.

Mario argued that we should form into a column and head southwest. We objected on the grounds that we didn't have a single compass and were practically unarmed.

The major followed behind our small group of subalterns, meek and silent as a lamb; we were also followed by about one hundred soldiers.

All the others, more than one thousand, were lying on the snow in black flocks. A good many, exhausted and utterly deprived of willpower, kept their dark faces raised toward us as they watched us go by.

The gully, all bends and zigzags, was slowly getting narrower. It was only then that we realized it was several kilometers long.

We walked on, shrouded in a ghastly silence.

The beaten surface beneath our feet told us that others had come this way, perhaps not long before us.

I did my bit to ensure that we made for what was certainly a German battery. On coming out of the main valley, this battery suddenly started firing a rearguard barrage back in the direction of Arbuzov—the flames bursting forth as it fired lit up the sky in the very place our feet seemed to be carrying us.

All was white and opaque in the dead of night; only at those points where the gully walls were steeper could we discern the dark hue of the exposed earth.

My thought was all prayer.

Eventually the walls became very low, and the gully came to an end.

On emerging, we encountered first one, then other Italian soldiers incapable of following us, lying dejected on the edge of a wide track of beaten snow.

By pure chance, we had found ourselves on the road the column had taken! What is more, the column was very close! As we later learned, it had halted a few kilometers farther ahead.

In my heart my pity for those poor creatures lying there on the ground struggling uselessly against death was stifled by a frenetic exultation at what their being there signified.

I know how swimmers must feel when, dragged again and again under the waves, finally, when they have lost all hope, they find something to cling to!

Meanwhile, we walked on.

And, one and all, our thoughts raced back to the men who had remained there in the gully. But none of us mentioned them.

So in the end I reminded the major about them. But he didn't dare send anyone back.

From Arbuzov, which was well behind us by now, we could now hear the sounds of desperate fighting.

Suddenly I stopped and told the major that someone simply had to be sent back.

"I've already sent an officer," he replied. Then he took a closer look at me and, as if recognizing me for the first time, muttered: "Ah! . . . It's you . . ." and went away without ordering anyone to do anything.

I had to make up my mind.

My whole being rebelled and cried out against such a decision. Try telling a shipwrecked man to abandon the plank he is clinging to, even for an instant!

"Help me, Lord!" By a supreme effort of will, I managed to get a grip on myself: "I'll go."

Mario Bellini took me by the arm, intent on dissuading me.

"We're officers!" I reminded him. He got the better of himself and fell in beside me. Vincenzo Candela, the medical officer, came too: out of a spirit of generosity, unwilling to let us go off alone.

Back we strode through the night, doing our utmost to cover those few kilometers in as short a time as possible.

At last we reached the flocks of men. We shouted and tugged them to their feet and got them to form into columns so they could be dragged away to safety.

The only men now remaining were those two hundred or so stationed at the mouth of the gully with the young captain in the cold silence.

They were four or five hundred meters from us.

I told myself (though how true this was I don't know) that we couldn't go and call them, because if we did the men we had gotten to form up (many of them inert and distinguishable from the dead only by the fact that they were now on their feet) would break ranks again.

In ragged file with the others a soldier was sitting astride a shaggy-coated Russian horse. I made him step out of the column, explained things carefully, and entrusted him with the mission of reaching the young captain.

He pretended to obey and, turning the horse around, set off; but a few days later I learned that he didn't carry out my assignment. And so all those men died.

On the move again; our souls trained on the snow to see if the enemy had—as we very much feared—blocked the road.

At last we were able to get the men following us to merge with the main column, which we finally found—a huge black, immobile blob—on a hillside.

My joy at having once again come through unscathed was mixed with that of having been the instrument chosen by Providence to save so many other human beings: "A thousand men snatched from the grips of death," I said to myself. "Even if I do nothing else in my life, I will already have done enough! . . ." I didn't yet know that my warning had failed to reach the young captain and his company.

*

And that is how we came out of the Valley of Death. The village was semidestroyed, many isbas were ablaze, and many civilians—old people, mothers, children—had been killed in the battle or by the Germans' hatred. Behind us we left a valley strewn with corpses. Along with the Germans who had died from listlessness, and the Russians, who had been lined up here and there in regular files and shot, there were our own dead. Ours, who were far greater in number:

ours who had been killed by enemy bombardment, or had fallen in waves in the bayonet attacks, or had starved to death, or had frozen to death.

Perhaps still more harrowing than the thought of the thousands of dead was that of the hundreds and hundreds of wounded abandoned on the snow, on almost no straw.

I later heard that a chaplain had insisted on staying behind at a dressing station. I vaguely heard his name—Father Celestino, probably of the Fifty-second Artillery Regiment. (I had no idea at the time that this chaplain had already been dead several days, stabbed to death by a Bolshevik while—almost blinded by grenade shrapnel—he was groping his way among the wounded, giving the last rites.) It was also said that his superiors should never have allowed the chaplain to remain, since the Russians were sure to murder him. This was my view too.[10]

I learned as well that many wounded only just able to stay on their feet had desperately attempted to follow the column, so that just outside Arbuzov, for a kilometer or two, the route was littered with poor wretches unable to go any farther.

Reader, do you know what that meant?

Who knows what fate they met . . .

Senni, a second lieutenant from the Eighty-second Torino Infantry Regiment, one of the last out of the village, informed me that fires were rising here and there behind the advancing Russians. And these fires were more or less where our wounded were lying on the straw by the hundreds.

Word also had it that wounded Germans who couldn't be brought away, or hadn't been loaded up, possibly because they were doomed to certain death anyway, had been systematically shot by their officers.

* * *

First with Candela, then on my own, I went in search of the Italian command.

I intended to report on the state of affairs at our rear. My main concern, admittedly, was to escape danger, since I reckoned that, in no time at all, the Russians would engage us.

At the head of the throng of Italians there was Consul Vianini from the Blackshirt M Battalions. He said that our command (which meant General X) was some distance ahead with the German command. There was no way of reaching him.

Thinking back to that night, I have the glimmer of a suspicion that we had been abandoned in the gully quite deliberately, so that, by acting as cannon fodder, we would make things easier for the others to disengage. It was not for nothing that the route followed by the column leaving Arbuzov ran near the gully . . .

I waited motionlessly by the baggage wagons for the column to get moving again.

Particularly in the last few minutes—as I was making for the consul's sleigh—a great deal of snow had gotten into my shoes. I took them off and turned them upside down: each contained half a glassful of water. I wrung out my socks, then put them back on. The cold gripped my feet so much that I found it impossible to stand still.

So I started springing up and down on the snow and stamping my feet—though this was really no more than what I had been doing for days. How much longer would I be able to do this?

Many others were springing up and down like me or clapping their hands together or against their crossed arms; and many were walking a few steps back and forth. Most, though, stayed stock-still, as if bent beneath the weight of the cold.

There was no sign of our leaving.

Then, at last, the enormous mass of men—Germans first, then Italians—got going.

FROM ARBUZOV TO CHERTKOVO

15

At first the cold was so atrocious that I was compelled to keep the blanket over my still capless head and face. So all I was able to see was the beaten snow at my feet.

Walking got our circulation going again, and we suffered less.

All our balaclavas bore masks of ice. The horses and mules proceeded, emitting clouds of steam from their nostrils.

Our pace was very rapid, and we kept it up throughout: in normal circumstances we would have maintained it for only a few hours. But this march was to last three nights and two days.

At a crossroads we discerned in the darkness several bullet-riddled Russian trucks. Around them lay a good many corpses.

I later learned that not long before they had been blocked by German tanks, while blithely taking ammunition to the troops besieging Arbuzov. Not a single Russian escaped the massacre.

Two Italian drivers in partly Russian uniform had been saved, though. Someone who had had the chance to speak to them told me they'd been taken prisoner a short time before and had been immediately enlisted in the enemy army.

Several drivers and a number of other specialists met the same fate. They were not treated badly and were assured that they would be repatriated when the war was over. The Bolshevik army, which largely comprised people of unbelievable ignorance, was sorely lacking in specialists.

Dawn of December 25 was slowly breaking.

Immense, gently sloping plains, usually white with snow, broken here and there by stretches of dried grass.

Throughout the march I kept at the head of the Italian column, behind Consul Vianini's sleigh.

Every so often I fixed my eyes on the sleigh, or the animals or men that were closest at hand, because the landscape, though not flat, had such enormous contours as to overwhelm and oppress one's soul.

When we got to the top of a rise I looked ahead of me at the long, straight, never-ending white line of the German column, then behind me at the black Italian line, which was still longer.

I couldn't help reflecting with horror on how many Italians must have been caught up in this tragedy because those who had been left dead, or dying, and the still greater number dispersed along the roadside far surpassed those who were still marching.

The five or six remaining German tanks took up our flank, leaving wide crawler tracks in the snow. They also patrolled the advance guard.

Hour followed hour, and there we were marching at the same brisk pace.

A thin, tenacious sleet began to fall.

A village—consisting entirely of thatched shacks.

Many men left the column in search of food. Somewhere around there must have been a shelter with some hens, because I soon saw them hanging from the shoulders of the famished soldiers, who couldn't, however, cook them.

A flowered woman's apron, abandoned shortly before on the snow. It made me suspect that some obscene deed had been committed by the Germans up in front.

I myself decided to enter one of the roadside shacks in search of food.

I went in, pistol in hand, preceded by a big, frightened, bucking calf.

The rooms were deserted: who knows where the inhabitants had hidden themselves . . .

I rummaged everywhere; all I found were some small raw potatoes.
I stuck them in my pocket, then . . . out.

The sleet continued to fall; it had been falling for a few hours now.

Near the end of the village we crossed a low wooden bridge over a wide, ice-covered stream.

In the middle of it there was a German truck that was partly burned, surrounded by pools of water mixed with gasoline and traces of fire.

Here the Germans had perpetrated one of their wickedest crimes.

Some partisans had fired at the truck, setting fire to its precious cargo of gasoline. They had been surrounded in a house, and taken alive—six or seven of them in all. The Germans had doused them in the flaming liquid, then left them like that.

Eyewitnesses told me that the poor wretches had started running and leaping about, screaming desperately. They had then ripped off their flaming clothes and thrust themselves completely naked into some pools that appeared through the ice on the stream's surface and had gone on screaming until they were dead.

I didn't see those corpses.

I did, however, see, a few hundred meters farther, other naked corpses, covered in a light layer of snow.

I thought they were Russians, recently murdered by the Germans, who knows in what manner.

In those few days how many episodes there were of German (though it would be more correct to say Nazi) barbarity! A soldier, who had entered an isolated isba in Arbuzov with a German had this tale to tell:

In the house there were women, young girls, and children. From the group, which was cowering in the corner in terror, the German had chosen the prettiest girl, then sent the others out. No sooner were they out the door than he had killed them all, including the children, with a few machine-pistol volleys.

He went back into the isba, threw the girl down on the bed, and raped her, inviting the Italian to do likewise. Our soldier had replied with a gesture of refusal: he only wanted to stay in the house because it was warm.

The German had gotten the poor girl to prepare something for him to eat and had then compelled her to sleep beside him during the night, raping her another three times.

The following morning he had driven her out of the house: she was no sooner through the doorway than he had shot her dead with his machine pistol.

How many times, for that matter, had we ourselves had to endure the bestiality of our allies!

And we were to endure it still more in the days ahead. Among other things, I heard of horses being unhitched from our isolated sleighs, which were loaded with wounded men, then hitched to some of their innumerable ones. And there was not a thing our soldiers could do because they were unarmed.

One distinguishing feature of the Germans was that they performed deeds of this kind with utter impassivity, as if it were all in a day's work.

As for the Russians—prone as they are to excesses under that systematic incitement to hatred that is Communism—when all is said, they were certainly no less murderous than the Germans. In the various discussions we had in the days to come, we found that we agreed more or less down to the last man on this point.

That we were not mistaken was borne out by the fact that only 20 percent of the Italians who were taken prisoner by them—one in five—managed to survive and return home.[11]

The march continued.

Russian tanks abandoned on the roadside. For some time now probably. Some Germans—mainly from the reserve panzers—had themselves photographed on top or in front of the tanks.

One after the other, I ate six or seven small raw potatoes. Not bad. A colleague asked me what I was eating: I had to give him the remaining six or seven.

Consul Vianini saw and chuckled, teasing us a bit for finding raw potatoes appetizing.

My prejudice against the Blackshirts of the M Battalions—whom before the retreat regular army men hadn't been able to abide and had even despised—had vanished since I had seen them fight.

Now, too, while our own generals were nowhere to be seen, their consul was trying somehow to keep at the head of the Italian column.

Finally, a halt. A couple of hours, which I spent next to a huge isolated construction: some of the time on my feet, some of the time lying in the snow.

Then, on the move again.

I was as relieved to depart as I had been to halt because my soaking feet were driving me almost out of my mind: better to keep walking until you dropped from exhaustion.

We walked on for many more hours without halting.

It stopped snowing.

It was afternoon by now.

I again found myself with Captain Varenna and with Carletti, Bona, and Sanmartino; we continued our journey together.

At a crossroads we saw some road signs that restored hope to our hearts because, as Varenna explained, Millerovo was near, and we ruled out any possibility of Millerovo being in Russian hands. I don't remember exactly, but it must have been about sixty to seventy kilometers away.

The tanks roared powerfully by, still patrolling our flanks, and every time they passed, our eyes lingered on the mighty furrows left in the snow by their tracks.

On the tanks there were squads of assault troops resembling motionless white owls.

In the afternoon, as in the late morning, German triple-engined aircraft flew over the column, parachuting down ammunition and gasoline.

Vainly, we waited for some Italian planes to appear.

Vaguely, words I had heard as a boy at school or who knows where came back to me: "The wings of our planes, are the wings of the *Patria.*"

Rhetorical no doubt, but in that dreadful isolation those words seemed to me to be profoundly true.

Darkness fell, and we were still walking at the same brisk pace.

Who knows how many men, already exhausted at the beginning of the march, had been left behind . . .

We went through a village smothered in snow and darkness.

Possibly without realizing it, [ ], who had been expecting for hours to be out of the pocket as soon as possible, started trembling and whimpering like a baby.

Finally, in one of the next villages, the column halted.

※

The soldiers burst into the houses frantically seeking warmth and food.

Our small band of officers also entered an isba: there were civilians in it.

The first thing we did was to send a Russian lad to fetch water, because, though we had swallowed a lot of snow, we were still tormented by thirst.

We then asked for something to eat. The civilians pointed to half a barrel of pickled cabbage, which I found disgusting.

I forced some of it down. The Germans, who had entered the house with us, wolfed it down. Our soldiers too I saw filling their caps with it, then thrusting their faces in voraciously.

But how warm it was in there!

I had sat down against a wall, on a stack of empty sacks, in peace; I intended to get as much rest as I could. Beside me was a sack containing wheat flour: I started eating small handfuls, which stuck to my palate.

An oil lamp shed its peace among us.

How infinitely sweet it would be to be able to spend the night here, without horseflies pestering us at every instant! It was too good even to bear thinking about.

Some women, wrapped in their customary old-fashioned clothes, watched us motionlessly, with their hands on their laps, without speaking. Their looks bespoke compassion rather than fear, because they understood our sufferings.

We too looked at them without rancor. For some time now we had learned to distinguish the Russian people from the Communists, even if under the threat of blind German ferocity, the Russians had rallied down to the last man behind their rulers in order to defend themselves.

Above all we became acquainted with the naturally good character of the folk in the small country villages, as yet untouched by Communism; of the poor women, who had the air of an age-old resignation and who, after the churches had been assigned for profane uses, huddled into the corners of their houses where the sacred icons were hanging.

A German corporal came up to me. Politely, first in his own language, then courteously in good Italian, he asked me to make a little room for him.

He then told me his story. He was Austrian and had spent a few months in Italy at the home of some relatives. He offered me what he had to eat: some crusts of Russian bread and small pieces of Italian biscuit, which we call *galletta*. I declined his offer. We conversed a bit.

We asked the Russians in the isba for news about the situation: they said that the zone was traversed "by the Russian *katyushas* by day, and at night by the German tanks." Millerovo wasn't far away (some forty kilometers, if I remember correctly), and it was in German hands.

It was good to know that.

After lingering awhile with the other officers I left the isba to fall in with the main body of the column, which was still flocking in and spreading above through another part of the village.

We thought we were about to depart again.

But time passed, and we were still there among those low shacks and wretched low stone walls smothered by snow.

The moon was up, and it cast shapeless shadows. The freezing wind blew.

It was killing us. We couldn't resist much longer. We forced our way into a stable with thatched walls, which was unbelievably crammed with people.

Here, in the pitch-dark, the cold was slightly more bearable than outside; yet I had to come away from there too, because the shouting, the perpetual bickering, and the swearing made the place resemble one of the pits of Hell.

All the buildings near the roadside were reduced to that state.

16

Finally, after what seemed an eternity, the column moved off again—the Germans still at the head, the Italians (led by Consul Vianini's sleigh) at the rear, and the tanks at the side, jolting forward several hundred meters at a time.

I have a confused memory of the first stages of that night.

Finding myself without my colleagues, I walked among soldiers from every division, behind the consul's sleigh.

I vaguely recall that a short distance out of the village the Germans took the wrong road, or possibly decided to change direction, and that for a while we were left standing there motionless on a ridge, where the cold was horrifying.

From there we could see innumerable ridges and valleys gleaming with inviolate snow, stretching as far as the eye could see, beneath the moon.

The wind lashed the uncannily clear sky. And the cold grew, and grew.

I seem to remember that we went back to the village, or perhaps it was another village we entered, and I remember that, try as I would to avoid it, I fell asleep and walked on in a state of slumber; every so often I was awakened by the protesting soldiers whom I bumped against as I walked.

Suddenly the world around me changed. All of a sudden I found myself in the drawing room of a Swiss hotel high up in the mountains: its walls were panneled in shining wood, and magnificent crystal globes illuminated it.

Delirium transported me to such an elegant setting, while for months all I had had around me were tents, earthwork shelters, and thatched shacks.

It was, however, extraordinarily cold in that drawing room. I summoned the servants and asked them why it wasn't heated, and they were immediately transfigured into soldiers, and replied that they didn't know.

So I got angry: I had had this hotel built. Where was the heated underground room for sleeping? It wasn't there. For a while I couldn't make up my mind whether or not to bed down on the shiny, polished floor and go to sleep right there.

If I had made that decision, I would have been one of the multitude who lay down to sleep in the snow, to be all too often transformed, in a matter of a few hours, into blocks of ice. Many, hundreds perhaps, died in that manner that night.

Instead, I decided to step out of the hotel and head along the street of the small Swiss village, in search of the parish priest's house. And finally I entered it. Providence would have us in a Russian village (later, when I tried to reconstruct things: Gushed or Manipol, though I wouldn't swear to it) and would have me enter one of the very many thatched shacks.

I was in fact astonished to find not a priest but an old Russian couple and a great many soldiers; but I was in no mood to trouble myself about this. There was a double bed, only one half of which was occupied by a soldier: I gave him a tongue-lashing because that bed "I had had prepared for me," then, softening somewhat, I propped my musket against the wall, removed my shoes and socks, and, settling down in the other half of the bed, spread my blanket over me and fell asleep.

I think I must have slept three or four hours . . .

I was awakened by a soldier I didn't know who was shaking my arm: "*Signor tenente!*"

I sat up with a start: "What is it?"

"The column left several hours ago . . ."

That shook me to my senses: the halt in the village; my fainting spell (every detail of which I now remembered), and all the rest.

In the house there were a good many soldiers. I rallied them: "Quick! Quick! Get ready—we're off."

I put on my shoes; in addition to my own, I threw a Russian blanket over my shoulders.

We went out into the snowy streets of the village; it was some time before I realized that I had left my musket in the house.

*

Though it was still pitch-dark, we could feel dawn approaching. We called out imperiously.

Gray figures then emerged from the isbas and from every direction: all of them Italians.

The swollen torrent of men had certainly flowed through the village, because vestiges of it lay clearly in the snow.

In a sort of small square (I had no memory whatsoever of having seen the place before), I stopped and got the men milling around there to form up—two hundred or thereabouts.

During this operation, I also saw a major with frostbitten legs coming out of a shack on a sleigh driven by his orderly.

I presented myself, saluting in regulation fashion.

Saying hardly a word, he put himself in my hands; I then got the sleigh to join the squad.

It was imperative to catch up with the column. There was a track all right, but which direction were we to go in?

Again and again I scrutinized the prints in the gray, cold snow, beset by an atrocious dilemma: one way lay safety, the other way slaughter.

The snow told me nothing: try as I might, I was utterly unable to decipher which way the column had gone.

I felt the responsibility for so many lives weighing upon me: the gray-haired mothers behind those men, and their wives, and their poor children.

So for a few seconds and with extreme intensity, I invoked the Madonna: "Enlighten me! Enlighten me!" Then I called out to three or four handpicked soldiers, who seemed to me the brightest, to step out of the lines and asked them what direction the column had followed. They all agreed with me but were also somewhat baffled.

"Good. We agree then. Back into ranks." And placing myself at the head of the short column, I raised my arm by way of a marching order.

We hadn't gone more than a few steps when a marshal stepped out of the lines with a couple of soldiers: *"Signor tenente,"* he exclaimed mournfully, "where are you taking us? I'm sure that the right direction is the opposite one."

It would have been sheer folly to appear uncertain! Everyone would have lost confidence in me, and that little column would have broken up.

So I stopped and said to the marshal: "You do what you think best. You're free." Then turning to the others, I shouted: "Everyone is free to go in whatever direction he wishes. I and the column will continue going this way," and I walked on.

The marshal moved off disconsolately; just one soldier followed him. Were they in good faith? Or mightn't they be exiles playing the enemy's game? This is another of the many questions I asked myself during those days that I shall never be able to answer.

Early on in the march I was in danger of losing my wits again: at certain moments I felt I was among medieval soldiers fighting over their own disputes, and I was there more out of curiosity than anything else.

But I took an energetic hold on myself, aided by the intensely sharp morning air, and became myself again.

That was the last time I was delirious.

We walked with the same quick step, possibly too fast for men who had failed to keep pace with the main column.

At times, I thought, as I trudged forward: short of a miracle, we're well and truly done for!

But my face was set, and I prayed to the Madonna fervidly.

How little we were and how few of us, in the dark endless solitude . . . Ants in the immensity.

And there, after no more than half an hour's marching, from the top of a snow-clad knoll, between folds in the land, was the black smudge of the main column, which, after a halt, was now on the move again. How frenziedly everyone burst out shouting: "The column! The column! . . ."

We later learned that it had taken the wrong road, thereby losing two hours; it had stopped for about another two hours' rest and was now moving on again.

That was the only night that one could afford to fall behind: any other night of the march, and we would almost certainly have been cut off for good.

We joined the column, several of us at a run. I let my squad merge with the column.

A few days later I was to learn that, furthermore, the advance guard, going through a small village, had been attacked fairly heavily by partisans that night.

On my own again, I walked past several trucks loaded with wounded. The drivers were having great difficulty getting the engines started. By this time they were the only trucks left, and in the course of the day they too would be abandoned. In fact, not a single Italian truck made it to Chertkovo.

When the vehicles ran out of gasoline, the few wounded men still fit to walk got off them and, crumpled and ragged down to the last man, fell in with the column. Those unable to walk at times shouted for help from the trucks and at times, particularly in those last few days, observed a terrible silence.

I also heard of cases of suicide.

17

And so, after this strange interlude, the interminable march continued, in the interminable cold.

After passing the trucks, I ran into a squad of soldiers and officers from my battalion.

On the understanding that it mustn't only be for me but "for everybody," one of the officers, Lieutenant Bona, handed me a small canvas bag containing sugar mixed with coffee beans. I passed the packet to Biddau, a Sardinian gunner from the Second Battery—one of the *vecchi*. Every so often, as we went along, Bona or I asked for the packet so that we could eat a small handful of that precious food.

A little farther ahead our small group was joined by Corporal Vanoglio, a tractor driver from the Second Battery, who told me that he had been one of the two hundred or so left behind with the young captain at the mouth of the gully near Arbuzov. Imagine how I felt asking him to fill me in on every detail! This is how I learned that, after killing a good many Russians, those soldiers had been massacred down to the last man. Even the captain was dead; the man on horseback whom I had sent to call them had never shown up. Finding himself alone, Vanoglio had miraculously saved himself by making off like a madman across the snow, until he had come upon the tracks of the column.

He too gave me a biscuit: he had a lot of them; where he had found them I no longer remember.

Landscapes with big hills, some with fairly steep slopes.

From a ridge, we spied, down below us, jagged in a fold of land, the thatched, snow-clad roofs of a village, possibly Khodokov.

After a while the column halted.

It began to get lighter. Day was breaking. It was December 26.

Down in the village there were large squads of Russian soldiers, and in order to force a passage the Germans, and above all the tank assault troops, were cornering them among the houses, then systematically eliminating them.

Beyond the village, we could make out our road going uphill, in the direction of Sheptukhovka, a distant, larger village on the railroad, as yet invisible to us.

Quivering tracer bullets, still glowing against the early morning sky, pursued each other insistently along that slope.

I don't remember why but we were all convinced that the new German front passed before Sheptukhovka, which meant only a few more kilometers and we would be out of the pocket.

Little by little we edged forward.

Among the first houses in the village.

I managed to quench my thirst with freezing-cold water drawn from one of the usual rustic wells at ground level, using a balancing pole made of trunks.

From bare branches, sparrows with ruffled feathers watched us forlornly. I seemed to be able to feel their poor little naked feet pressing against my heart.

Forward again in short jerks. A longer halt. It was then that I met Borghi, the gun artificer of the Second Artillery, of all my soldiers the one who was perhaps fondest of me. He was walking without shoes, just socks, but didn't have frostbite.

He recounted some of his vicissitudes. For example, in the Valley of Death during the bayonet attack he had collapsed exhausted onto the snow, and some Russians, who were in momentary retreat, had passed him: they hadn't touched him, believing him to be dead. When our men came back that way he had managed to get to his feet again and return to the village. There an old peasant woman had saved his semifrostbitten feet by massaging them with snow and had then advised him to walk shoeless like that.

The halt showed no sign of ending, and the Italian column was becoming a formless mass, pressing into the village from every direction.

How we had to shout, that morning too, to hold the men back until the Germans had opened the passage up completely! We bawled ourselves hoarse, losing our voices in the process.

Little by little, the tide of men passed through the village. Numerous Russian soldiers lay dead in its streets. Nearly all had already been deprived of their high felt boots or their shoes; on the front flap of their caps, smothered in the fur, you could make out the red star.

Finally the march was able to move on quickly.

I was now with Mario Bellini and Vincenzo Candela, the medical officer.

We learned that not far from the village, high up on the left, there was an abandoned Italian warehouse.

Leaving Candela behind on the road for a moment, since he was exhausted, Bellini and I reached the stores, which had by now been pillaged by the Germans. We got there in time to catch one of our men in the act of making off with a sack of biscuits—the last sack.

I stopped the soldier at gunpoint and confiscated the sack. I gave him five or six rations and distributed the others among the knot of starving men who had lost no time in congregating around me. Five or six rations I kept for Bellini, Candela, and myself.

We commenced the long ascent toward Sheptukhovka.

We were joined by thin, lean Antonini. We lost contact with Mario Bellini.

Candela, who was semidelirious, beseeched me not to abandon him.

I gave him my word and, to ease his plight, had him tied to the tail of a mule that was carrying a wounded man.

Soon I realized that I had lost sight of him.

So I started anxiously scouring the column for him. In vain.

Eating ravenously, Antonini and I were almost halfway up the slope when an order suddenly came from the head of the column to turn back; Sheptukhovka was German property; the Italians were to stay where they were in the village they had just left.

A car went by behind us. Leaning out of it was a sublieutenant shouting at us to turn back: "General's orders."

A lot of men did so. Antonini and I, together with many others, continued to press forward.

But were we out of the pocket? Once again we were tormented by uncertainty.

Up there ahead of us, at the end of the ascent, some Russian planes came flying over the column as it entered Sheptukhovka and dropped bombs. Furious billows of smoke and explosions.

Thankfully there were no further attacks.

Just before the village we passed a long, awesome formation of German light artillery pointing toward us and riddled with enemy bullets. They were positioned in the snow straddling the road for the obvious purpose of blocking it. The guns seemed to have been literally ripped to pieces by Russian fire.

They brought home to me our whole painful predicament: here too, then, awesome Soviet forces had passed a few days earlier, overwhelming all they encountered . . .

So when would our calvary be over?

Better not ask such questions. Better keep moving.

٭

We were now among the houses in Sheptukhovka, largely abandoned by the population and in ruins.

All of them were already occupied by the Germans.

I wandered about with Antonini in search of a heated corner; everywhere, as usual, the Germans blocked our entry to the houses, yelling violently.

We got to the railroad station: the first one since the beginning of the retreat.

We had to make do with a huge construction that had formerly been used as a railroad stores. There were several of them: reduced to semiruins, with shapeless cracks instead of doors and windows, and completely exposed to the wind.

There was already a crowd of Italians in ours. They had lit some fires that gave off not the slightest bit of heat, and the place was filled with pungent smoke.

Here we met up again with Candela, the medical officer. He had managed to eat some chicken cooked by a compatriot and seemed to have revived somewhat.

There was still the widespread conviction that it was Christmas Day: so, deferring the calculation of dates to a less painful moment, I too chose to believe it, and to celebrate.

This was the third day running that I had believed it was Christmas . . .

My Christmas festivities consisted of a piece of biscuit and some canned food (obtained from a soldier with whom I bartered some biscuit). I ate this seated next to Candela on two slippery, ice-cold beams.

In front of us we had a little fire around which many soldiers clustered. This fire overheated the part of our bodies that was exposed to it, leaving the rest completely frozen.

It was close to noon, and my memory of those hours is becoming somewhat confused.

I seem to remember that a wounded officer was brought to Candela, who examined him but was unable to give him any aid. If I remember correctly, the poor wretch was unconscious, and I had to assert my authority to obtain a little room for him among the soldiers beside the fire. In the end I succeeded.

I also remember that Candela, with the generosity and profound sense of duty that distinguished him, wanted to go out on his own initiative to examine some of the wounded men bedded down under a small nearby shed.

Mortar shells exploded on the open snowy spaces of the station, but none of us were prepared to bother too much about them: they did however remind our ever vigilant spirits that the Russians were not far off and that they were reorganizing.

Then, for some reason, Antonini and I found ourselves with Colonel Matiotti, the commander of the Thirtieth Brigade. With him we made our way slowly down some streets. Then he invited us to come with him to the station in search of Mario Bellini.

A pale wintry sun lit the village, into which growing numbers of men were pouring.

We skirted the railroad and headed back toward the station. Besides its group of buildings, more imposing than the usual Russian isbas, it was distinguishable by virtue of a gigantic, squat water tank on which the name of the place was written in big letters.

Along the road we stopped at a quaint little house, where an NCO had billeted himself with a few soldiers. We sat with them on a neat veranda, incredibly embellished with curtains and vases with plants in them. We gazed enchanted at all that order and cleanliness. We had scant hope of finding our friend Bellini.

The soldiers offered us some butter, which they had pilfered from the Germans.

After about an hour, with heavy hearts, the two of us plunged back into the immense cold.

Word was going around that we were due to leave at once for Millerovo. Very soon things started moving.

We rejoiced to see several German tanks that had not previously been in the column filing past in the precincts of the station. They were not the usual low, gigantic ones; they were smaller, many of them French war trophies—but tanks all the same.

The armored columns as such had never shown up, but now at least something could be seen.

I heard that, like us, these tanks had been trapped for some time in the pocket and that there were twenty of them. There seemed fewer to me.

The column began to form up again along the railroad.

The last specter of sun was vanishing.

For hours we stayed where we were in the snow.

This was certainly a blessing insofar as it meant that our compatriots who had halted farther back in the village were able to catch up with us and join the column, but in another respect it was a dire misfortune for the cold began to reduce our chances of resisting, on the eve of the most terrible night we were to spend on Russian soil.

Standing motionless in the snow for hours is unbearable. So I moved several times.

I went and drank water at a well.

I listened in for a bit to what Colonel Matiotti was saying, from the top of a wagon, to whoever was within earshot. Driven, like all the best of the men there, by the urge to explain this disaster to himself, and by the intention to escape it, our old colonel seemed to have lost his sense of reality. He spoke of noble sentiments, of valor, of amor patriae. His words rang so oddly in that savage clash between barbarians in which we were entangled that more than one of his listeners appeared perplexed.

I managed to sneak into the former railroad stores for a while and sit, among the crowd, on a beam lying on the floor not far from the fire.

At dusk the column got on its way.

The new arrivals from the village farther back were already complaining that they had had to run several kilometers under Russian mortar and machine-gun fire and that lives had been lost.

And sure enough, unbeknownst to us, the Russians had attempted to cut them off from the column. I learned this later from Captain Pontoriero, who had been there with them.

I myself had heard nothing more than insistent mortar fire.

18

I left Sheptukhovka with Bellini, Antonini, Varenna, Bono, Candela (the medical officer), and a group of soldiers from the Thirtieth but after a while found myself alone with Candela, who took my arm because he was feeling weak. His fine, intellectual face looked exhausted.

I, on the other hand, was in excellent shape; this may have been a nervous reaction or because of the food I had eaten or the few hours' sleep I had managed to snatch the previous night.

Total darkness descended.

We kept up the same rapid step. The sky above us was becoming astonishingly clear.

The temperature continued to drop, so much so that after a while we felt that we had never known it so low. (Those who were able to look at a thermometer at the end of this stretch told me that it read -47 degrees—and that was only in town.)

A light freezing wind stirred from the right, gradually gathering strength, until it blew gusts of powdered snow on us.

Our faces wore masks of ice and frost. On our entire right-hand flank a huge crust of ice was forming. The cold was such, and the wind so sharp, that it felt as if we were walking completely naked there on the snow: we could feel the whole surface of our bodies battling against the cold.

The column slowly became twisted and thinned out; our step became quicker and quicker, and the wounded, the frostbite casualties, those whose resistance was lower got left behind.

I had given the small Russian rug to Candela, and he had wrapped it around his head. I too had pulled my blanket over my head, since it was poorly protected by the balaclava alone. So all we could see was the beaten snow at our feet.

Off on the double, leaning on each other's arm, forcing ourselves not to think of the cold and obsessed by one single idea: to walk, to walk, to walk.

Candela started groaning and dragging his feet. Come on, keep moving!

We passed a long line of magnificent Italian trucks that had been abandoned several days earlier. They looked as if they were made of glass: heaven help anyone forced to touch them with a bare hand!

Down there, almost straight in front of us, the moon began to appear from the crystalline stretches of snow.

It was an immense, ruddy moon.

But there was no time to think about the moon or about anything else. Keep moving!

The march was fast becoming a race.

Candela implored me to slow down.

I made sure to keep him on the left of the column so that those trudging along on our right could shield us a bit from the wind, which seemed to me capable of killing him.

At a certain point we began to pass men who had collapsed onto the snow. It was pointless trying to move them; stopping meant death. All we could do was keep moving!

Every so often someone became delirious: he would stop, look around him, then possibly turn back. There were those who thought they were entering their own houses, and were walking open-armed toward their children, or heading for the bar on the corner.

I could hear disconnected, meaningless sentences. One man walked like an automaton, ceaselessly repeating: "A little soup, a little warmth . . . A little soup, a little warmth . . . ."

I myself felt ferociously well. I almost wished that the march would never end. I was furious with the desire to walk; I felt warmth throughout my body because the horrible wind was lashing my limbs relentlessly without managing to undermine them.

Being from Palermo, Candela was unaccustomed to temperatures below zero and was beside himself by now.

Suddenly I needed to relieve myself. Stopping was no problem for me, since whenever I wanted a single dash could get me to the front of the column; but heaven forbid that I should let Candela lose ground. If he fell too far behind the Germans and their tanks, this could, I thought, have meant death for him.

I therefore decided to entrust him to one or another of the soldiers who were passing us and eventually found one who took him by the arm. I repeated Candela's name several times to the soldier, so as to be able to track him down later.

When I had stopped to relieve myself, I had made the foolish mistake of washing my hands with the snow. Immediately I could no longer feel them: I felt no more than a slight swelling on my wrists. I tried clasping them together, clapping them against each other, but this did no good; it was as though they didn't exist. So I frenetically slipped on my threadbare gloves, thrust them in my pockets, and was on my way again, with this anxious invocation on my lips: "Lord, Lord, don't let me lose my hands! . . ."

Soon afterward I felt, with violent joy, that my hands were coming back to life.

I immediately started trotting along at the side of the column, loudly calling out my friend's name: "Candela! Candela!" My voice, which was very loud, bounced vainly along the dark, frenzied swarm of men, receiving no answer.

To some I must have given the impression of having lost my wits. Then, finally, when I'd already given up hope, Candela answered me in a low voice.

I took his arm again, and on we went. But he could hold out no longer. He suddenly started trembling: "My heart . . . My heart's had it . . . ." He also uttered garbled sentences; he said he could see ambulances, that he could see his refuge back on the Don and wanted to enter it.

I slowed down a little, remembering that Candela had two children at home.

I tried to find him a place on a sleigh. To no avail. He lost his glasses and wasn't able to find them.

Beyond all my expectations, I managed soon after to hoist him onto a huge mule, behind one of the wounded. The mule staggered forward.

I kept to the left of the animal to shield myself from the wind. Meanwhile, to the exclusion of every other thought, my mind was being hammered by the thought of how that mule must be suffering from having its right flank completely bare and exposed. And by the thought of all the other, if few, remaining mules and horses still sharing our journey with us.

After a while Candela asked to get down from the mule.

We did another stretch of road on foot; then he gave out again.

By an act of Providence, I found a horse with no load: the wounded men it had only just been bearing were attempting to walk: if you stayed on horseback you did in fact freeze before very long.

I noticed that Candela no longer had any gloves on. I slipped mine on him, and thrust my own hands in my pockets.

He wanted to get off that horse too. He had lost all powers of reason. I treated him like a child, scolding and browbeating him. And to think that this was a man who just two evenings earlier, at Arbuzov, had risked his life when he turned back with Mario Bellini and myself so that we wouldn't have to go off on our own.

That night I got him to change horses two or three times, so that some stretches of road he covered on horseback and some on foot.

The moon was now strongly illuminating the road and the white immensity of the steppe all around it.

Finally, after hours of marching, there were some isbas to the right of the road.

I heard a solitary voice, calling out to a sergeant again and again, just I had been calling out to Candela a short time before.

News had gotten around that we had crossed the German line and were now in friendly territory. Millerovo, someone said, was not far away. I decided to stop with Candela at the first small house we came to. I was very much loath to do this, because I would have liked to have gone on at all costs.

The house was so crowded that it was impossible to get in. But there, attached to it, was a lean-to cowshed with reed walls, and this was worth a try.

I made my way through and, pushing the door, eventually managed by a great effort to get Candela through it. He stood there waiting speechlessly, head bowed, oblivious of the din the soldiers were making around us.

I realized that the cow was still in the cowshed, which was unlit. I ordered it to be shoved out in order to make more room, but no one paid me the slightest notice.

The cowshed was crammed to the point of bursting.

So I myself grabbed the beast by the horns, forced it around, and, kicking it in the shins with my hobnailed foot, pushed it as far as the door.

But an old Russian couple suddenly appeared in front of it, weeping, wanting to push it back. I yelled that I would kill them then and there: this got them scared, and they fled; and I pushed the cow outside. We occupied the place and tried to get settled as best we could by the light of wax matches that the soldiers lit for us.

The first thing I did was to sit Candela down on a small stool in a corner.

Every so often he addressed meaningless sentences to me such as: "This place is for the soldiers, for us officers there's my hole, which is well heated . . . ."

I then succeeded in spreading my blanket on the floor, on the cow's still fresh excrement among other things, and we lay down.

"Now I'm all right," Candela said, and nodded off.

I too dozed for a few hours amid the din of the constantly bickering soldiers and others hammering on the door to be let in.

The cold still troubled us, though, and an attempt by the soldiers to light some straw did no good.

In the end I decided to move on. Candela seemed to have rallied somewhat; I took him outside again into what was still deepest night.

The road was still filled with stragglers hurrying along it. Basically it was still the column, but it had thinned down greatly.

After a while Candela began to give out again.

I found a burdenless horse, mounted him on it, and refused to let him get off.

So here we were once more in the white desert. We pressed on, leading the horse by the reins—a poor, exhausted animal, doing its utmost to slow down with every step it took, so that the soldier leading it beat it from behind with a jagged stick.

Several times I myself urged him to beat it, shuddering all the while at the thought of the pain the animal must be suffering. At that temperature, if you touched the metal of your musket, your fingers stuck to it painfully.

We covered many more kilometers in this fashion, in that endless night where all was possible.

Candela now claimed to see nonexistent houses along the roadside and wanted to enter them. I shouted at him roughly, and on we went.

Then, through the darkness, we saw a truck coming the opposite way. It pulled up beside us; a German got out and went behind it to check something. *"Scolca chilometr tú Millerovo?"* ("How many kilometers to Millerovo?"), I asked him. "Zwei," he replied. Thank God for that! Candela was truly on his last legs.

I myself was now beleaguered by a pain in my heels, naked inside my shoes, which were rigid as if made of iron. I mean it: they were literally as rigid as steel.

Down there, to the left, was a large, dark, distant building: the clearing station.

Then, at last, some lights. The houses of the town.

I had no choice but to head for the first lighted window, because Candela was dying. His delicate face, completely covered in ice and frost, had stiffened into an appalling grimace.

At the front of the house there was a porch made of wooden planks. I knocked on the door.

It was opened by some fellow Italians. In the middle of that narrow hallway they had lit a small, putrid-smelling fire, around which they were sitting. I sat Candela down on the floor next to them.

CHERTKOVO

19

In the stone body of the building there were Germans. I knocked, and they too opened the door to me: two rooms filled with men lying in every kind of posture in their soiled white uniforms.

I spoke to some of them, explaining that I was an officer and that there was a medical officer with me at death's door. Would they take him in for a while? Meanwhile, I would make it my business to find somewhere else for him.

I managed to get him accepted.

I brought Candela into the room and sat him down near the door in the only free space. I stayed with him for a while, sitting at his side. I caressed him and spoke to him gently, as a friend.

When I stopped talking, the silence was filled with the animal, yet somehow reassuring, breathing of the sleepers. A Mongol, in the service of the German army, was staring at us, his large yellow face turned our way: all the while he was calmly eating, without stopping for an instant, something he was pulling out of his pocket. (I wonder to this day what became of that man and the others of his race who were present in quite sizable numbers in the units of the 298th German Division.)

Candela dozed off quite soon. So I went out in search of a house and, more pressing, headquarters.

It was beginning to get lighter. Meanwhile, more and more soldiers were entering the town.

Which was not Millerovo, but Chertkovo.

Its disastrous siege, which was about to begin, is the only episode in the winter war explicitly referred to in the proclamation for the repatriation of the destroyed Eighth Army.

How many of us got as far as Chertkovo? We officers calculated at the time that of the thirty thousand men or thereabouts trapped in the pocket on the banks of the Don, around eight thousand of us must have made it to the town. The others had died or, a fate often worse, had ended up in enemy hands. Those who were taken alive by the enemy were undoubtedly more numerous than the dead.

That last night was horrible.

Giudici, a second lieutenant from the Eighty-second Torino Infantry Regiment, who entered the town several hours after me, told me that the road was strewn with dead bodies. Exhausted individuals who, on falling to the ground, had been turned into pieces of ice by the cold or had died delirious without even realizing it or had frozen to death as they dragged themselves forward on their hands and knees until their strength gave out.

Above all, I heard of cases of delirium. I was particularly affected by the story of one who, having removed his shoes and socks, sat on the roadside rolling his feet in the snow, barefoot and singing at the top of his voice. He had been seen by many.

When the Russians got there more than one day later, they laid into all those corpses with their bayonets. This at least is what the Germans claimed, after conducting a tank reconnaissance along the road.

✳

There I was, then, walking around the small town, among the eternal thatched houses, in search of headquarters.

I turned onto the main street.

An Italian soldier on patrol, dressed in white and well equipped, filled me in on all the details I needed.

Chertkovo was garrisoned by about five hundred Italians and at least as many Germans. On three sides it was blocked by not particularly powerful Russian strong points, while to the west it was free, and there lay the chance of complete liberty. There were large warehouses of provisions and clothing and an operational headquarters.

I asked where I could find it, thanked him, and set off. It gave me pleasure seeing him snap to salute, in perfectly disciplined fashion.

I pressed on toward headquarters but made slow going because my feet were smarting inside the shoes that were once again turning to steel.

Beside an isba a white-uniformed corpse, probably German, was lying on the snow with its skull split open. This meant that there were partisans in the town.

I passed several of our trucks, including a few ambulances, that had been abandoned for some time now along the roadside.

Seeing them took me back to the beginning of the retreat, to the fleeing trucks clustered with men. A few days later I learned that in Chertkovo, as in other towns on the supply lines, this phenomenon had assumed unbelievable proportions.

Russian tank forays had in fact penetrated deep, putting all the services to flight. There we were still calmly in line, while far behind us columns of vehicles, mixed with columns of men on foot, were fleeing, gripped by the most indescribable panic. People clung to the tarpaulins of the trucks, then, when their strength ran out, rolled to the ground and were sometimes run over.

Soldiers were trying to stop the trucks by blocking the road with outspread arms, and the drivers ran them down because any increase in the load would have prevented them from moving off again.

A twenty-year-old driver of a Bianchi Miles from Como told me that, in one case, after he had run down some wretches who were blocking the road, a hand with half a forearm had come flying up into the cab of the truck.

After rounding several snow-clad embankments, I reached a straight stretch of track that was overlooked by headquarters and a lot of other buildings.

To the right there were more shacks but to the left were large, solid buildings as well.

I traded my worn-out frozen rug for a fine new barracks blanket, issued to me by a soldier who pulled it out of a stack that had been set up on the roadside.

"Excuse me, *signor tenente*," he said. "Shall I give it to you now, or will you be sending your orderly to collect it?" I stared at him, wondering whether he was trying to make fun of me. No, it had never crossed his mind. On the contrary, he may have felt compassion and wanted me to feel that I had come to a place where order and calm still reigned.

"Yes, of course," I replied at first. "I could very well send my orderly." It was a pity to upset the order he still seemed to conserve in his soul . . .

But the softness of that big woollen blanket, so different from our small field rugs made of assorted materials, won the day. "Cut it out," I said to myself; and to him: "Hmm, no, just this once you can give it to me."

Finally, I got to the small building that housed headquarters.

I entered and immediately found myself in the kitchen; the two cooks (a tall, bearded soldier and a young lad) placed before me some cognac, canned meat, biscuits, and marmalade. Almost at once other soldiers too, including Bellini and Antonini, came into the kitchen.

We ate voraciously.

I drank some more cognac. I told my companions that I had left Candela with the Germans at the entrance to the village and that we had to find him a place in a house and call him, or send for him, as soon as possible.

Did we send for him? I don't remember.

What I do remember is that I suddenly felt sick and vomited. Then I drew up a stool by the big stove, sat down, and, taking off my shoes, moved my feet up to the fire grate, rested my elbows on my knees and my head in my hands, and was soon asleep.

I woke after about an hour. Candela!

I leaped to my feet. As I was putting on my shoes I realized what a fool I had been to expose my feet to such intense heat after so much cold. If I had been suffering from just the beginnings of frostbite, I wouldn't have been able to save them.

As it was they hurt and gave me trouble for a good many days.

Some soldiers from headquarters showed us to a nearby single-story building, consisting almost entirely of a single large room, where there were two rows of beds made out of rough planks with pallets made from tenting material. This was probably the dormitory of headquarters. It was bitterly cold in there, and we needed to light the fire.

Bellini occupied one of the beds, as did Antonini. I personally disliked the place (which was subsequently to become the "infirmary"). So I went out. Together with a sergeant major from the *Bersaglieri* of the Chertkovo garrison—who had offered to be our guide—I visited some of the huts facing headquarters on the other side of the track.

Among these there was a very low, white hut, containing a number of bunks with pallets and a small iron bed; a few soldiers were already tidying it. I decided to settle down there and, taking the small bed and a place in one of the bunks for myself and Candela, went out in search of him.

I ran into him almost immediately, staggering toward me along the road lit by the thin, early-morning sun.

On his face the mask of frost had already reformed; he was bent double and whimpering because I had abandoned him.

I dragged him into the house and tried to justify myself.

On waking, he had found himself among Germans who had hurled abuse at him; then a soldier had come along, pulled him outside, and accompanied him to headquarters. I can't recall whether that soldier had been sent by us.

Little by little in the freezing-cold hut, which consisted of four small rooms, a pleasant warmth began to spread because the soldiers had lit the stove.

I got Candela to eat something, helped bed him down on the bunk, and spread two blankets over him—his and my Russian one—then threw myself down on the iron bed.

All that day we did nothing but sleep and eat stuff that I had brought from headquarters or that the soldiers had spirited from the warehouses.

Who can express the enormous animal satisfaction of being able to sleep in a warm place?

Of feeling a blanket on top of you, holding the warmth. Of turning over occasionally, then sighing deeply, like a great bundle of bones and muscles flooded with blood.

And your mind no longer tensed from one moment to the next to send your body leaping to its feet to flee or inflict death, but itself relaxed—stretched out, as it were, resting.

Those hours are now long past and far distant; yet, as long as I remain on this earth, I shall never forget the indescribable sense they gave me that life was being made anew.

Every time I awoke, I ate and blessed the Lord for granting me that repose; but not for long, for I immediately dozed off again.

Other soldiers and officers settled in the house, occupying the bunks that were still vacant. By evening only the smallest of the four rooms, in which the garbage had gradually accumulated, remained cold and uninhabited.

That's how we spent December 27.

20

Night fell.

With the stove out, the room grew colder and before morning was very cold. But the stove was relit and, mixed with the acrid scent of smoke by now familiar to us, warmth returned.

We spent the whole of the second day as well eating and sleeping. Our main diet was biscuits and canned sardines: multicolored cans with writing in different languages, German war spoils from various nations.

We could feel life slowly flowing back into our exhausted bodies.

The night of the third day was marked by intense enemy bombardment: artillery, the odd *katyusha*, and above all mortars.

Those cursed Russians were reminding us that they were close by and would soon be hurling themselves upon us.

Several mortar shells smashed through the roof of headquarters and exploded inside; Lt. Col. Virginio Manari, the commander of the Chertkovo garrison, was seriously wounded; he died in a matter of hours.

What awaited us now?

Word went around that the Germans had been granted four days' rest: we would be on our way again as soon as that period was over.

Several times a question I had already asked myself earlier during the days of the march recurred to me: what would have become of us without the Germans? And regrettably I was compelled to admit that had we been alone, we Italians would have ended up in enemy hands. So while on the one hand I abhorred the Germans for their inhumanity (which at times disqualified them, in my eyes, from membership of the human family) and for the really trivial haughtiness with which they showed that they considered every other man an inferior being—born to be exploited and expected to be grateful to his exploiters—I also thanked heaven that they were with us there in the column.

And—much to the chagrin of my soldier's heart—during the fighting I prayed to heaven that they would bring us victory.

Much as I disliked them, I also had to admit that, without a shadow of a doubt, as soldiers they have no equal. Whatever my human aversion to them as a man, it is only right that, as a soldier, I acknowledge this.

I even found it moving, in the ensuing days, watching German soldiers in Chertkovo forming up in short files of five or six, with no need of a superior, and relieving their comrades at the line at the appointed time.

Later, however, after speaking to compatriots who had escaped from other pockets, I no longer felt that the absence of the Germans would have meant the end for us.

Just the opposite.

Apart from the vicissitudes of the Alpini (who from the very start of their time in the pocket proved superior to the Germans, so much so that the latter put themselves completely in their hands), if the Pasubio and the Torino had, like the Sforzesca, acted by themselves, I believe we would have gotten out earlier and with fewer casualties.

If we hadn't headed so far south (which meant remaining encircled for almost twice as long as the other Italian divisions), less than a week's march westward and we would have been out. We would have found shelter at night in the houses, and we wouldn't have found ourselves for days on end being pounded by the Russians: we wouldn't have been totally and pointlessly destroyed. My dislike of the Germans, whose treatment of us certainly helped increase our already endemic disorganization, thus became still greater than it already was. (I must, however, admit that if we had gone our own way once we were in the pocket, they would certainly have raised no objection.)

There we were, then, in Chertkovo, awaiting marching orders.

The town, divided by the railroad—one half Ukrainian, the other Cossack territory—looked much like most other industrialized Russian towns.

Long lines of isbas with mud walls and roofs of straw and only rarely of metal sheeting; only a small number of large brick houses; a few storied houses in masonry; large industrial sheds; and a number of very tall modern buildings in reinforced concrete, their ugliness accentuated by the mutilations of war.

A good deal of grayness.

The town rose on several folds of land that raised it in most places above the surrounding plain. Around it, at greater or lesser distances, were several small clusters of thatched shacks, smothered by the snow.

Among these, and far beyond, were expanses of snow, very often half-hidden in mist.

We Italians were heaped indiscriminately in the zones northeast of the railroad. In the southwestern sector, in more numerous and better buildings, were the Germans.

The Italian provisions and clothing depots (situated alongside the railroad) were in German hands: our catering units had apparently abandoned them when the first Russian tanks arrived, and the Germans who had stayed behind to defend the town had then taken possession of them. When we were there, however, they were regarded by the Germans as spoils of war. Only on the first day were Italian soldiers able to carry away a certain quantity of provisions. The second day, the German guard opened fire on whoever ignored the order to halt.

Two "provisions-distribution stations" (one for each "quarter" of the town) started operating, thanks to the efforts of a few senior officers.

But the rations, probably taken from a small storehouse belonging to headquarters, were meager. Only those who had managed on the previous day to pilfer from the subsistence stores (which were, thank heaven, plentiful) could eat normally. Several thousand were still left hungry.

All the more so for the fact that there were in almost all the houses wounded and frozen men who were completely unable to move, and the distribution systems were so inadequate that those allotted the task of doing the "shopping" had to stand outside in long disorderly lines for hours on end.

I reckon that even in those few days in Chertkovo there were men who died of starvation.

So the soldiers took to stealing again, often with their officers' consent. And the Germans fired on them. Quite a few lost their lives in that wretched manner.

And there were sections of those large warehouses devastated by Russian grenades and shells, where the pasta, mixed with rubble and snow, was putrefying. I saw it myself.

Word also went around that lying abandoned in the snow in front of the warehouses were the corpses of sixty or seventy soldiers who on the day they arrived in Chertkovo had found some cognac and gotten drunk. They had walked outside and collapsed on the ground, and the cold had killed them without anyone bothering about them—and many of them had fallen only a few steps away from the isbas occupied by our men.

Many of these things, in the first two days, I just heard about, since I only left the house for very occasional visits to headquarters, in search of news about the situation and of something to eat.

✳

The third day, December 29, I managed to overcome my fierce selfishness and decided to embark on a tour of the town. Who knows how much there was to do!

I had difficulty getting my sore feet into my shoes. I then plunged out into the great cold along the straight, white road—"the avenue", as we were to call it.

I walked several hundred meters toward the warehouses.

Here and there alongside the "avenue" there were now dead bodies.

In the snow there were black funnels mainly created by mortar fire.

In a small square some burned-out Russian tanks: possibly some of those that had sown panic in the supply lines.

Beyond the square the avenue got narrower and proceeded between two rows of low shacks.

In front of one of these my eyes met a heartbreaking spectacle: two men were writhing on top of a mountain of refuse covered in snow. One, realizing I was observing him, shouted to me in an anguished voice: "*Signor tenente!* Don't abandon me, *Signor tenente! . . .*"

I walked up to him. His legs had been smashed by a mortar; he said he had been in that state for several hours now.

The other man, who had been hit by the same shell, had one eye shut, his face was bathed in blood, and he was unconscious. His whole body, but particularly his right arm, was writhing incessantly, and he was puffing heavily.

Occasionally soldiers came hurrying along the road, unaware of them, or unheeding.

Around those two men there was only solitude—that glacial solitude which, from where we were, could be seen drifting away into the distant fogs. Not one of our close brothers was anywhere to be seen.

I assured the wounded man that I wouldn't abandon him. I asked him: "Isn't there anybody in the house?" "Yes," he answered "but . . . ," and from his troubled expression I could see that he meant: "but they couldn't care less about us . . . ."

But what was worrying him most was the fear that I too, after this momentary concern, would abandon him.

I stormed into the house, the door of which was three or four meters from the wounded men.

In the first room a dozen soldiers were gathered cheerfully around a big southerner who was preparing some pasta. They greeted me and even offered me some.

Without saying a word I walked out of the house. I had noticed that a major was coming along the road. I called out to him and told him what was happening. He gave the soldiers a dressing down and ordered them to take the wounded men to the infirmary.

I refrained from making a scene with those men, since I wasn't sure how things would have ended, given the blind rage that had taken possession of me.

By now we were capable of doing anything to each other.

I personally undertook to supervise the transport of the two wounded men to the infirmary, which was the building near headquarters where Bellini and Antonini were also to be found.

The less seriously wounded of the two was lifted onto the grating of a window made of wood and metal netting and carried bodily; the other was loaded into a wheelbarrow.

I accompanied them a good part of the way: but by now the soldiers had repented of their former criminal disregard, and my presence was no longer necessary.

I walked to the left of the wheelbarrow to make sure the wounded man didn't fall out. The latter, a very robust southerner, had gripped my forearm with his right hand and was shaking it rhythmically, with great force, still letting out that puffing sound: "Uff . . . uff . . . uff. . . ."

In the end I let that small company go on its way, and walked back the way I had come, toward the stores.

I was passing a one-room wooden hut (somewhat similar to one of our bathing booths back home, but lacking the façade) when I heard an imploring voice calling to me: *"Signor tenente! Signor tenente!"* I stopped.

Inside there was a soldier, whom I had failed to notice on my previous journeys past the hut.

He was sitting cross-legged in the middle of the hut, hugging his legs to his chest. He had a rug over his shoulders, and next to him, to his left, were his shoes. I went up to him. Tearfully he told me that he had been brought there during the night by his companions, who had deprived him of his gloves, then made off; both his feet had frostbite.

I noticed that his nose and part of his face were black with gangrene.

I assured him that I wouldn't abandon him and looked out of the hut in search of a vehicle and someone who could transport him.

Two Germans were coming across the square where the tanks were standing; one of them, in a snow-white uniform, was pulling a tiny sled.

Though I had no hope of being listened to, I begged him to lend it to me. To my great surprise, he agreed and even helped me lift the sick man onto the sled with his wretched belongings. Then, we each took one end of the piece of wood to which the sled cord was attached and began dragging it.

I decided to get the frozen man settled in the small house in front of which I had found the two wounded soldiers. I knew that the infirmary was full to overflowing, whereas in that hut I had glimpsed some free space (which was a rare enough thing).

The German helped me throughout the journey there; at a certain point he even urged me to get a move on, pointing to the poor wretch: "Kaputt . . . kaputt" ("He's dying . . . he's dying").

He also helped me carry him into the house. I thought the fellow must be an Austrian, who knows . . . even a seminarist, because a normal German would never have behaved like that.

This was what I thought then and there. I was incapable of believing that even Germans are capable of human sentiments: when all is said, they too have churches, mothers, children, poets.

But at the time I couldn't think in those terms: the Germans themselves, and the way they behaved, prevented me.

The small house consisted of three heated rooms: two were inhabited, while in the third I had glimpsed a single soldier stretched out on the floor with a blanket under his back; I had thought he was dead.

But when I started tugging the blanket from under him, the man let out a slight groan. He was still alive! Perhaps he was aware of what was happening around him, and this was his way of dying . . . I murmured: "Would you believe it, he's still alive!" and left him the blanket.

But I made no attempt to speak to him; I didn't stay to give him comfort in his last moments.

Before this new, unexpected horror, the selfishness from which I had broken free with such difficulty only an hour earlier got the better of me again. All at once I decided not even to go to the stores, but to return instead to my small house: above all, I told myself, to spare my feet further suffering . . .

Who knows how many other harrowing sights there must have been in the streets of Chertkovo and in the houses where so many were suffering from frostbite! But, in a wholesale massacre like this, I no longer intended to consume any more of my strength helping others, thus jeopardizing my own chances of future resistance. Again, every charitable instinct in me was fast dying: my soul was once again becoming stony, insensitive. To tell the truth, at this point I wasn't that much concerned even about my own fate: it was too much of an effort, too complicated to worry about, and even the very thought of it . . . We were all becoming paltry beings, with no inner stimuli save the animal instinct of self-preservation.

✻

That same morning we witnessed a formidable Stuka bombardment of several Russian-occupied positions around the town.

The wailing of the sirens cheered us, and the terrible rumbling of the explosions made us smile.

That day we finally had our first sight of Italian planes as well. They were twin-engine Fiat BR 20s, which flew very low over our heads, as if wishing to hearten us. We greeted their familiar forms with cries of joy.

From that morning on, practically every day, when the sky wasn't too foggy, the Stukas appeared on their skirmishes around the town, filling the air with their wailing.

The Italian aircraft also put in frequent appearances, always flying very low overhead, chased by a babel of portable gunfire the moment they were over the Russian lines.

When would we be leaving for our lines?

And how far away were those lines?

We had nothing definite to go on. Only the Germans had a wireless, and they gave us whatever news they wanted to.

The evening of that third day, when I went to headquarters to procure something to eat, I asked to see Colonel Matiotti, whom I had already met there.

This time I found him lying on some straw in the semidarkness of a room, in a row with other wounded and frostbitten officers. His feet, I saw, were covered with huge reddish blisters; his hands were also in wicked condition.

When I snapped to salute, he mistook me for Bellini and greeted me with an exclamation of joy. Nor did his welcome become any less warm when he saw it was me.

As I spoke I deliberately accentuated the "Yes, sir! No, sir!": I wanted him to feel that, come what may, he would always be our commanding officer.

He confided that he was no longer capable of walking and had therefore lost all hope. During our fitful conversation, outside we could hear the slightly muffled, snarling rosaries of opposing sub-machine-gun fire.

I tried to rally his spirits, then took my leave. I was to see him again only years later, in Italy. The following day some German planes were to land at Chertkovo and fly off again with wounded Germans and fourteen wounded Italians. Matiotti was one of them.

Meanwhile, at headquarters there was this news: German and Italian Alpini Divisions were marching on Chertkovo.

It was hard to know whether the town was now completely surrounded or whether the roads to the west were still negotiable.

News of the imminent divisions got around rapidly, gladdening the hearts of everyone. The most inert apathy gave way to hope . . .

And so the third day passed as well.

Later, as on previous evenings in our little house, we all recited the rosary together.

Even the small minority of former unbelievers. And not just out of confused fear; during those days in Chertkovo the supernatural seemed so close to the natural that to deny its existence would have been tantamount to denying the existence of material things that were there before our eyes: the snow outside; the fire crackling dully in the stove, making us nostalgic for a moment's peace; our very selves.

Above our gray emaciated figures, from the low ceiling, the light hung: a piece of telephone wire burned very slowly, producing a dense, small flame.

It only just penetrated the darkness, and many rapt eyes followed its movement. From time to time the insistent voice of a submachine gun came on the great wings of the cold to patter at our flimsy windows.

21

The fourth day broke.

As on the previous days, we ate abundantly in our hut because of the provisions pilfered from the stores, and because of the "shopping" we had managed to do, against orders, at both distribution stations.

But we were all increasingly eager to be on our way, and worried too: any moment now the enemy might tighten their grip, and then we would be done for.

That very day orders came through from General X to get ready to depart.

The Italians in Chertkovo were organized as follows. X was in command of all the fighting and nonfighting troops. As far as we could gather, he exerted his command by occasionally summoning the highest-ranking officers of each regiment to his house, along with the other generals who were there in the town (no more than one or two, after some of them, afflicted by frostbite, had departed by plane).[12]

Furthermore, headquarters had, officially at least, changed its name to *Comando delle Truppe Italiane in linea a Tcertkovo:* a sort of battalion command, which in effect still directed all the Italians deployed with the Germans in the defense of the town.

These soldiers, dressed in white German uniforms, were a mixed assortment of clerks, sappers, light cavalrymen, and *bersaglieri*. They had just arrived by train from Italy and were meant to be going to the supply lines. They had gotten off the train at Chertkovo in time to see the flight of service units who had been occupying the town since the summer, whereupon they had been promptly sent off to the front line by the commander of their troop train, Lieutenant Colonel Manari. The latter, an able, valorous man from the Third *Bersaglieri* Regiment, had died after the first heavy enemy bombardment. An infantry major had taken over for him.

At first these troops had been joined by volunteers; then all or practically all the Blackshirts from the Montebello and Tagliamento Battalions who were not wounded or afflicted by frostbite joined the line: the meager, haggard remains of great assault units, who still seemed to have preserved something of their fighting spirit.

Subsequently, companies—or, to be more exact, *centurie*—were to be created: mixed formations of infantrymen, artillerymen, sappers, and soldiers with specialist skills of every kind, who were to take turns up at the line. These too were fitted with German uniforms.

However, these *centurie*, which inspired scant confidence since they consisted of men who had been press-ganged at random, ended up being employed mainly as support troops.

All told, during the entire period of the garrison, the number of Italian troops in the line at Chertkovo ranged from five to seven hundred men.

The Germans were said to number around four thousand, but by my reckoning there were many more. To our knowledge at any rate, they had all the units still fit for combat and were commanded by a colonel who was said to be "a fortifications genius", and whose authority even extended to the lieutenant colonel who had led our column from the Don as far as Chertkovo.

Their main headquarters was in the basement of a solid reinforced concrete building in the German sector. They had branch headquarters as well, which were also underground. Later, I chanced to visit one of these: the building this time was in the Italian sector.

They kept a liaison officer at the *Comando italiano truppe in linea.*

Despite the warning to stand ready, the fourth day went by, and still we didn't depart.

Nor the following day.

We then learned why: the Germans, who had orders—personal ones from Hitler apparently—to hold the town as a fortress, were not prepared to put a single tank at our disposal.

And without tanks it was impossible to cover the sixty kilometers or thereabouts separating us from friendly lines—if, that is, genuine lines had actually been reformed. It would take just one Russian tank bearing down on us to wipe us all out.

And so, from then on, nobody talked any more about leaving the town: we would be liberated by troops coming from outside the pocket.

If such a prospect was alarming, since with each day that passed our numbers were diminishing under enemy bombardment, in one way we were pleased: it meant that we wouldn't have to leave our innumerable wounded in a stronghold occupied only by Germans.

Around the town a complete Russian line soon formed: many more enemy forces had arrived, and the ring was now soldered around us.

All we could do now was begin living as people under siege. Each man tried to organize himself as best he could.

*

After various comings and goings, six officers and about twenty soldiers remained in our house.

Except for Candela and Giudici, a second lieutenant from the Eighty-second Torino Infantry Regiment, who were older, we officers had all been born in 1921 and were thus twenty-one years old. There was also Valorzi, from the Eighty-second Infantry as well, who came from Rovereto; Conti, the Sicilian from the Eighth Pasubio Artillery; and his friend and fellow student at the military academy, Ballestra, a Milanese.

I still feel profound esteem for all those fellow officers. I shall never forget the way Conti made every effort to persuade Ballestra to go to the infirmary to get a back wound seen to—even to the point of losing his temper. But Ballestra wouldn't hear of it: his was a light wound, so he had no intention of depriving the seriously wounded of as much as a single drop of medicine, which was already scarce. (Complications set in, and on his return to Italy he spent a whole year fighting for his life.)

Among those who had gone, there was, by contrast, a despicable lieutenant from the command of [ ] Division, one of those utterly amoral individuals who always find a way of worming their way into high places. A toady to his superiors with the odious mentality of the supply lines—a mentality that he preserved to an astonishing degree—he actually kept back from us, his peers in rank, the few pieces of news that came his way through working with X. His soldiers claimed that in the course of the summer, in order to rid himself of a young Russian girl who had been his lover, he had denounced her as a spy and had had her shot.

At first, this person had attempted to expel us from the house. This wasn't the first time he had quarreled with Conti, the most nervous and touchy of us.

For all his close contact with X, however, he would have difficulty getting his way with our group, for we were united down to the last man. The moment he realized this he made his exit with the few men he had.

With the departure of the intruders, who had in any case kept to themselves even when they'd been there, a mood approaching intimacy reigned.

Even the room in which we had accumulated the garbage was cleaned up by newly arriving soldiers, who then occupied it: with all the internal walls heated, and the two stoves now working, the temperature in the house became more regular.

At dawn, our teeth no longer chattered with the cold until someone finally decided to get up and light the fire.

The firewood came from fences, poles, beams from ruined buildings, and the like, which the men foraged for daily in the immediate vicinity and broke up into pieces.

Meanwhile, the enemy were making their presence increasingly felt.

Their automatic weapons were now almost continuously in action against the German lines, and the German machine guns (ultrarapid MG 34s) never failed to respond. Russian mortar shells plummeted down more or less everywhere: by now it was practically impossible to go one hundred meters without spying their blackish funnels on the ice or beaten snow surfaces of the roads.

The German cannon and mortars, positioned among the houses, returned fire, with sudden, almighty blasts that made the few remaining windowpanes vibrate.

A couple of German mortars must have been positioned just in front of our house, inside a large building whose roof had been brought down by cannon fire months before.

Their shells rose into the air with a strange, shrill, and at the same time mournful wailing sound unlike that of any other projectile. The Russians, who managed to identify roughly where they were being fired from, often tried to return fire.

How many shells fell around us there!

And so after the brief respite of the relatively calm very first days in Chertkovo, death was again constantly in our thoughts; once more we had to accept its company, as we had during the days of the ferocious marches and the nights spent out on the snow.

At times, when we heard the frequent sound of shells coming over, we artillery officers (Conti, Ballestra, or myself) nonchalantly said that they were departing German shells, in order to spare Candela needless anxiety.

The poor fellow, who could only just manage to walk, had the tip of his nose frostbitten, as well as three or four fingers that he reckoned would have to be amputated. He had become something of the center of our concern and attention.

Those days saw the creation of the armed *centurie* that I mentioned earlier. Of the many thousand Italians who had made it to Chertkovo, the number of muskets and rifles amounted to only about five hundred (the officers and the few specialists there were had pistols, and the rest were unarmed: it was in those conditions that we had covered the last leg of the march amid the Russians!).

In all, two or three *centurie* were formed.

I didn't intend to return to the line until (as I said repeatedly to myself and others) I was sure my feet wouldn't end up with frostbite the first night out in the open.

At times I went so far as to justify my selfishness. Why, of all the hundreds of officers there, should I be one of the ten or so about to face those monstrous hours of watch in the intense cold? If one had to die, better to die the victim of a mortar shell, indoors, in the warmth . . .

The truth of the matter was that within us our indifference to the horrors in which we were immersed was being accompanied by, and becoming practically one with, indifference to the call of duty.

So—this at least is what I believe today—God was punishing me for my past presumption.

As in everything we did, the formation of those *centurie* was a very messy affair. It confirmed my previous impression: efficient as we were in anything regarding individual organization, we Italians were hopeless to a degree that astonished even ourselves when it came to collective organization.

It seemed impossible that good order could be restored . . .

When I thought of life in Italy, which was undoubtedly well organized, and of our civil discipline, I found it hard to understand how we had ever managed to attain such levels.

Of the officers in the house Valorzi volunteered for one of the *centurie* that were being formed.

He later expressed indignation and anger at the thought of all those who should have volunteered before him but who preferred to spend their time in the general's company doing nothing.

But he didn't go back on his decision. As in everything he did, he was an efficient platoon commander.

The soldiers in the house were included almost down to the last man in his platoon.

I had gradually found many of my fellow officers and men from the Thirtieth Brigade scattered here and there.

There was Captain [ ], more ruthlessly selfish than ever, together with the medical officer, who pretended to be ill in order to save himself the effort of looking after the countless wounded and frozen with whom the town was swarming.

What we lacked most at Chertkovo perhaps were, in fact, doctors: while the few conscientious ones worked to the breaking point, others, like this one, lay as low as they could.

Nor were they beaten out of hiding by a circular of General X's, which later ran the rounds from house to house, aimed at re-establishing order in this sector.

I had found Sanmartino again, as well as Carletti, a Marchegiano, my bosom companion of so many days on the front. He was lodging in a wing of the huge building behind headquarters, together with many *vecchi* from the Second Battery, including the former mess officer, Catturegli. Captain Pontoriero, the commander of the Third Battery, was also with them.

With what silent rejoicing did we find one another again!

Even if the grave, emaciated faces of most of them bespoke scant hope of coming out of this alive.

From Carletti, I learned the whereabouts of Bona and Zinzi.

So, little by little, we succeeded in getting an idea of how many of the Thirtieth were living barricaded in the town, and in exchanging a few visits.

✻

In those last days of the year Bellini and Antonini, to whom I paid the occasional visit at the infirmary, were transferred to our house, along with the "university" sergeants Braida and Pillone from Bellini's patrol.

Life had become impossible in the infirmary. Its rooms (one very large room, a few small ones, and a corridor with the entrance at the end of it) were overflowing with wounded and frozen men heaped on top of each other. Only one of the small rooms was kept free, so that there the sole medical officer could administer the so-called medications.

The truth of the matter was that there was no sanitary material at all: the few knapsacks of medicine dropped by our planes were used up immediately, so immense was the need for them. (None of the wounded, during the siege in Chertkovo, received medication more than two or three times, with only rare exceptions: and in these cases with airdropped material procured by friends.)

Practically all the doctor could do, therefore, was disinfect, or try to disinfect, the wounds and sores with a mixture of cognac and water.

The few service troops were barely able to distribute provisions and thaw the snow—which was often not that clean—for drinking water; so when you entered that bedlam, you were immediately hit by the nauseating stench of the excrement of the many who were in no condition to go outside.

The place was perpetually filled with smoke, and almost incessantly there resounded the plaintive cries of those asking for something. Some shouted for water for ten or twenty minutes on end.

The spectacle outside the infirmary was no less depressing. The snow was strewn with excrement, and invariably there was some poor fellow intent on satisfying his bodily needs.

Near the entrance, and in the open spaces between the surrounding buildings, several deep ditches had been dug by the Russians who had been captured by the troops on the line (these prisoners were a sorry sight too, with their tattered uniforms and their faces blue with cold). Here, every day, layer upon layer of corpses were deposited, one beside the other, after being dragged out of the infirmary, and very probably from the surrounding houses as well.

I stopped several times to look at them.

Beside the heads of one or another of the dead men some friend's compassion had fixed a wretched cross made of two small strips of wood nailed together. On the cross stick, written, more often than not in pencil, were the man's rank, name, unit, and often too the phrase that, in those circumstances, made such strange reading: "Caduto per la Patria".[†]

As an ever larger number of corpses were deposited there, those crosses had fallen and lay mingled with the dead, so that you could no longer tell who the names referred to. In the holes lay a multitude of oblong forms, wrapped in frozen clothing, with blackish faces that were hard to distinguish as faces. Over them, every so often, the snow attempted in vain to spread a veil of pity.

The only officer from the Sixty-first Battalion to remain in the infirmary was Lugaresi. During a bayonet attack, a bullet had gone through both biceps, digging a narrow tunnel beneath his chest muscles.

He preferred to stay there in the hope of being treated when real medication arrived.

He was being cared for by his extraordinarily devoted orderly, Bozza, an Umbrian peasant with an eternally embarrassed expression on his face, who had received a bullet through his left shoulder in the same bayonet attack.

Lugaresi lay speechless in the filth amid the oppressively foul smell and the lice on a pallet made of small rough planks. I tried to relieve his suffering by bringing him a little cognac—which he wanted and which I managed to obtain at headquarters—and by giving him all the news I could gather.

He was grateful and smiled at me forlornly.

†Tr. note: "Died for his Country".

22

With the arrival of Antonini, Bellini, Braida, and Pillone, life in the small house picked up somewhat, but didn't change.

It got dark around three in the afternoon. After eating and saying the rosary, we fell into a sleep that, from listening to others, often sounded restless and interpolated with nervous moaning. We got up at daybreak—which meant at about seven.

Most of the day we stayed on our pallets, our minds racing wildly. Will the Alpini arrive? Will the German panzers arrive? Or after so much suffering, will the only arrival be death?

It was only natural that we also talked about those troops whose arrival we could no longer count on. Each of us, however, tried not to voice his anxiety too openly.

Quite often we joked and recounted comic episodes we'd been witness to in days less desperate than these. Bellini kept us entertained a whole evening re-evoking, in his sonorous voice, the deeds of the Albanian Lieutenant M[ ], from group command, and of several other characters who had been sent home on leave some time before. We laughed heartily.

More than once—strange as it may seem—we seriously discussed a theoretical overhauling of our army.

We all agreed that an Italian army reconstructed, in the light of our experiences, according to specific criteria, could be a good army—a match for any other one and free of all the major pitfalls we had encountered.[13]

We drew up a list of those criteria, discussed each of them in turn, and studied them. The result was a sort of complete, organic picture, which I shall not go into here.

Physically, we were all still fairly debilitated. Nor did the unvarying ration of biscuit and canned food, and the occasional minestrone, do much to restore our strength.

That is why, to spare the soldiers further fatigue, I, who almost inadvertently had come to assume, to all intents and purposes, the direction of things in the house, eventually tolerated the presence just outside the door of two corpses, discovered there on different mornings.

They were the bodies of a German soldier and of a Russian serving in the German army. The German's eyes and mouth were wide open: we often went past him in the course of the day, and each time I was affected by his expression of terror, frozen by the cold.

One of the two had his clothes open and his lower abdomen indecently exposed. I made a point of covering him, buttoning up his greatcoat. I think he must have been killed by partisans.

All I did was order that the door of the house be kept shut at night by means of a small hook on the inside, and for anyone going out during the night (a common occurrence, given a widespread need to urinate, resulting, I imagine, from the cold), to take the necessary precautions.

In fact, in the town, where the inhabitants were keeping such a low profile, there were certainly partisans. Near the line a German officer had been butchered together with the entire Russian family with whom he was lodging: the only survivor was the father, who had rushed to the Germans to tell them what had happened.

We observed once again how the Russians were no less ruthless than the Germans.

Of the officers I was the one who went out most often: to seek news and to visit acquaintances.

During one of these walks, beside the abandoned tanks in the small square I found the still-fresh body of a fellow Italian, equipped with a reasonably good pair of knitted gloves. I took those gloves, since mine had lost some of their fingers, but didn't use them for long because someone stole them.

On one of those days (it must have been the penultimate day of the year—Sant' Eugenio, my name day) I was finally able to have two handkerchiefs. I was given them by Califano, the former mess officer of the Second Battery, and now chief cook in our house, who at the start of the retreat had found a small supply of them in an abandoned pack. So I no longer needed to tear pieces of lining from my greatcoat to wipe my nose.

*

The fifth day came—San Silvestro, the last day of my first year of war.

Waking that morning after a twelve hours' sleep, we were unsure whether it might not be the first day of the year.

I had to go to headquarters to check that it was December 31.

As I was on my way back, a request arrived from Colonel Casassa, commander of the Eightieth Infantry (billeted almost directly opposite headquarters, in the house where the inhabitants of our quarter did their "shopping") for "two officers for a special task."

Valorzi and I decided to volunteer. What was involved was a sort of patrol to intercept soldiers who were walking off with provisions from the stores—those caught in the act were to be shot. Given the state of real starvation that some groups of soldiers were in, it was clear that we would never be able to bring ourselves to denounce anyone.

Nevertheless, we started making the rounds of the streets and, after a pause for lunch, went out again in the afternoon.

We came across people carrying off half-crates of biscuits, sacks of flour, pasta, and the like.

After removing everything that served their needs, thereby creating their own stores, the Germans had given the old ones back to the Italians. And now, with the aid of the guards, it wasn't hard for the more enterprising, or the more famished, to procure something for themselves.

We told everyone about the grim punishment they could expect to receive and got them to hand the provisions they had purloined back to the stores of headquarters.

I remember that as we were rounding a bend in the street, one of a German truckful of loaves fell at our feet—a huge two- or three-kilogram loaf. It was picked up by a soldier, whom we immediately stopped since he also had a sack of flour on his shoulders.

We asked him to hand it over to another soldier—ragged, wretched, with frostbitten feet—who was slowly approaching along the same road, looking in all probability for something to appease his hunger.

The first soldier refused. So we ordered him to follow us, intending to denounce him for having taken the flour. He obeyed. Hearing about the bread, the second soldier, a southerner, started hopping along some distance behind us, crying all the while to the other: "Comrade, a bit of bread . . . Comrade, a bit of bread . . . ."

Valorzi and I shook our heads knowingly, as if to say: "They're all alike, these southerners!" For not even the Russian front was proof against that trite backbiting between northern and southern Italians, which had in fact flared up again since southern recruits had started rotating shifts up at the line with the northern infantry divisions. Although we northerners had little reason to be proud of ourselves, we had a very shabby opinion of the southerners. We didn't know how wrong we were; but this was only to come home to me several years later, when I saw, from the statistics, that in the postwar period it had been the southern vote that had prevented Italy from falling into the hands of the Communists. The southern electorate proved in the end to be more civil than certain highly regarded populations in northern and central Italy.

Eventually we came to a compromise: we split the bread between the two of them.

We saved another soldier from summary execution by a German guard from whom he had tried to steal some potatoes.

But what we mainly did that day was visit a great many houses, on our own initiative, to get a better idea of the condition the soldiers were in.

Luckily, almost all had reserves of food, particularly biscuits; I don't know how they would have been able to keep going otherwise.

In every house there were several men suffering from frostbite or wounded in the recent bombardments. All of them complained about the food-distribution system.

Some men, moreover, hadn't yet found suitable shelter and were compelled by the acute shortage of rooms allotted to us to sleep in unsuitable buildings that were exposed to the cold and the wind.

This was nothing new: not long before, a group had installed themselves in a hovel close to headquarters. For some days now I had seen them through large rents in the wooden walls, which were badly patched with sacking canvas, seated permanently amid the smoke, around a reddish, restless fire.

As we did those rounds, I noted, once again, how almost all my fellow countrymen had eliminated from their language the trivial expressions and oaths that are so frequent in military jargon.

And that day we also saw a noble and goodly scene. In an isba some distance from the center, a sick second lieutenant was being tended with genuine solicitude by six or seven of his men. They had brought him into the town on a sleigh and declared that they were determined not to abandon him, come what may.

Thus, in the besieged town good and evil, and misery and generosity, commingled.

But the goodness and generosity were far outweighed by the misery. We tried offering a word of comfort to the worst sufferers—meager drops on an enormous sweep of sand, which went all but unnoticed by the grains they fell on.

At the end of the day we reported back to Colonel Casassa and attempted to outline the situation to him.

The colonel (who had several wound bands on his sleeve and had just been wounded again) listened benignly; he then asserted that four thousand men drew provisions every day.

I took the liberty of saying that there must be about eight thousand Italians in Chertkovo at the time. Precisely half of them weren't drawing provisions because of the faulty distribution system.

The colonel heard me out, shaking his head incredulously: he was convinced that there were only four thousand Italians . . .

Several days later, when we assembled in divisions, and it was possible to take a census, if I remember correctly, there turned out to be seventy-six hundred. Bearing in mind those who had died in the meantime, my figure was accurate.

That evening Valorzi and I turned in with heavy hearts. We had talked about our studies, and he had also mentioned his fiancée. Around us, in the endless lines of wretched houses that made up the town, other Italians—hundreds and thousands of them—were watching their limbs slowly going gangrenous, their wounds putrefying, and were dying, dying.

Almost hourly, the enemy shells, falling almost continuously, were adding to the death toll.

As evening approached, a shabby-looking German, carrying some cakes in his arms (San Silvestro meant the distribution of "special rations" to the Germans), had addressed us in his language. Valorzi—who could speak German—had answered him correctly, and the latter, laughing, had insulted us.

When we answered him back we didn't mince our words. But what could we do—shoot him? Valorzi was very sore about the incident.

Inside our hut we too celebrated New Year's Eve.

Conti suggested we go to bed late: and so we agreed to turn in at eight in the evening.

We laughed at the lateness of that hour.

Gathered around the tiny yellow light of the burning telephone wire, we ate the minestrone flavored with a few cans of meat, recited the rosary, then talked, taking good care to keep off the most distressing issues: the armored columns and the Alpini who were meant to be arriving; what we would have liked to be eating; our distant loved ones.

But try as we would, the thought of our distant families wouldn't stay away. Were they, at that moment, worrying anxiously about us? Or perhaps cheerfully seeing in the New Year?

When we turned in, and silence reigned, all we heard were the occasional submachine guns from the opposing lines, mechanically pattering out their short, staccato rosaries.

I fell asleep, though I was itching from the lice (large, whitish ant-sized creatures, with which the whole town was crawling) that had recently started keeping me company. We hadn't changed our underwear for about a month and at night slept fully clothed, except for our shoes.

23

Dawn broke on January 1, 1943.

As usual we awoke one after the other, and in the half-light someone started munching a piece of biscuit, taking care not to make a noise for fear of waking the others. As usual I said my morning prayers and prayed to the Madonna of my people, the Madonna of the Wood.

With a heavier heart than usual, perhaps. Despite the fact that I sensed Her assiduous protection, the fruit of my mother's untiring prayers. I now had an almost physical perception of this protection: I felt it as I felt the heat from our fire and the rattle of the submachine guns out there. Nor was I the only one to have such a singular experience: others too were having similar sensations, because somebody far away was praying for them. Mario Bellini (the least suggestible of men and, though a believer, of a very "secular" cast of mind) had spoken to me more than once in puzzlement about the strangest of redeeming encounters—probably not natural but transcendental— that he had had on the night of the march toward Chertkovo.

That morning too, however, I thrust melancholy and brooding of every kind from my mind and reverted to the state of deliberate atony that ensured that I remained indifferent to everything.

On that first day of the year we received greetings from Gariboldi, the general in command of the Eighth Army, and along with his greetings his incitement to reorganize and "continue resisting".

Resist? Did the general have any idea at all of the state of utter ruin we were in?

We bore him a tacit resentment, since he never put in an appearance except by sending the odd wireless message over German headquarters' radio.

The remains of his three army corps were surrounded at Chertkovo: couldn't he fly over to us at least for a few hours? If he did (and this is all we wished) it might bring home to him the condition of the countless frozen and wounded men, among whom gangrene was relentlessly gaining ground. And then perhaps surgical instruments and sanitary material would be sent.

This was the way we saw things. We were, however, unaware of the problems besetting him: not long after, a son of his would be trapped with the Alpini.

Who knows how much he must have suffered!

I heard that in the course of the first week of the siege German heavy aircraft landed at Chertkovo three or four times, Italian aircraft a couple of times. On one of those occasions General Enrico Pezzi, commander of the Italian air force in Russia, and Bocchetti, the medical colonel in charge of the hospitals at Kharkov, flew down to see us. During the return journey their plane was discovered to be missing: it was obviously shot down. No one informed us of this, and our indignation with the medical colonel, whom we believed to be safe and sound, steadily grew at the sight of the pitifully small quantities of sanitary material that continued to be airdropped to us.

A soldier from our house gave me an eyewitness account of the horrifying scene of some of the wounded first being loaded onto an Italian twin-engine plane, then dumped again because the aircraft failed to take off. Those unhappy men had seen safety within a hair's breadth, only to be thrust back into that bedlam, where all they could expect was death . . .

The soldier who told me this had been particularly struck by the behavior of an all but demented elderly major, in tatters, with both feet and parts of his legs wrapped in pieces of blanket tied with metal wire: the poor fellow had flung himself to the ground and rolled about in the snow screaming.[14]

From the first days of the year the heavy aircraft ceased landing because the Russians were pounding the large landing strip with their guns. From then on only a few "storks" were to land—tiny German reconnaissance planes, which needed only a few dozen meters of airstrip to land and take off. The heavy aircraft confined themselves to dropping material: the Germans in great quantities, by parachute; ours, in invariably modest quantities: mainly medicine, in packages resembling padded haversacks and without parachutes, since they clearly didn't have any.

As I said, to make sure we got the material, the Italian pilots, in a spirit of great self-sacrifice, flew incredibly low over the town, harried by a tremendous uproar of machine-gun and rifle fire as soon as they crossed the Russian line.

When I was out of the pocket and happened to stop off at the airport of Voroshilovgrad, which those planes had used as their base, I learned that nine of the twelve Fiat BR 20s that made up our heavy aviation had been shot down in those flights over Chertkovo.

At the time we had been completely unaware that this had happened.

*

January 2.

This day was marked by two events: the attempt to organize all the Italians into *centurie;* and the creation of a large emergency hospital.

We had been talking for some time about forming into *centurie*, to bestow a semblance of order on the immense chaos in which we were living. From January 2 it was established that provisions were to be drawn per *centuria:* that way whoever hadn't gotten himself enrolled would go hungry.

As those in our house were quick to observe, it was a grave error lumping together in the same *centuria* men from disparate units.

Rather, it should have been patently clear that to achieve a little order the houses should have been distributed among the various regiments, thus ensuring that the survivors from the old units would find themselves together again.

But our senior officers didn't dare take this step, because there were scarcely enough houses to go around, and they were afraid that if any changes were made, the men would no longer fit into them. There was, besides, the problem of the wounded and frostbitten, who were present in every house and were receiving at least some kind of nursing.

And so the half measure of mixed *centurie* was adopted, and chaos continued to reign, because whoever had reserve provisions thought twice about joining the *centurie.* Most of them feared that once they were enlisted, they might be sent back to the line.

In the end, a total of three or four *centurie* were formed out of some eight thousand Italians.

Conti and Ballestra joined the *centuria* that already included Valorzi, as platoon commanders. A few days later, a small house was assigned to each of their two platoons, and they moved from ours to the one closest to Ballestra's platoon.

Giudici, however, was suffering from the beginnings of frostbite, so he stayed behind in our house as "standby officer" of the *centuria* command.

Bellini, Antonini, and I volunteered for another *centuria*, forming under Captain Pontoriero of the Sixty-first Battalion, which was to include Carletti and a good many soldiers from the Thirtieth.

Since, however, no place was to be had with Pontoriero, we stayed where we were, pending fulfillment of his promise to get us placed. This confused things: Pontoriero regarded us as his men, while Valorzi, Conti, Ballestra, and Giudici's centurion (who gave us provisions) also considered us his "standby officers".

What with the general disorder and the failure of the plan to organize us into *centurie,* the little goodwill that we had recovered vanished. So from that moment on we took good care to confuse matters further and stayed calmly where we were until the remains of the Thirtieth Brigade decided to regroup as before.

Zanotti, the adjutant of the Sixty-first Battalion, found himself in the same situation, having given his name to Pontoriero as we had, and then, of course, immediately regretted his decision.

With him and, I think, Mario Bellini, I went one afternoon to Y, who was now the highest-ranking officer in the Thirtieth, expressly to urge him to reunite the brigade.

At that time Y wasn't occupied with the brigade (of which he had become commander after the colonel's departure) but was running a "provisions-distribution center".

He gave us very short shrift.

Like most of the subalterns, I intensely disliked him, particularly since the night of our exodus from Arbuzov, when, after staying late with us in the gully, he had vanished without giving the slightest warning.

I therefore gave him a piece of my mind.

A row broke out, and he ordered me out of his house.

So things stayed as they were.

Corporal Navoni too, who had been in Zorzi's patrol and often spoke to me about my dead friend with affection and devotion, had moved from our house to a neighboring one, allocated to Conti's platoon.

But he often came to see me and—like other members of the Thirtieth—urged me to send for him at his present *centuria* as soon as our old brigade had reformed.

In an attempt to somehow organize the nursing service for the wounded, General X had decided to create a large emergency hospital.

In northeast Chertkovo, in a relatively low position compared with the center, a gigantic modern building rises. It was a school before the war and, I think—given its immense size—also housed public offices. Several rooms in that building (which was by far the largest in the town) were occupied by Germans, who vacated them to make way for our hospital.

We started clearing the large rooms of the scraps of metal and the filth of every order cluttering them. Countless windowpanes were broken, but since the windows were double glazed, the unbroken panes were taken out of the inner frames and fitted into the outer ones, and this made the rooms habitable.

Temistocle Ruocco, the efficient captain from the Medical Corps, a southerner and a man of untiring goodwill, directed operations: he was certainly one of the best Italian officers there in the besieged town.

On January 2 several rooms were ready, and orders were given to start transferring all the wounded and frostbite casualties.

That day, the next day, and in the days to come (as the rooms gradually became ready for use) along the frozen streets, under the misty sky, long processions of wretched men, accompanied at times by friends, at times alone, could be seen wending their way toward the hospital.

On the ground floor there were some rooms reserved for the officers.

I advised Candela not to let the opportunity slip. He moved in there, and Bellini's two "university sergeants", Braida and Pillone, moved out of the house with him, since they too were suffering from the beginnings of frostbite.

Transportation of patients to the infirmary also got under way.

This was done using one of the three or four trucks that head-quarters had at their disposal on our arrival in Chertkovo.

For an hour or two I watched them being loaded outside the door of the infirmary. Terrible scenes met my eyes.

Twice orders came to suspend operations because there was no more room in the hospital, and all that could be done was wait until other rooms were ready.

Meanwhile, a lot of wounded and frozen men billeted nearby, who were not up to covering the six or seven hundred meters separating them from the hospital, were dragging themselves as far as the infirmary so that they too could avail themselves of the truck. Some of these men's uniforms were literally in shreds, and they themselves were in the most lamentable condition.

On one occasion orders came to suspend operations when on the ground around the truck there were three or four of these wretched, incredibly ragged, dirty men. On hearing this, they didn't wait for an explanation but started howling and shouting to be loaded onto the truck. The soldiers detailed to transport the patients left them where they were, so they started crawling over the snow toward the front of the body of the truck, moving like broken-backed animals.

One of them had lost almost all human features. He managed to get to his feet and lean against a pole: his eyes were strangely devoid of movement, and all the life in that poor body seemed to be concentrated into his blackish, hirsute jaw that spat out words that were hard to make out: insults and attempts at coherence.

I enjoined the soldiers from headquarters (in their white uniforms and orderly) to load both him and the others onto the truck and made sure they obeyed the order.

Among those soldiers the driver of the truck distinguished himself for his kindness and conscientiousness. Later, in his attractive Veneto accent, he complained to me about the lack of organization and told me that his back was broken from having performed too many loading and unloading operations.

Those poor wretches too were taken to the hospital, where room was found for them.

The infirmary was still full, though.

In the afternoon I went along to the hospital, to make sure that Candela had been accommodated adequately.

Unfortunately, the rooms reserved for the officers (all on the ground floor) were bitterly cold, and there seemed to be no way of heating them.

In only one of them was there anything resembling warmth. On the floor of this room, among the sick officers, but some distance apart, lay a soldier in agony. Most of his body was naked and filthy, and he was near his last gasp.

As I came in, the officers implored me to take him away: some of the soldiers had rushed him in there, ignoring their protests, seeing that they couldn't move.

I got ahold of some of the men in charge of cleaning the rooms and, with my usual energy verging, if need be, on sternness, got them to lift the poor fellow up. He did actually inspire disgust. I had them carry him upstairs to the first floor. I went ahead to find a place for him but failed to find one.

Finally, at the end of a corridor, I found a heated room, filled with a pile of rags more than half a meter high.

Some men afflicted with frostbite lay there; I had the dying man laid there and settled him among the rags with my own hands.

Then—determined not to be paralyzed by emotion—I descended again to the ground floor.

Among those I knew there, besides Candela, were Captain Lanciai and Ricò (the medical officer), both from the Eightieth Infantry, Second Battalion. Although he had several pieces of shrapnel in his legs, Ricò was making his way slowly among the others, giving them what assistance he could. Usually he hid his profound sense of duty beneath a gruff exterior; his face, which had been pale enough even when we were on the Don, now appeared chiseled, even striated, by suffering.

I had no intention of letting my friends stay on in those cold rooms.

So I took the matter up with Captain Ruocco and learned that a small one-story building was being made ready for the officers, some hundred meters across from the hospital, almost directly opposite it. I immediately checked it out: the place, which was heated, seemed just right, so I accompanied Candela there at once. With the help of his orderly, I also carried Captain Lanciai over there, since besides having a bullet in his right shoulder, he was not up to walking.

Having settled both men in the best part of the best room, I walked back again across the snow-covered square between the small building and the hospital.

A graceless, and to our eyes incredible, cement statue in modern dress—of which there are many in Soviet Russia—seemed to follow me with its black eyes in my comings and goings across the square. Alongside it was the plinth of another statue—representing a better-known, and thus more heartily detested, figure—which had been wrenched away: iron spikes were sticking out of its cement shoes, which had remained in place.

This was not the first time that statues of this kind had made me reflect how, parallel with the loss of God, Communism's victory over the Russian people had led to an all but total loss of their artistic sensibility, which had once been so considerable.

The misty façade of the hospital, beyond the inadmissible statue, bore the scars of numerous shell attacks. And at that very moment shells were falling, far off, among the houses of the town. As always.

Killing whoever chanced to be there.

I also had an unknown centurion from the M Battalions carried away from the hospital: his feet were semigangrenous, and he had asked me not to leave him there in his freezing room. I found a place for him too in the small building, next to Candela.

It was late by now, and I left them there, on the floor, promising to come and see them the next day.

As I came out, the same truck was pulling up outside the door, loaded with wounded and frozen men of every rank whom it had brought from the town center. Before long the few rooms of that small building would be full too.

24

One day followed another.

We still received frequent news of the arrival of our troops from outside—news deliberately invented and promulgated by the German command.

Sometimes we were told that the panzers were arriving; at other times it was the Alpini; then at others German infantry divisions.

After so many disappointments, no one would have believed it any longer, if something new hadn't happened.

During the night we began to make out among the noises of war around Chertkovo, other far more muffled noises that could have been those of distant combat.

We didn't give it much thought at first; then some of us began to listen with bated breath. Little by little those noises began to make themselves heard during the daytime too.

It was clear before long that fighting was going on thirty to forty kilometers west of us.

But were these really troops who were on their way, or was it a besieged garrison like ours? We started to hope once again.

Those days witnessed several duels in the sky over the town between German planes, which were often present, and Russian ones, which, by contrast, showed themselves only rarely. The soldiers in our house saw a German aircraft being shot down. The pilot parachuted out; unluckily, he landed behind Russian lines.

Why on earth wasn't the enemy coming over in large formations to bombard us? From my experience of almost seven months' campaign, I reckoned that the Russians didn't possess many planes and had to use them in other, evidently more important, sectors. Which sectors? That was a mystery.

No less of a mystery was exactly how much territory they had succeeded in winning back. We knew only that, like us, they were holding out at the strongholds of Kantemirovka (sixty kilometers north of us, up the railroad) and Millerovo (sixty-five kilometers south, again on the railroad leading from Millerovo itself to Voronezh, and so passing through Chertkovo and Kantemirovka).

We also knew that Starobelsk—about one hundred kilometers west of Chertkovo—was free as yet, since ARMIR headquarters were still there.[15]

Morale was boosted somewhat by the news that the Italian mail, which had accumulated at headquarters, had suddenly left for Kharkov in a German "stork". With it there were also some of my postcards, in which I had written home that I was "out of harm's way" and told my parents to enroll me for the third year at university.

I later learned that only one of these postcards reached its destination and after a considerable time. It bore only German postmarks.

Subsequently, an enormous quantity of post accumulated at headquarters, but no plane descended again to collect it.

During those few days I also had the joy of meeting up again with Borghi, the gunner from the Second Battery—one of the *vecchi*—whom I was extremely fond of.

I felt remorse at observing that my old soldiers still bore me their former respect. But under my hobnailed shoe I still repressed any impulse to take any further noble decisions worthy of their respect.

Borghi, I remember, had a small tin basin in which I was finally able to bathe my still smarting, and also very dirty, feet in warm water.

In all our time in Chertkovo, only once did I give my dirt-encrusted face and hands a really good wash with soap and hot water. It didn't seem right that one of us, simply to satisfy his own personal needs, should use the little stove that was always laden with food containers or filled to the brim with snow for drinking water.

And last, I was reunited with Reginato, my orderly.

If only I could find Zorzi! . . . But for him there was no hope left.

Reginato, a shortish fellow from Veneto, had been my orderly since shortly before the retreat, when his predecessor had gone home on leave.

He brought me back my camera. How many terrible photographs there were to take . . . But on careful reflection, I refrained from doing so: I was repelled by the idea that one day someone might derive any kind of satisfaction, even of a documentary nature, from images of such endless suffering. So I used the camera at Chertkovo only to have a couple of snapshots taken of me standing in front of the house. Reginato stayed with me until the end of the siege. His feet, and one in particular, were plagued with frostbite sores, but he still managed to walk reasonably well.

I had to reconcile myself to the painful absence in the town of Gimondi and Giuseppini, the two men who had fallen in at my side the first night of the retreat, determined to share my lot if I were no longer fit to walk.

I was unable to obtain any news at all of Gimondi, the Bergamask.

On the other hand, I learned that Giuseppini—a gray-haired peasant from the Lodi plain who during the summer had always worn some nonregulation peasant handkerchief around his neck—had fallen in the Valley of Death during a bayonet attack.

A Russian machine gun had been keeping our men nailed to the ground: there was no way of getting past it. In a fit of fury, Giuseppini had made a lone forward sally, with a dagger between his teeth: he had been seen falling as if snapped in two by a volley.

This was how Giuseppini, the fierce, silver-haired corporal, is said to have met his end.

I also learned of the death of the sergeant who had been the factotum NCO of our battalion command. Before the retreat, this lad had been treated—because it had suited us to do so—as extremely capable, but this was an exaggeration: he appealed to more or less everybody's sympathy as he went about his tasks, smiling with a strange air of mutual complicity.

The last, or penultimate, day in the Valley of Death he was just beyond the main agglomeration of houses in Arbuzov. He had put a cigarette between his lips and, having nothing to light it with, had asked a passing soldier. The latter, having lit the cigarette, had continued on his way.

A few steps on, the whistle of an impending shell, then the explosion.

The sergeant's head, severed clean from his body, had rolled away across the snow.

The soldier had hurried back and bent over the headless body in horror: he had seen the whole thing with his own eyes, and the sergeant's stripes were still there on his arms; yet he had difficulty, he told me, convincing himself that that headless trunk had until only shortly before been his sergeant.

*

On one of those days I also accompanied Lugaresi to the hospital.

I had turned up at the infirmary with Antonini at the very moment that Lugaresi—who had been taken to the small room allocated for the purpose—was about to have his wound dressed. He hadn't been medicated for six or seven days. The wound on his right biceps seemed to have completely healed: I pointed this out to him, and he looked at it in surprise; until that moment he hadn't realized that he had had a bullet through that arm! . . .

The wound in his left biceps, by contrast, and the one under his chest muscles were oozing pus abundantly. I supported him while he was sitting up having his wounds dressed: the medical officer washed his lacerated flesh with a mixture of water and cognac. Then he bandaged it.

At a certain point I was compelled to ask Antonini to take over for me and went outside for a few minutes.

As I helplessly watched that rose-colored, soaking flesh and, still more, the contractions of the yellowish face of Lugaresi, who seemed to me to be at death's door, it was all I could do not to vomit.

Luckily, this didn't last long.

When his wounds had been dressed, Lugaresi seized me by the arm and beseeched me to make sure he wasn't taken into the bedlam of the large room of the infirmary.

First I had him taken to the hut, where I gave him my small iron bed. Bozza, his ever faithful orderly, went along with him.

We all gathered around Lugaresi, who, sitting up with his head against the headboard, looked at us in silence. If only we could have healed him with our eyes.

He made an effort to exchange the occasional calm word with us, but his face, beneath the bristling hairs of his beard, and with all that yellow both in his eyes and on his skin, seemed to be that of a man who was done for.

After a few hours he seemed to pick up a little.

I therefore went down to the hospital. That very day they were getting a second small building ready, which this time would really be for officers only.

The larger construction and the other small building were now filled to overflowing: some of the big rooms were beginning to assume the same bedlamlike appearance as the infirmary.

There were about seventeen hundred patients: nevertheless, both in the infirmary and in the houses there were still hundreds and hundreds of frostbitten and wounded men.

Some mortar shells had plummeted into the main building, smashing the windows and wreaking havoc among the bodies stretched out on the straw.

When the corpses had been removed and the walls and windows repaired as well as possible, the space vacated by the dead had been occupied by other wounded men.

And to think that there were many people in the town who would have liked to have gone to the hospital.

I decided without more ado to take Lugaresi to the small building that was being prepared.

Conti got ahold of a sled and sat the wounded man on it; then off we went along the ice and dirty snow of those dismal streets.

Two soldiers pulled the sled; Bozza (who had a bullet through his shoulder) and a few other soldiers followed behind us with Lugaresi's few belongings and my dismantled iron bed.

When we got there, the small building was already completely occupied. Luckily, I managed to get the bed wedged in between two others.

Bozza found a place in a lumber room, into which I had first tried unsuccessfully to fit the bed. Lugaresi told me later that two or three officers were to die in that room in the space of a few days. Since he too was an officer, he said, that room would only bring him misfortune.

*

At dawn on January 4 the Russians launched an extremely violent attack.

This was the second large-scale offensive unleashed against the stronghold of Chertkovo. Oppressed though the town was by so much wretchedness, it continued to hold out, isolated in the glacial whiteness of the plain.

This time there were far more enemy troops than previously, and they had a dozen or so tanks as well. They were not only determined to take the town but certain of doing so.

A Russian major captured by the Germans declared that when they crossed the Don he and his men had been assured that they would encounter no resistance as far as the Donetz. (As I heard the story, he was then immediately killed, which was standard German practice.)

The Russians didn't get through this time either. When their tanks came into the range of the antitank guns, they were all annihilated, save one or possibly two, which managed to pull back just in time.

A small valley extending ahead along a stretch of the German lines was now literally filled with Russian corpses. This was the second Valley of Death; "the Valley of Death of Chertkovo".

The Blackshirts distinguished themselves admirably in this action. A tank was knocked out by the large Russian antitank rifle of a Blackshirt, a certain Dino Betti. I was also told by "M" that they had even climbed up onto the tanks to slip hand grenades down through the embrasures.

The only advantage the enemy gained was that now, to west and south, their lines were no longer a couple of kilometers from the German ones but very close indeed. To the west the German line even passed through the stores.

The din of gunfire, persisting throughout the day, diminished in the afternoon and at night faded quietly away.

*

On the morning of January 5 I was with Antonini in Captain Pontoriero's house when orders came to take the whole *centuria* quickly to the stores, to extinguish the fires that were devastating them.

So the stores were burning as well! There was a risk of our starving to death . . .

We went out, and mustering the men as best we could, dragged them back, struggling over the leaden ice.

It was unspeakably cold that morning. As we proceeded slowly, our heads down into the wind, it occurred to us that the same wind that was shaking our clothes and tormenting our flesh must also be fanning fires.

Sticking close to the railroad, we crossed part of the town. We passed the first stores, where we saw heaps of pasta mixed with rubble, beneath roofs riddled with holes and likely to collapse any second. Finally we passed a few Italian guards and entered the inner courtyards.

Here we found a few platoons already at work.

The fire, thank God, wasn't threatening the biscuits or the cans of meat. It had destroyed a long stack of packing material, the rolls of which appeared intact but had been reduced to white ash.

It had destroyed thousands and thousands of woolen blankets and the storeroom containing sleeping bags (a certain number of which had thankfully already been distributed, mainly to the officers in the hospital, and a good number stolen), and devastated a supply of pressure lamps.

When we got there stacks of dismantled wooden huts were burning. It wouldn't take long to isolate the flames if we worked windward. Banishing every other thought, I set to work furiously, assigning each man a task.

Not far from the fire, under a roof, some Germans were manning a submachine gun: so the line passed there. Some others went around in massive groups, scouring the ground for ammunition. We had already seen them walking around the town: maybe they too were short of ammunition?

Volleys of swift, hissing Russian bullets flew over our heads. If the enemy started firing mortars—apart from the risk we ran from being out there in the open air—there was the danger of other fires developing . . .

Here and there some German cartridges, which the flames had gotten to, started bursting and crackling.

It was a job to keep the soldiers at work. I worked alongside them.

In the intolerable cold, the minutes succeeded each other slowly and laboriously.

Seeing so much apathy in the soldiers, the grievous insensitivity of the Germans impassively watching us at work, and a sort of impenetrable sphinx's face in everything around us, a fearsome doubt all at once wound its way lazily into my heart: the vision of reality that guided my every action and movement was a meaningless castle in the air.

And did the distant world of Italy, as I remembered it, really exist? I had to force myself not to think any more about it, to keep ahold of my wits.

Deep down I kept hoping—coyly almost—that one day I would be able to return to that world.

One would have said that none of those present wanted to return to that world; and that morning, perhaps, no one really wanted to return, for fear of suffering such sorrow.

Despite the confusion I felt within me, to all appearances I was my usual self-confident and energetic self.

We isolated the fire.

By midday we were back at the house. It was still infernally cold.

25

January 6. Epiphany.

Our families back in Italy must undoubtedly have been very worried about us.

A few evenings earlier, before moving to a new house, Conti, who had managed to find a sleeping bag, and, stripping completely, had slipped into it, happy to be free from the torment of the lice, had suddenly started sobbing his heart out in his sleep.

Again and again he moaned: "No, no, mammina . . . No, no, mammina . . . ."

I was sleeping on a bunk next to him. I stretched out my arm to wake him. We made light of it, but he was nonetheless shaken. The thought of our loved ones at home was fast becoming an obsession.

Each time Mario Bellini breathed out in his sleep, he started with a gentle moan.

I was told that I too moaned one night.

Lanky Antonini kept silent but turned over continually in his bed and never took off his shoes so as to be all the readier to leap to his feet when the Russians invaded the city. He kept saying: "Only one thing I ask of God: not to fall alive into the hands of that lot. Nothing else matters."

The soldiers in the house were in a similar state.

One of them fell ill one day. We went back and forth under the low ceiling, tending him as best we could, but there was very little we could do: almost all we did, we did with desire alone.

He rallied by himself.

With those men we also shared the spoons, which were the only cutlery we had. At first there weren't even these; then someone found a few, and a number of others were made by carving away patiently at some pieces of wood. But there were still never enough to go around.

So while some ate, others waited—holding vessels of various sizes in their hands—until their companions were through with the spoons and they in turn could eat. Meanwhile, we joked.

On the afternoon of Epiphany, Valorzi received some white German uniforms in which he clothed himself and his soldiers; then he left for the line. Conti too, armed with a Russian submachine gun (a personal war trophy, which he always had dangling from his shoulder), went off with his platoon and, if I remember, Ballestra too.

As evening approached, on my way back from visiting Lugaresi and Candela at the hospital, I met a soldier who'd been sent by Pontoriero to look for me. I at once reported to the captain. He had orders to send a platoon up to the line and—failing to find Zanotti, who had left the house a few hours before—wanted me to command that platoon. Not Bellini, or Carletti, or Antonini, since they were in poorer physical shape.

While Pontoriero was briefing me (what bothered me most was the prospect of spending nights outdoors) Carletti spied Zanotti making his way slowly back home along the avenue and called out to him.

The beast in me rejoiced.

Meanwhile, in Captain Pontoriero's house the soldiers were getting ready, putting on their greatcoats and our brown Italian helmets.

How well I knew those preparations! They reminded me of earlier days, before we had lost our pride.

Zanotti started to get ready too. He seemed nervous; his usual Milanese cheerfulness had vanished; it was as if he had a premonition. I had never seen him like this before. I sank so low as to reproach him for being so nervous!

I was unaware that within him, and in spite of himself, his youth was rebelling against the prospect of death. Yet there had been a time, before things had come to this pass, when I had felt great affinity with him. He was, after all, a Milanese student, like myself.

For a few moments I tried steeling myself to resolve to go in his place. But something instinctive and obscure—perhaps no longer just the worry of spending the night outside—prevented me. I just couldn't bring myself to do the generous thing.

Finally, Zanotti set off—young, tall, and distinctive despite his crumpled clothes—followed by his platoon, as night's shadows began to lengthen along the sullen roads.

Back I slithered into the house, crying within myself: "I just can't right now, I just can't. . . . But when this horror's over," I told myself, "I do want to be generous and valorous again . . . as I once was!"

Then the usual apathy set in.

We were a small-enough company the evening of Epiphany: Antonini, Bellini, Giudici, and I in the deserted house. Polito, the orderly whom, that evening at least, Valorzi hadn't wanted with him, prepared the meal. He made a very abundant minestrone.

Seated on the only bench and on a few rolled-up pallets, we ate until we were full. We ate by the small light of a few drops of oil— taken from the trucks—burning inside a sardine can.

We exchanged the occasional word.

All around us darkness had drowned everything. Only occasionally was it rent by the sudden flare of a rocket, shooting up from the line, and, for a few seconds, illuminating the entire spectral town.

That was Epiphany.

*

On the morning of January 7 the Germans launched a violent attack aimed at driving the Russians back from the positions they had gained a few days earlier.

And after a whole morning's fighting, the Russians had in fact been beaten back. Their line was again in its former position, a few kilometers from the German line.

Nevertheless, the distant, scattered, and tiny outlying villages of the town were still in Russian hands, and, though encircled—by relieving each other continually, as the Germans did—they were able to take turns at warming up, and thus resist.

Word ran around that during those days, and still more so in the previous days of marching and struggling through the snow, frostbite had taken a fair toll, even among the Siberian troops.

The tanks inside the town took part in the German attack. Two were lost, and several of the others returned in a sorry state. Our platoons up at the line were used for mopping up operations. That was the third and last major battle fought around Chertkovo.

In the besieged town, however, not so much as an hour went by without mortar shells plummeting down and our hearing the volleys of nearby or distant automatic gunfire.

That day, while Antonini, Bellini, and I were in the house, a soldier came from the line, saying that an "artillery lieutenant" was dead. We immediately thought of Zanotti. After a while Polito came back from seeing Valorzi and gave us the news: Zanotti was dead.

Awakened by an alarm during the night, he had left the shed that his platoon was using as a shelter with seven or eight soldiers. As he was making for the trench, a mortar shell had fallen at his feet and exploded, killing him outright and ripping his face to bits.

Behind him, Corporal Oronesi, a Sardinian, one of my *vecchi* from the Second Battery, had been wounded, together with another soldier.

✳

The following day I went up to the line to photograph Zanotti's remains. If ever I managed to return home, I intended to give the photograph to his mother, who lived in Milan.

But Zanotti had already been buried, and, in any case, Valorzi told me that his facial wound made him unfit for any kind of photograph.

I went to see where he had been buried. They hadn't dug a grave as such, but had placed him, along with a soldier, under a wretched layer of earth and straw, against the wall of the shed where the *centuria* was quartered. There was already a light blanket of snow over the straw, giving that mound the same appearance as all the others scattered around.

Suddenly two Fiat BR 20s flew very low overhead, dropping crates of ammunition. Filling the air with the clamor of their engines, they wheeled around immediately, and there they were again flinging down other crates. Our pilots, with their customary daring, were risking their necks in the attempt to help us! This was why—though we didn't know it at the time—all too often they didn't make it back to base.

Many of the crates smashed into pieces on hitting the ground, scattering the submachine- and machine-gun cartridges over the snow.

Several Germans who witnessed this made an eager dash to where they fell, hoping to find something to eat.

The centurion and Valorzi had to send soldiers to gather the material up in blankets.

Both men were thoroughly depressed: it now took more than NCOs to get the men into position. Each man had to be personally dragged off his pallet and thrown out of the shed.

On my way back to the town I again passed a gigantic German tank, abandoned on an escarpment. It looked intact. It was obviously one of those that had been hit during the last bout of fighting.

As the number of tanks decreased, our already tenuous chance of being saved was further diminishing.

No one said as much, but this was another reason that most of us had lost all hope.

*

In the days that followed, being very closely acquainted with the officers working there, I spent more time at headquarters.

Since becoming *Comando truppe in linea* it had changed appearance. A lot of tall, slender tree trunks had been propped up along the outside walls of its most exposed sides—to give it some kind of protection from the shell fragments. Inside, in the office of the deceased lieutenant colonel, our commander, Russian prisoners were busy digging an underground room. The entrance was now at the back, in the same square as the infirmary and Carletti's house, and a sentry stood permanent guard outside.

I spent a bit of time with the adjutant captain—an original fellow, who on one occasion told me nonchalantly that he had just had two soldiers shot because they'd been caught stealing in the stores. Who knows whether he was telling the truth? I met the German liaison lieutenant and others, including a journalist who was serving as a clerk.

It was around that time that General Gariboldi, the commander in chief of ARMIR, granted General X permission to award medals for gallantry in combat at Chertkovo. At "Troop Headquarters" there was a great coming and going to make sure that medals went to the most deserving of the five hundred men who had been on the line since the first days of the siege; but X allowed only very few men to be decorated.

I was there when the adjutant captain, getting a courier to give him the names, listed the recommendations for several members of the only Italian battery present in the town, a 75/46 antiaircraft battery.

That battery had quite a tale to tell.

Before our arrival, the guns had been positioned at certain road junctions by way of antitank defense. When we got there, one of these guns had ended up beyond the resistance line. The captain in command had then gone to such great efforts as to obtain four German tanks, and, with assault troops, his own men and one of his gun-commander sergeants had managed to get them hooked up and towed into town. He lost his life in the process, though. The battery was now commanded by the lieutenant who had been his second-in-command.

If only we too could have had a couple of guns in Chertkovo! How often, in my artilleryman's heart, did I find myself wishing for them. How different life would have been then . . .

Sometimes German gunners would drag a cannon to a crossroads or the edge of a square and open fire. They generally fired at very close range, with the sight set almost at zero: the smoke from the explosions could be seen rising as little as one kilometer away, or less, among the wretched houses outside the town, where the invisible enemy was nesting.

Occasionally I stopped for a while and watched: the gun shuttled violently back and forth on its cradle, between formidable crashes and lashes of blackish smoke. How well I knew the prompt obedience of that steel!

At other times I would stop to survey the land around me with a now-expert eye: look, a line of guns might be positioned there . . . and the observation post, there . . . and so that must be where the telephone line ran, hung haphazardly from the poles and the edges of buildings.

Little by little my eye would lose itself in the dirty, indifferent whiteness, so that I found myself no longer caring and, beneath the weight of the cold, proceeded on my way.

*

I also went along fairly frequently to the hospital, where they eagerly awaited the little news I managed to bring with me.

Candela greeted me with open arms, as did Captain Lanciai, whom I found more than once with his head in a small Bible. For days the bullet in his shoulder had kept him from sleeping, and he seemed very run-down indeed. I was given a hearty welcome as well by the centurion whom I had had brought to the small building along with my two friends.

I also met other officers who'd been admitted there, including Second Lieutenants Scotti and Triossi.

Except for Captain Lanciai—who had managed to procure himself a wretched iron bed—all the others slept on the ground on pallets or in sleeping bags.

During the day, those not compelled to spend their whole time lying down folded up their pallets and sat on them. The floor (and this was the main difference between the officers' and the soldiers' room) was kept constantly clean.

At times, while I was on one of my visits, mortar shells exploded in the open space between the small block and the large hospital building: when this happened, everyone waited in silence for the enemy to suspend or adjust fire.

If ever anyone was in God's hands it was those sick men.

Sometimes Captain Lanciai's orderly, who had become pretty much everybody's orderly in the room, started singing as he went about his chores.

Since nobody sang in Chertkovo, we fell silent and listened.

His low, limpid voice traced gentle patterns of love, or nostalgia, or regret; or else tripping, carefree patterns.

How those words took on new meanings—words we might at other times have considered stupid!

Into our hearts there crept a wistful memory of less luckless days in the war, when there was always somebody singing, and of our voices in the evenings rising in chorus from our encampments. And this in turn brought a hankering for our homeland, and nostalgia for smiles, and peace, and love—things denied to us, surrounded as we were by death. Even the gray figures we saw going past outside the window, bent double by cold and adversity, brought vividly home to us the contrast with the colorful world of those songs.

Then the man's pleasing voice died away, and, speechlessly, each of us relapsed into apathy, in order to keep going, in order to endure.

*

On one of those days—January 7 or 8—so as to have some reliable news to bring my wounded colleagues, I decided to go and ask the Germans. They had put around the most astonishing news: the Russians who had broken across the Don had themselves been trapped in a massive pocket. Boguchar was now in German hands. Even Moscow and Petrograd had been caught unawares.

I presented myself at sundown at a branch headquarters located in our zone and was accompanied beyond the railroad to the underground quarters of the main command, where the radio was functioning.

Working there as an interpreter was a soldier from the Ravenna Division, wearing a white German uniform: Conti, a modern-languages student at the Bocconi University in Milan. He gave me all the news he had and translated that day's German bulletin. Unfortunately, nothing new: the bulletin only spoke about German counterattacks on the central front.

So we had to rest our hopes exclusively in the sounds of distant fighting, which we heard mostly at night whenever we woke up, held our breaths, and started listening.

Conti came outside with me: it was dark by now.

In front of headquarters a bespectacled German sentry was trudging back and forth over the beaten snow.

"Password . . . ," he asked, and on receiving the password, asked for it again, obtusely. Possibly he wasn't convinced by the foreign accent in my companion's German.

Finally he shut up.

To make sure I didn't lose my way, Conti, with goliardic solidarity (we were both Milanese students), insisted on accompanying me through the German sector as far as the railroad, then through the Italian sector almost as far as headquarters. All about us, among the ruined buildings the impenetrable darkness of the sky pressed down on the snow, which seemed to be forcing itself—quite uselessly—to push it back with its feeble reflections.

I called again on Conti a few days later: he still had no news about the progress of operations.

He did, however, give me a piece of information that surprised me: the King had conferred our highest decoration for valor on General X: the military order of the House of Savoy. Gariboldi had radioed this through.

The news hadn't been circulated and wasn't supposed to be.

At those headquarters I got a glimpse of the German colonel in command at Chertkovo. He was an elderly fellow, not tall, thickset, stern featured. He treated his subordinates haughtily.

Shortly thereafter, he was to be flown off by a "stork", summoned to some German army command. He was promoted and didn't return. Another colonel was flown in to take his place in the besieged town.

26

Meanwhile, enemy shells continued exploding, day after day, in every quarter of Chertkovo. The leaden sky of the town was rent by the hissing of shells, shells, and more shells from the mortars, artillery grenades of various calibers, and *katyusha* rockets, each with its own distinctive sound. The projectiles from the portable arms smashed against the more solid walls with dry, little explosions, like violent whipcracks.

We were so used to the explosions that we now regarded them as an integral part of our environment. Thus, a 50-mm mortar shell, bursting just one meter outside the window under which I was lying, did no more than make me turn over onto my other side.

Not all those shots, not even most of them, but some, naturally, claimed victims.

One evening, as I was on my way out of headquarters, some 82-mm mortar bombs exploded in the square between the latter and Pontoriero and Carletti's house.

One exploded a hair's breadth from two soldiers who were standing by a horse harnessed to a sleigh. While the horse reared, the two men staggered about in the smoke, then fled, both of them wounded.

Carletti told me that another shell had exploded a few hours before just outside the door of his house: the windowpanes had shattered, leaving huge rents in the wooden body of the door; one of two Germans who had been walking by at that moment had been killed, and the other had been left lying wounded and bleeding on the ground.

What horror those evenings brought with them!

And deep in our souls we had to add all these things to the tally of our earlier experiences. Who could tell what the final count would be?

That badly sundered wooden hovel, mentioned above, faced the short, shapeless square between Carletti's house and headquarters.

186

Ragged compatriots, finding nothing better, were still residing in it, exposed to the cold and the wind.

Outside, in the grubby snow illuminated by the wavering glare of the fires that those poor wretches kept perpetually lit, some horses, skinny and frost encrusted, were lying. One wasn't dead, though, but dying, and had been out there in the merciless cold for days writhing in interminable agony.

I went up to examine it. Possibly the poor animal heard me; I got the impression that in its fidgeting it was attempting to stretch its ice-bound head, with those blind eyes, toward me.

I had to put it out of its agony. Sparing with my bullets, I walked around until I was facing its forehead, and gave it an almighty kick with my heavy shoe. I hoped to kill it, as with a club, but the animal was now doing all it could to avert its head from me.

Again and again I kicked it, but it was still no good.

In the end I whipped out my pistol and put a bullet through its brain.

There were mortar holes practically all around us. Scattered matter gone to rot. Corpses that had lost all human form. Ragged frostbite casualties dragging themselves along. And just beyond, the infirmary graves brimming with dead bodies. War!

Again I thought of those who had blithely filed through the streets clamoring for the war . . . and the scenes of luxury and indulgence in the cities and at the seaside resorts also came to my mind: it almost seemed then that there was no way of checking the flood of corruption; but here was the other side of the coin, here was the dam.

The horror of the martyred and rotting flesh on those live bodies, a punishment in kind for the inexcusable inebriation of the flesh.

As in the valley of Arbuzov, again we had before us God the castigator.

*

One dismal morning the Russians began systematically bombarding us with all their heavy armaments. This lasted uninterruptedly for nine hours.

The whole town fell under the rake of enemy fire. From that day, one could safely say that there was not a building in Chertkovo left unscathed in one way or another.

Shortly after Epiphany the senior officers, summoned by General X, had finally decided to split the Italian part of the town into zones and to allocate each zone to what remained of a regiment.

The Thirtieth Artillery ended up with a group of thatched houses on the northern outskirts of town.

The very day of the bombardment, Bellini, Antonini, and I were off to see how things were coming along in our future billet (a group of Blackshirts were taking their time vacating it). Bellini led the way. He was just about to step through the doorway when he stopped in his tracks, then swiveled around, and shoved us back inside.

For some time now I had noticed that he had an incredible ear for *katyusha* missiles. And sure enough, all hell at once broke loose as sixteen missiles exploded one after the other, bursting around us in rapid succession.

We flung ourselves to the ground, clutching our heads between our arms. The house shook to its foundations. I muttered a prayer through clenched teeth.

A hair's breadth away all the windowpanes suddenly smashed to smithereens; their slender wooden frames slammed screechingly to and fro again and again.

Eventually we were able to get up, still in one piece.

I saw then that Providence, working through Bellini's fine ear, had saved us from death yet again. Had we left the house we would have passed immediately in front of a wretched house a few meters away to the right of ours. Well, this house—which was made almost entirely of wood—had been literally split in two by a missile, and nailed to the pavement along which we had to pass was a heap of large sheets of metal roofing and beams.

What was most astounding was that out of this ruin came Lieutenant Colonel Rossi of the Eighth Artillery, completely white with rubble. Before our eyes he shook the dust off, adjusted his holster belt, then ambled off along the avenue, without so much as a word.

There were several other people in the house at the time: none died.

Since the bombardment was still so close, the three of us, along with my orderly, Reginato, left our habitation for the time being and moved over to Ballestra and Conti's, which was set some eighty meters back from the avenue.

Giudici stayed on in the house a few minutes longer; then he too left with his men, though I don't know where he went. (I was only to see him again back in Italy, years later: he had managed to get away with a few small amputations of his fingers and violent nervous tremors.)

The bombardment was formidable.

Above and in front of us the air was perpetually rent by the enemy shells and grenades hurtling down, invisible and swift as lightning, then smashing to earth with enormous bursts.

The huge shell fragments howled their lamentations, which wavered after a bit and finally died away.

From the position close to us, incessantly—with that strange, drawn-out wailing of theirs—rose the shells of German mortars firing back.

Through one of the windows of Ballestra and Conti's house, we could see the smoke of frequent enemy shells among the nearby houses surrounding the small square where the tanks were standing.

Some rose just over our heads, and then we stopped joking and looked each other in the face, then smiled: God's will be done!

Midmorning we had to return to the house because Reginato, whom I had sent to fetch something, reported that it was being pillaged by soldiers.

Mario Bellini stopped one of them, and was barely able to resist killing him. Seeing my friend's indignation brought me close to laughter: how could one still fly off the handle like that over such a thing? He took the pillager's first and surnames, determined to report him.

Now that the windowpanes had been destroyed, we had no alternative but to move.

We carried our pallets to Ballestra's house, where we were put up until the following day.

In the afternoon, in the continuing bombardment, a 76-mm cannon shell skimmed the roof of the low house we had left and penetrated the one to its left—where the soldiers from Conti's platoon were billeted—exploding in their midst.

Scared out of his wits and white with rubble, Corporal Navoni came to tell us this: the dust on his face was mixed with blood dripping from where he had been cut.

We dashed to the house.

I was the first to get there. Soldiers were coming out; I could hear cries of pain.

I immediately arranged for the only two who had been wounded to be transported to Ballestra's house. (All the others—about a dozen—had no more than scratches.)

As he was being carried on the back of a companion, who held him suspended by his arms, one of the two wounded men let out a scream of agony.

We then realized that he had half an elbow missing.

On his side, he also had a gaping hole in one of his thighs, at the level of the top of his thighbone.

We laid him down on a makeshift cot.

We couldn't take the two men to the hospital without dressing their wounds first: given the shortage of doctors, it would be three or four days before they were looked at, which meant they would have bled to death.

I decided to dress their wounds myself.

Luckily, one of Ballestra's soldiers had a first-aid kit and some cotton wool, which he immediately handed me. Surgical instrument: an iron-colored pair of Russian household scissors. Disinfectant: melted snow, which was, I seem to recall, salted.

The main thing I did was to fill the two cavities in his arm and thigh with cotton wool, then bandage it up. I also washed a number of deep scratches, encrusted with ceiling plaster and blood, that the wounded man had on his face.

The poor wretch kept repeating in a Tuscan accent: *"Il mi' bambino, signor tenente . . . Il mi' bambino . . . ."* To give him heart I cheerfully scolded him: Had he ever seen anyone die of an arm wound, or a leg wound? What was he worrying about then?

And all the while I knew that certain death awaited him!

The other wounded soldier had a reddish cavity just below one of his armpits: almost a third of a grenade head had penetrated there and was now sticking out of his back, with its short serrated edge near a shoulder blade.

He was a mere boy. From what I could gather, he had already been wounded a few days earlier.

One of Conti's corporals, Brighina—a sort of thickset Sicilian brigand, whose devotion to his fellow countryman, Conti, I had noted, as well as the brutal stories I'd heard him recount about his exploits in the Valley of Death—never left the wounded lad's side, anguished at not being able to assist him.

He was from the same village: he continued calling the boy by his first name and spoke to him in Sicilian dialect, comforting him with a strange impulsiveness that was overbearing but that also bespoke fright.

The wounded boy, who had lost buckets of blood, had difficulty staying on his feet. With the scissors, I cut away his shirt, which was incredibly saturated. Then, still using the scissors, I extracted the large grenade splinter that had threads of shirt sticking to it. When I had cleaned the wound in a fashion, I placed the cotton wool at both the entrance and the exit of the cavity, then bandaged it up.

In the semidarkness of the room the other officers stayed at my side, ready to come to my aid.

Suddenly [ ] asked me if the scissors cut well: "I want to clip my nails," he explained.

We were going to pieces. I looked at Mario Bellini, who shook his head.

The two wounded men were loaded onto a German sleigh drawn up alongside the house, and Conti, getting soldiers from his platoon to drag it, took them to the hospital.

A couple of days later Brighina, on a visit to his *paisan*, reported that he was still alive. That was the last I heard of them.

27

The following day, January 10, we moved to the isba in the sector assigned to the Thirtieth.

Of the seventeen hundred men who had formed our brigade on the banks of the Don, we realized that there were only about three hundred of us left. We heard the memory of those others weeping to us silently in our hearts; we did what we could to stop that memory from taking full possession of us.

The zone we were now living in, somewhat lower down than the center of the town, was, as I have said, on its northern outskirts. Apart from the isolated metal carcass of an aircraft engine, which overlooked it, it had the usual uniform appearance of Russian villages.

Single-story isbas, with large, thatched roofs and uneven walls, not at all solid, built without bricks: they were generally painted white and had small windows, which were often double glazed. In some of them—a rare ornamental touch—above the door or the odd window there was a small, crudely carved wooden plank, a sort of mantelpiece.

Between one building and another, only a few bare plants.

Many of these isbas were inhabited by civilians. But since, like most Russian peasants' houses, they had an external underground cellar or storeroom, the civilians all lived hidden away in those holes, coming out of them as little as possible.

Here, however, it was a good deal easier to encounter them than in the center, especially the women: wrapped in large dark shawls, drawing water from the wells or walking alongside the frozen roads beneath the leaden sky.

Sometimes they were followed by children whose heads were wrapped in large scarves. These women and children stirred our Italian hearts to pity.

Our new dwelling place consisted of three rooms, two of which were heated, while the third, which had wooden walls, served as an entrance hall against the cold.

Some soldiers from the Thirtieth were already there, having laid claim to it as the Blackshirts were moving out.

The first day we shifted for ourselves as best we could; but on the second day I had the few pieces of furniture moved out into the entrance hall, thus clearing the two heated rooms completely, and got our places into some kind of rational order.

Three iron beds, one beside the other, on which we officers arranged our straw mattresses, and two orderly rows of pallets on the ground (straw mattresses, or simply straw) for the soldiers.

I had a list of the occupants put up on the inside of the door and a single ration card for drawing provisions.

Provisions were no longer distributed in just the two places. There were sectors and subsectors: provisions were collected for each regiment by a specially appointed officer, who issued them in turn to the houses of his respective regiment. We of the Thirtieth drew ours from Captain Varenna, who had also been transferred to our zone.

The service was on the whole fairly well organized; but unfortunately the provisions themselves were now becoming scarce, since the general had decreed that they were to be made to last until the end of February.

On some days all each man received was a biscuit, half a can of meat, and a handful of pasta. Also, the distributions of wine—which the soldiers went to collect with sacks, since it was issued in badly hewn blocks of ice (rare enough at the best of times)—had, as I recall, ceased some time before.

Since the water from the nearby wells—located along the roadside, with their mouths at ground level—was oddly salty, we were still using the water obtained from melting the snow. We did, however, get into the habit of sending someone to draw water near the hospital: it was invariably green, murky water, but some of us found it less disgusting than the water from our wells. What we didn't know was that there, at the bottom, three or four meters from the surface, lying one on top of the other, were the corpses of two Russians. I later learned that they were perfectly aware of this at the hospital; nevertheless, it was the only water anyone drank.

A family of civilians inhabited our isba as well, living and sleeping in a small underground room. But since they cooked their food on the stove of the isba, they were often with us.

There was the seventy-six-year-old grandfather, the grandmother, a man of about forty who had been the manager of one of the town's factories and who knew a smattering of German, two or three women, a small boy, a babe in arms only a few months old, and I forget who else.

We bartered some food with them and spent some time in conversation. Mario Bellini acted as interpreter since he had learned Russian during the summer, on the supply lines.

I remember that the simple little landscapes and seascapes that Simonetto, one of our soldiers, enjoyed painting, won their admiration—and not just the boy's.

It's not at all easy to make out the Russians; and I don't think just for those in a predicament such as ours. They are extraordinarily elemental. The impulses that drive them arise like the natural phenomena on their immense, fenceless land: excessively and uncontrollably. Positive and negative impulses alike, which seem to alternate indiscriminately within them, just like the natural phenomena on their land.

All of us, to a greater or lesser extent, had noted their fundamentally good character; but we'd also noted their fatalism, and their consequently alarming inertia and carelessness, and a dense materialness, which made them generous one moment and ferocious the next.

This was the terrain on which Communism had taken root, systematically inciting the Russians to hate and thus butcher one another by the millions. If we were terrified by the prospect of ending up in their hands, above all it was because we knew that we were automatically bracketed by their leaders among the enemies of Communism.

The common folk, though—the people—didn't strike us as being remotely Communist . . . but more like its victims, particularly the peasants.

But for that matter, what a tragic pass we had all come to—ourselves no less than they!

The kindheartedness of their countrywomen, and particularly the mothers, also needs recalling, and their compassion for any suffering being. Wherever we encountered them, in whatever village, they were always the same—monotonous and marvelous.

All of us knew how, during the halts on our ferocious marches, more than one of our compatriots (including Corporal Borghi of the Second Battery) had been rescued from frostbite, and thus from death, by the maternal, selfless care of poor women.

Humble women, like those in our isba who, when a shell exploded nearby, crossed themselves repeatedly and mumbled prayers.

Some of my *vecchi*—veterans from the Second Battery—were billeted in two isbas near ours: Corporal Borghi, whom I've just mentioned, Pedrollo, Catturegli, Gola, and one or two others.

Every so often I went to visit them and always got a joyous welcome.

On one occasion they gave me some half-burned honey that Pedrollo had managed to purloin from a burning German warehouse: "Try putting it in the 'surrogate', as we have, *signor tenente;* you'll see how good it makes it . . . ."

Often they were the ones who paid the visit, listening carefully to everything I said. After backsliding on so many occasions, I always felt I had no business to be the object of the trust they still had in me.

In an isba just outside our sector, I unexpectedly met up again with Second Lieutenant Montresor, the head of my department at the officers' training school in Moncalieri.

Since they were partly frostbitten, he had swathed his feet and legs up to the knee in pieces of blanket, then stitched sacking canvas tightly over it, so that he seemed to be wearing boots.

One afternoon, while I was over there with him, heavy Russian shells exploded in the sector of the Thirtieth, sending up huge billows of smoke among the shacks.

No one was killed, luckily. Wide shallow craters, black with earth and cinders, were left in the snow.

It was during those days that the sad news reached me of the death of Califano, the mess officer who had given me the two handkerchiefs I was still using.

He was killed, along with others, while going about his business as a cook, by a grenade that exploded inside Valorzi's shed up on the line.

The same shed next to which Zanotti lay buried.

One after another we were all disappearing . . .

*

From January 10, things changed: the Russians suddenly ceased bombarding the town.

One day went by, then another, and the enemy stayed calm.

Despite their customary impassiveness, the Germans didn't know what to make of this. This I was told at headquarters by their liaison officer, who spoke Italian: they thought some nasty surprise was in store for us.

The Russians' silence, however, had the reverse effect on us Italians: it reimbued us with hope. The rumor going around might, then, be well founded: that the Russians who had crossed the Don were themselves about to be encircled and were therefore beginning to fall back northward.

General X, normally so stern at these senior officers' meetings, now appeared to be good-humored and optimistic. News began to circulate, and to be believed, of the dates when our men would be arriving and opening up the road: in seven days, in five.

I too began to hope more ardently, above all because the sounds of combat to the west could now be heard more distinctly and closer to hand.

And so the fierce seesaw of hope and unease got going again in that part of our souls that still remained alive.

One morning a carabiniere responsible for guarding the stores came into our isba, saying he had seen a long line of enemy wagons and trucks crossing the railroad a few kilometers from the town, heading north. Was it actually true then that the Russians were in retreat?

Under the dark sky, the German antitank guns fired on that silent procession of ghosts.

The carabiniere—a friend of one of our soldiers—also told me about a strange thing that had happened to him at Arbuzov.

He was standing in a group with four or five soldiers when a *katyusha* shell had exploded in their midst, knocking all of them over, except for him, who managed to stay on his feet. This had dumbfounded him, for the others seemed to be have been literally torn to pieces. One had had the front part of his chest completely ripped away by a shell-fragment: his lungs, heart, and stomach were visible, all intact: "as if someone had opened a book," was the way he put it.

Shock had driven the carabiniere out of his wits, and he had become convinced that he was dead. He himself was no longer alive, only his soul. This belief had persisted for a number of days, until, finding food, he had managed to recover some of his strength. In the interim he went into attack with the Italians, spurring them on with his voice and with gestures; he didn't shoot though, and he didn't take cover from enemy bullets, for a dead man can neither kill nor be killed.

❊

Valorzi had returned with his platoon to the house we had abandoned, patching up the broken windowpanes as best he could with planks and rags.

Every so often I visited him, as did Conti and Ballestra; or the three of us went along to see Candela and Lugaresi in the hospital.

It was a pretty act of penance even for us, who were now past masters at this sort of thing, to linger in Lugaresi's room. There was an almighty stench, coming from the neighbor to his right, who was unable to move from his bed.

Lugaresi was wounded in the stomach and already well beyond the boundary line separating the living from the dead. To this day I can see his emaciated face, in which the only living things were his eyes.

He looked at us with those intent eyes of his and seemed to be following our jocular talk and listening to the words that we often addressed to him too, though who knows whether he understood them.

After January 10 Italian night work for the Germans on the line was stepped up. Initially the latter only made use of Russian civilians and prisoners. Every so often, in the evening, we would see Germans roaming the streets in search of men. They even dragged off old men of seventy. On one occasion I managed to salvage the grandfather in our isba from the hands of one of the Germans, who had come to get him. It was a wickedly cold night, and the poor old fellow might well have died before dawn.

Later, since there weren't enough Russians, the Germans also took to using Italians, whom they treated all too often in the same fashion as the Russian prisoners.

At the request of the German command, they were currently being dispatched in shifts by the different regiments, through headquarters: every night the Germans took delivery of a batch of two, three, or four hundred men.

The men had to dig communication trenches, shelters, and weapon pits.

For two evenings running I too found myself having to accompany forty men or so to headquarters, where German couriers were awaiting them.

I don't say we should have refused to do this job; but it was, to say the least, humiliating.

On January 11 the Thirtieth received orders to form four armed platoons, each consisting of fifteen men.

The old hybrid *centurie* had been disbanded. The idea was to form new ones, all consisting of members of the same regiment. Bellini, Antonini, Regazzoni of the Sixtieth Battalion, and I were each assigned the task of getting a platoon together.

I went along to an isba housing some twenty men and a sergeant—a student called Marcello Martano. I took him on as vice platoon commander and picked out fourteen of the men. These I split into two squads, each with its own commander and vice commander.

The only one of the men I already knew was the gunner Carrara, who belonged to the First Battery of my battalion. Unlike the other officers, I actually preferred using soldiers I didn't know: more than likely I would be taking them up to the line, very possibly to their deaths. I couldn't abide the thought of being the one to lead those last wretched remnants of the large family of my men to their deaths. Better to leave them in peace as long as possible.

I armed the men in my platoon with rifles and pistols commandeered from men who had not been enlisted and supplied them with helmets found in one place or another.

In my platoon hut I imposed a modicum of military discipline: on my entry, the sergeant called the men to attention and every two hours sent a man along to me to ask if I had any orders or news to communicate.

*

Meanwhile, the hours and the days followed each other over our isbas: we were living in a perennial state of expectancy for some new event that never came to pass.

I tried to keep the soldiers' morale up by relaying the few scraps of positive news that came my way.

But by now we had been in this pocket for almost a month; we had had too many all too fervid hopes snatched from between our teeth; and we were haunted by the constant knowledge that the vast majority of us were missing or dead.

And others were continuing to die every day.

Very few, I think, made any effort to believe—as I attempted to believe—in the possibility of salvation.

In the mornings, made crystal by the frost, all the thatched roofs in our quarter smoked identically, in a sort of rapt silence. This is perhaps the vision of Chertkovo that most often comes back to my mind today.

Every time I stepped outside, my eyes met a number of large mules, their coats shaggy with dew, eternally, agonizingly standing there in the snow and on the ice outside a neighboring isba.

Although they were not tied up, they stayed there night and day, never once receiving anything to eat, their poor heads bowed.

They must have saved some man's life by carrying him into town; but now they had huge, lumpy, frozen wounds and were no longer of any use to anyone; and the men who had used them, even if they were still alive, no longer bothered with them.

Every time I came out of the house I hoped that, next time, I wouldn't see them. I hoped that someone would decide to lead them off somewhere; if not, I myself would eventually take them into some sheltered place. In the end they died.

We too received some of that meat.

Much of our time we spent sitting or lying on our pallets.

One of our main occupations consisted in removing our filthy underwear and examining it carefully for lice.

Hour followed hour.

In the isba of my *vecchi* from the Second Battery, Catturegli, the former cook, a Tuscan, suddenly fell ill.

He lay on the straw, shivering ceaselessly with fever. What could we do? We waited for him to pull through by himself, or die.

What troubled us most, however, was the thought of the patients in the hospital buildings, who now amounted to two thousand.

One of the three doctors working there had a dark view of their fate, and said as much: "A week more like this," he said to me on one occasion, heedless of the poor wretches who could hear his words, "and half of them will be dead." He had become very gloomy, opening his arms and shaking his head; he then returned to his rounds.

Both he and Captain Ruocco were working in appalling conditions: at times they amputated gangrenous legs and arms with knives and razor blades.

Conditions were becoming particularly disastrous in the main building. It was a job getting up the stairs along the unheated corridors, because there was a razor-thin layer of ice (mainly frozen urine) permanently covering the floors and steps. On entering some of the rooms, you were greeted by dense smoke descending in a thick mass from the ceiling to a mere meter above the floor: beneath this smoke the rooms were filled with men heaped on top of the straw, ragged, crawling with lice.

Many had been lying there in that condition for weeks. Around them they could see death—the mower—going tirelessly about his business; each day their eyes silently followed their dead companions as they were carried outside by the soldiers appointed for the task . . .

I remember the face of a soldier with a fine red beard, who came from a village not far from mine. He had been brought to Candela's small building, and I never failed to linger a while with him as well. He trembled incessantly and violently.

His neighbors said that he had a *"febbre fredda"*—a cold fever. The last I saw of him, he couldn't stop crying, desiring something that nobody could give him.

I remember another patient as well, though he was a stranger to me. Driven by thirst, he had walked out of the hospital—despite the fact that his feet had frostbite and possibly gangrene too—making for the hole in the ice from which both soldiers and civilians of the zone drew drinking water, the water that had two Russian corpses lying at the bottom.

Suddenly he could walk no farther and burst into convulsive tears, shaking a German flask that he held in one hand. His whimpering extended but a short distance around the frozen patch of wasteland.

I went up to him: a very characteristic—and very agonized—southern face, his long teeth bared in a grimace.

Poor infantrymen of Italy!

I had no containers with me; I filled the flask with water from the bucket that a little girl was doing her level best to carry away.

*

Around January 12 Mario Bellini, together with Regazzoni, left our isba on a liaison operation with the Germans.

He went off one evening, with some hundred soldiers and his two "university sergeants", Braida and Pillone. He seemed edgy and worried. What did "going on a liaison operation with the Germans" mean? We didn't know.

Who would have thought that we would only see one another again several years later in Italy?

His place in the isba was immediately taken by Captain Magaldi, from the army corps artillery command: a young captain (of twenty-five or twenty-six) in good condition but with a delicate constitution.

He settled down in Bellini's bed, against a wall that had on the other side of it a stove that worked for us by day and by night for the women of the house.

Too much heat made him feel very unwell, giving him a headache and fever. I was duly compelled to reorganize the room in order to bring his bed closer to the windows.

The captain's orderly had moved into the isba with him—Bellagente, one of the *vecchissimi* of the CSIR, who had found himself in the pocket only a few days before he was due to return to Italy on leave. (Like others in a similar predicament, he had had to embark on the retreat in his summertime, canvas uniform.)

He took Mario Bellini's place as interpreter with the Russians.

The two men's arrival brought no change to life in the house.

And so January 15 came as well.

Recently, the Russians had given very little sign of life. Many of us thought it possible that only a few units had stayed behind to keep us encircled until the bulk of their army—which, after leaving Chertkovo behind them, must still be well to the west—had pulled back toward the Don.

FROM CHERTKOVO TO OUR LINES

28

~

On January 15, at six in the evening, the news came out of the blue: we were to get ready to leave the town within a few hours.

I hadn't yet gotten wind of anything when I was sent for by Captain Varenna, who distributed provisions to us. It was already pitch-dark.

"Draw two days' provisions. Major Y will fill you in. Go to him. He wants to see all the officers."

I went to Y, then went back to Varenna so that he could fill me in on the details. All Italians fit enough to walk had been ordered to be ready and drawn up into columns by eight o'clock. The Germans were going to attempt to break out of the Russian circle that had been strangling us for days: once a passage had been forced, we would march in the direction of Belovodsk, westward. Before Belovodsk—which was about sixty kilometers away—we would meet up with the new German line.

But how far would this be from Chertkovo? No one knew. Not twenty or thirty kilometers for sure, as rumor had had it a few days earlier; let alone eight kilometers, as the Germans had led us to believe one morning.

So once again the long-awaited columns hadn't arrived. Was there, for that matter, a German line to the west? We no longer believed anything; our hopes rested only in the distant sounds of combat—these, at any rate, were not the mere work of fancy. And what if those sounds too came from a garrison that was besieged as ours was? That possibility didn't bear thinking about.

And another thought had to be thrust aside as well, if we wanted to save at least ourselves, the wretched remnants of that fine army corps that had been the old CSIR: the thought of about two thousand men—the frozen and the wounded unable to walk—whom we'd be leaving behind us in the hospital, in the infirmary, and scattered here, there, and everywhere in the houses of Chertkovo.

Our life had been theirs as well; they had been tormented by the same hopes as ours; they had fought with us and for us in that wicked climate; and now here we were abandoning them to the hands of the enemy . . .

I banished the thought of them as well.

Varenna gave me the task of doing the rounds of every single isba of the Thirtieth, without exception, to order the men to draw two days' provisions immediately and warn those "who could walk" to be on the ready "to go and work on the line for a few days." They were to assemble in front of Varenna's house. Every house was to dispatch a courier to him every two hours, to maintain contact.

Since we had drawn a plan of the zone a few days earlier, I had no difficulty finding individual isbas. I was joined on these rounds by my vice platoon commander, Sergeant Martano, who some time ago had recounted to me—ascribing great importance to it—a strange dream he had had that portended good, decisive news for January 16. He recalled this to me now with emotion.

In some isbas, where the soldiers of the Thirtieth were mixed with those from other corps, news had already gotten around of our imminent departure, and this time it wasn't veiled by the pitiful phrase "work on the line", which Varenna had coined to prevent those unable to move from abandoning themselves to despair.

In the last, or penultimate, house, we came across the *Caporalino,* the little wireless operator from the Second Battery, for whom I had managed to procure a sleigh back in the Valley of Death. He greeted me joyously: "I can't go up to the line, *signor tenente;* as you know, I'm wounded." "Listen: It isn't work on the line, but something altogether different. Get ready and go off with the others. You can take that as an order." "Yes, sir. Whatever you say, sir." That was the last I saw of him. I do, however, know that he made it back to Italy.

When we had finished our rounds, I went back into my isba.

Martano, back from a fact-finding mission to headquarters, reported that there too preparations were proceeding fast and furiously: our departure, of which Varenna had left me not altogether convinced, could now be taken as a certainty.

One of the soldiers who had left with Bellini came back, reporting that in the afternoon the Germans had thrown away their old uniforms and donned new ones.

We ate abundantly that evening, then, as always, said the rosary— the last of those rosaries thanks to which (I was, and still am, convinced) our previous house had been left intact, while all those around it had been hit or destroyed.

We then rubbed our feet with antifreeze ointment and prepared ourselves as best we could. I now had a pair of new socks and a really precious pair of long stockings with snow gaiters (these, which were a present from Valorzi, had freed me once and for all from the torment of wet feet). I also had a pair of army gauntlets that, when I wasn't wearing them, hung, German fashion, from a cord tied behind my neck.

We spent our last hours in the isba stretched out calmly on our pallets.

The men were preparing a huge bowl of pasta with the abundant provisions we had drawn. But they didn't have time to finish cooking it, because we had to be off; the Russian civilians were left to complete the cooking.

Captain Magaldi, who was still in bed with a violent headache, decided to come with us and got ready.

Finally, my watch told me the hour had come: it was about quarter to eight in the evening.

I ordered the men to finish dressing and to form up in a column on the road in front of the isba.

Would we manage it this time?

Would we attain the freedom that had so constantly slipped our grasp?

I invoked Heaven's help, then turned my mind elsewhere.

Reginato, my orderly, had worn the camera around his neck as far as Chertkovo, and seeing me now putting it around mine, said: "This time, *Signor tenente*, you've decided to carry it because you know there's no hope of my making it"; and he looked down at his blistered feet.

"Don't be a fool," I exclaimed, removing the camera and holding it out to him: "What makes you think you won't make it? Go on, take it if you like." Then: "But no. Why on earth should I listen to such drivel? I'll hang onto it"—and I withdrew my hand. Silent and shy, he didn't answer, but there was a painful leadenness in the way he looked at me; my words hadn't completely convinced him.

And in fact he didn't make it.

*

Once the men were in file, Antonini and I took up the head of the column and set off. The frozen snow squeaked beneath our feet; the cold lost no time in hurling itself at us and immediately got busy biting and devouring us from every side.

Captain Magaldi, who was walking at the rear, on the arm of Bellagente, his orderly, suddenly asked the latter to take him back to the isba. He said he was certain that he wouldn't be able to manage it. After vainly beseeching him to come with us, to make a supreme effort, Bellagente eventually gave in. He fervidly enjoined the head of the Russian family to accompany the captain to the hospital at dawn the next day; the Russian promised he would do so.[16]

In an isba near ours Second Lieutenant Salvador, a Triestine from the Sixty-second Battalion, who was seriously afflicted with frostbite, had also been abandoned.

Outside Major Y's habitation several scraps of column were waiting. We let our soldiers join their friends. I joined my armed platoon.

We stayed where we were for more than one hour.

We could see the road leading to the town center thronging with columns of men; the main column was reforming. It easily fit into the small town, though. A far cry from that endless river during the first days of the retreat!

We shuffled around a bit, then joined the column.

Finally, the column moved off: the Torino Division at the head, then the Pasubio, and finally the army and army corps units. Being the artillery brigade of the army corps, we took up the rear.

The Germans led the way, together with a few Italian units, including Bellini's, who were to help them when the time came to break through.

Very slowly—halting continually—we crossed the small square where the tanks were standing and marched through the center of the town. In the snow's reflection we gave those places a last look. I tried to fix them in my memory as accurately as possible.

Shortly before we crossed the railroad, an officer hailed me from a sleigh. It was Triossi, whom I had met at the hospital. I immediately asked him about Candela and got reassuring news: "He's up in front, on another sleigh."

One halt after another, some lasting an age.

The Russian submachine guns fired frequently; they seemed nervous. Their volleys of golden tracer bullets could be seen traversing the darkness.

The odd tracer bullet hissed by in the gelid air, skimming our heads at times.

No flare rose any longer from the defense lines, tracing its half parabola, splashing about it that familiar whitewash color, which brightly illumined everything for a few seconds. Very likely all, or almost all, the defense lines had already been abandoned.

Time passed, and there we still were in the town.

The cold was very intense, about -30 degrees by my reckoning; we had difficulty bearing it. The houses by the roadside were just too enticing.

Groups of soldiers began entering them. Things got more disorderly with every hour that passed. Eventually all that was left were the subdivisions between the Torino up ahead and the Pasubio with the remaining corps behind.

With Antonini and Martano, I went into a house that had been inhabited by the Germans and then into one of their underground shelters.

Here we came across a soldier who had lost half a foot: he was determined to try his luck leaning on a long splinter of wood.

Soon after leaving the shelter, in the middle of a dark road, we came upon a group of five or six dead men. A mortar shell had chanced to fall on the column. They looked small, and close to each other, and the white beaten snow beneath them was black with cinders. Here then were others who wouldn't return home!

A second house abandoned by the Germans. In it we found the stump of a candle and lit it. There were plates with the leftovers of honey, butter, and apples.

One odd thing: on the table there was a large collection of numbered metal buttons, which had, however, been turned over so that the numbers couldn't be seen. Only one number was visible: 13.

Out again.

The cold, more atrocious with every minute that passed, was martyrizing us.

Abandoned German trucks.

A small uphill stretch and the town was finally behind us. Around us now, only the odd isba or cattle shed.

We had the impression that we had marched south, or southeastward out of the town.

In a cattle shed, crushed together terribly in the darkness.

Then the column lurched forward again, and once more we were outside.

We entered one of the very last isbas, before the endless waste of the steppe, drowned in darkness.

We stopped here for a very long time. Every so often, Antonini and I fought our way through to the door (because the room was crowded) to check whether the column was still ahead of us.

About an hour after we had gone in there (I was propped somehow on a windowsill inside the room, my head bowed, my eyes closed), I heard someone calling to me from the middle of the shed.

I had already had the feeling that someone was unwell: it was Lieutenant Maestri, of the Thirtieth Brigade command, who had a violent attack of heart palpitations brought on by the cold. He was completely done for. When his men told him that I was in the isba, he wanted me at his side.

Sitting there on the ground, hedged in by the men, Antonini and I kept him stretched out on a patch of straw, his head resting on our legs.

From one of the walls some candles cast a dim light. Maestri spoke slowly, sporadically. He complained about Y, who had made excessive demands on him. We were to leave him to his destiny by now. If, however, the column took time about moving off, he was sure he would recover.

His orderly—numbly at our side, wearing a lambskin cap—got into a state. He couldn't take the idea that Maestri was urging us to abandon him.

Luckily for Maestri, we stayed where we were for up to three or four hours, and this gave him time to rally.

Finally (since the tail end of the column was now some hundred meters ahead—a wide, gray, immobile mass in the darkness), Antonini and I decided to fall in again.

The cold was literally unbearable. How much longer would we have to wait there, as if paralyzed, taking one or two steps every ten minutes?

Far away, behind us, we could descry the flames of the German warehouses burning in the immense silence.

Our own stores had been spared by the fire: a medical officer with multiple wounds, who possessed a smattering of Russian, had stayed behind at the hospital with the task of telling the enemy that we had left the stores intact for our wounded.

What would become of them? I shuddered to think. Perhaps the Russians were already overrunning the town.

Time passed, painfully slowly, but it passed.

Heaven help us if we were still in this condition at dawn!

Meanwhile, among us—among our motionless, bowed figures—there was that cold, still making us suffer unspeakably. Little by little, I was beginning to feel that I was no longer a distinct unit, with my own identity—no, I was an atom of suffering humanity, a minute part of endless human pain and sorrow.

Later, I was to think back to that sensation, which I had felt so vividly, but I find it hard to put into words, given our individualism. What I had felt was that man, in me as in others, was paying for his sins. It was as it should be. But the pain of it!

When we finally set off at a brisk pace, to our left, eastward, we could see the first glimmerings of daylight.

Our constant fear was that we would have to stop again, but we didn't.

There was an abandoned German truck, then another, and another —an array of "mud-clogged" trucks abandoned in the snow.

Rumor had it that the Germans had made us wait so long for the express purpose of using us as a sort of shield while they attempted, uselessly, to clear the mud from those trucks. The main body of their men was already well up ahead.

29

With the first light of day we crossed the Russian line, which consisted of snowbound weapon pits. In these pits, all around us, on the road we marched along, more or less everywhere, there were Russian corpses. Already they were reduced to pieces of ice, and some were in strange postures. One was on his knees and his arms were raised as if to point his rifle; but he was lying on his side on the snow and had no rifle.

Everywhere were the mighty tracks left by tanks.

Off almost in a rush along the now downhill road, wishing, longing all the while to see other enemy corpses.

On an abandoned truck, a wounded German: a big blond, blue-eyed youth, who anxiously scrutinized each of us as we rapidly showed our faces at the body of the truck to take a look inside it. He was wearing a new, spotlessly white uniform. Who knows with what hope he must have donned it that afternoon: and now, before long, it would be his shroud.

Keep moving! The cold had increased again: it must have been around -40 degrees, I reckoned. Our faces were covered with crusts of ice. A small slab of ice and frost had formed on our balaclavas, at the level of our nostrils.

Uphill.

Suddenly in front of us the close, slow rumble of cannon fire split the still air.

Day was breaking.

Over a hump and downhill again: the road was to be up and down all the way—like a switchback railroad—as far as Belovodsk.

Down below, at the bottom of the slope, a group of thatched shacks straddled the road. Those nearest the roadside were on fire.

From one spot among the shacks, we could see Russian tracer grenades being lobbed slowly up and striking the column on the opposite slope, where the Torino and the Germans were marching. In response, antitank shells flew up from the column.

We would have to go through that village . . .

Volleys from enemy automatic weapons. Almost all those Italians who were armed were up at the head of the column with the Germans, who had promised two rearguard battalions, then failed to supply them. Possibly they hadn't had them to supply.

Antonini and I were at the head of the Pasubio. The senior officers wouldn't allow the Pasubio to mix with the Torino; but when our stretch of the column was hit by automatic fire, there was no holding the mass of soldiers from careering off down the slope: whoever ran faster, went ahead. The whole column now was running.

Off I went on the double, with Antonini.

The rising and falling hiss of the *katyusha:* down there, just past the shacks, billows of smoke rose from the long line of explosions. The *katyushas* burst furiously astride the road, perpendicularly to it; but none exploded on the road itself, so not a single man was hit.

After a while, we heard the hissing once more, and again saw the clouds of smoke—to the right of the road this time, at an acute angle to it, but falling short; again missing their target.

What I feared was that "that witch" Katyusha would come up on the column from behind and rake through it: if she did so, who knows what havoc she would wreak!

A stray mortar shell hit the middle of the track at the foot of the slope beyond the small village. Some men fell to the ground.

Our part of the column was practically unarmed and lacked organic unity: by the houses there could have been only about thirty enemy troops, possibly fewer, who had managed to dodge the Germans; yet for us (who numbered one thousand) they might well spell the end.

Panic is invincible. Fear is the normal expression of the survival instinct and can be dominated, according to one's character, with the force of reason or a powerful surge of feeling. Not panic. Whoever it seizes is no longer master of himself: obstacles he might otherwise take in his stride become insurmountable.

How many of us, I thought, had once fought courageously, what difficulties we had overcome; but at that moment it was quite impossible even for those who were still armed to pull together and fight. What a disaster!

Just as we were entering the village, the column halted ahead of us. Those in front had suddenly slackened their pace and were crowding together cautiously behind a shack, because enemy bullets were whistling along the stretch of road that went through the bottom of the gorge. Didn't they realize how dangerous it was to linger like that? That it was the worst thing we could possibly do? I called out to them: "Quick, or it'll be too late! Get moving! Get moving!"

Everyone moved off on the double. We made it unscathed. Behind us, the column started flowing again.

On we hastened up the white, spotless slope. For the time being my sole wish, my sole concern, was to get beyond that stretch of road on which, from one second to the next, the *katyusha* explosions lay in wait for me. The terror of death still had me by the throat.

Several dead and wounded men, Germans and Italians, were lying on the road in the place where the mortar shell had exploded.

A German, propping himself up on a hand and kneeling, was groaning and stretching his other hand out toward us, as if wishing to grasp us and be dragged away.

An Italian, also propped on an arm, was staring at us with horror-stricken eyes. As I passed him, I heard him say, in his shattered Lombard voice: "*Signur . . . Signur . . . .*"

After a while, we came across dead Russians strewn along a considerable stretch of the road.[17] Wrecked enemy sleighs: they had tried to escape the Germans, but a tank must have caught up with them. A dead Russian officer.

Against the whiteness, the small black bead of a rosary, obviously lost by one of our compatriots. And to think that I should chance on it just as I was invoking the Madonna.

I picked it up and slipped it into one of the pockets of my greatcoat among the pieces of biscuit. It would be my memento from the retreat.

Keep moving!

Antonini was hurrying along even faster than I was. It was all he could do not to leave me behind. I actually warned him: "Be careful . . . we still have at least fifty kilometers to go."

Ahead of us and behind us, the column stretched as far as the eye could see. Behind us it was all black, ahead a mixture of black and white: Italians dressed in gray-green; Italians (mainly Blackshirts) in white uniforms; and Germans.

We began overtaking some Germans.

To the side of the road, on a ridge, some abandoned German trucks.

When we turned around and looked back down there in the direction of the village (through which the column was still passing), we could now make out on the left, a short distance from the houses, some khaki puppets: about twenty of them. They were the Russians, who appeared to be observing our flight in puzzlement and amazement.

We passed some Germans blithely relieving themselves against an isolated haystack at the edge of the road.

But in the column there was the odd exhausted German, trying as best he could to run, but falling behind.

Every so often the din of gunfire still reached our ears from the village.

Down to the last man—and not just Antonini and I—we still expected to be hit from one second to the next by *katyusha* and mortar shells. Many therefore shifted to the left, opening up a new, slender trail in the snow, which converged again with the main trail after a couple of kilometers.

We passed one or two Germans who were trudging along towing a light Finnish-style sled shaped like a rowing boat; lying on it was a wounded comrade of theirs, possibly a brother. Everyone was passing them. Every now and then one of them stretched out a hand to us in vain supplication.

There was no more *katyusha* fire. We started to breathe again. But still we walked on, and still at a double-quick pace.

The snow had become powdery, and deep, even on some stretches of the road. Here we tried to walk in the tracks left by the tanks.

Until, having surmounted two more switchbacks, all we heard was the tiny pattering of our shoes over the snow.

✣

It was a very clear day. On either side of the road endless, gently undulating wastes, all white. We could see across incredible distances.

Not a house, not a sign of life.

Every now and then, here and there dreary gusts of wind sent up plumes of powdered snow.

What were our steps in that immensity?

As we walked on relentlessly, I felt that Nature was utterly indifferent to all these feverish comings and goings of ours. Compared to her, what were we men but a ridiculous sprinkling of ants? It was right that we counted for nothing when measured against her. It was what we ourselves ought to wish for: she was so immeasurably big, we so immeasurably small! I had never had that sensation back in Italy.

And then I thought: That's why the Russians build such fragile houses and cemeteries that vanish in a matter of years—they submit to Nature's will; they don't even wish to compete with her.

Far away, ahead of us, a few silent planes appeared, and began circling in the sky. Were they Russian? Or German? They were nose-diving, so they must have been German! Around them appeared little red clouds from antiaircraft shells.

Onward, at a normal pace now.

At one point where a small bridge bore the road across a rift in the land (one of the usual *balkas*), we were greeted by an unexpected sight: in the *balka* a German tank, one of those gigantic ones, abandoned. Near it, on the snow, a bloodstained tanker's jacket.

Beyond the bridge, positioned on the side of the road, was a German antitank gun pointing our way: this too was abandoned and had no dead men around it.

It must have been used by the Russians to annihilate the tank. But what had become of its gunners?

Onward, again.

And now, for the first time, there were clear signs of panic and confusion among the Germans in the column: their equipment abandoned here and there along the road, above all loaded submachine-gun belts, of the type they normally wore around their necks.

What had happened?

Keep moving! Now it was Antonini who had difficulty keeping me behind him; but we just had to try to get toward the head of the column, within the operating range of the tanks.

Meanwhile, we wondered how things had turned out in the village that had been the scene of all that shooting, just outside Chertkovo.

Only later did we learn that the Russians—some thirty of them perhaps, with two submachine guns—had finally succeeded in cutting the column in two. First of all, with the odd volley, and a sparing use of ammunition, they had severed it, and then, by placing the two guns on the road, blocked the stump of the column.

Eyewitnesses told me that four or five hundred of our compatriots had fallen into Russian hands, mostly wounded and frozen men at the rear. They were all herded into the isbas; a guard was placed outside every isba.

Some managed to escape, though, and caught up with us later. I also heard about a Russian tank—immobilized amid the shacks—firing with a single machine gun.

As we walked on, the gelid east wind was getting stronger and more persistent.

Every so often it assailed the road with huge gusts of snow. The cold was bitterly intense. Only on very few days had it been as rigid as this during our stay in Chertkovo.

Not so much as a second's halt. Antonini asked me to slacken my pace.

Suddenly, ahead of us, at the foot of a slope, we saw a village. We decided to stop there to drink a little water.

Pistols in hand, we entered an isba. A mixture of warmth and the stench one usually found in Russian houses with fixed windows. Wordlessly, a woman set down some water before us.

Out we went again. But look: The Germans in the Italian column had come together once more and formed into a sort of platoon. They were preventing the Italians who were behind them from passing them.

There was no way of getting past them.

Bellagente, Captain Magaldi's orderly, was walking behind the German platoon. He joined us.

※

We reached the foot of a wide, steep, and very long slope. Halt.

The whole column, stretching as far as the top of the slope and beyond, was now still. There must have been fighting up in front.

216

Midday.

The Stukas were flying overhead in the pale, clear sky. In no time at all, the sky filled with the mighty shrieking of their sirens: we watched one of them going into a dive, then gaining altitude again. We could see the bombs clearly rolling through the air, then bursting with enormous billows of smoke. Their terrible bellowing shook the wilderness.

All were dropped around the head of the column, beyond the summit of the slope.

To our left a slight rise in the ground kept a valley hidden from us. Small, white groups of Germans headed for it; they positioned their submachine guns there and stopped, some standing, others kneeling behind the weapons.

Over this valley too, shrieking Stukas came diving down. They released their bombs, then regained altitude and flew off.

Others came fast on their heels. There were five or six in the sky almost constantly.

When I was later able to reconstruct the action, I realized that if the Stukas hadn't intervened in strength that day, we would have been done for. The Germans too were at the end of their tether.

The slope ahead of us led to a village—probably Petrovskiy—around which stretched a vast plateau, broken occasionally by woods.

Here, on a line that had been drawn up some time ago, the Russians, on discovering that we had left Chertkovo, had immediately moved a considerable number of troops along the shortest route. They had also hidden four tanks (some of which were T.34s, then considered "the best in the world") among the isbas, and an armored car.

When the German vanguard, with most of the village behind them, had opened fire with their tanks in an attempt to break through the line, the Russian tanks behind them had hurled themselves on the column, leveling away all and everybody.

The German troops up at the front scattered, but not before they had relayed news of the attack rapidly down the column from one man to the next—a sort of human telephone. Three of their tanks, including one or two small ones, French war trophies, had immediately returned. Crushing their own infantry in their wake, they hurled themselves on the Russian tanks.

In the lightning action that followed, four Russian tanks had been eliminated; the armored car, which had taken flight, had been pursued and stopped by gunfire from a German tank. Not a single German tank had been damaged. One of the Russian tanks was unhitched, and dragged away as a war spoil.[18]

At last, slowly, the column moved on again.

I was told that the Stukas that I had seen nose-diving in the main valley to our left had given chase to other enemy tanks, smashing them as they attempted to assail us from behind.

Not knowing the people who told me this, I can't vouch for its reliability: my own view is that it was true.[19]

On the slope there was now a massive throng of people running uphill: the Italian column, quickening its pace all the time, had turned into a sea of men. The sun made the powdery snow gleam faintly among so many trampling feet.

Suddenly mortar shells began plummeting down in quick succession among the sea of men.

Only one mortar was firing, and a low caliber one at that; but in some places the men were so tightly packed that every shell claimed its fair share of victims.

In the case of one man, I saw what looked like the upper part of a skull with a full head of hair fly up into the air.

The Stukas spotted the Russian mortar: two nosedives, four bombs, and the hollow in which it was hidden was hit head on.

Years later, Second Lieutenant YY told me that one of its shell fragments had completely carried off one soldier's testicles. The soldier had thrust them in his pockets, then having feverishly bound the wound with a piece of string, hurried on his way again. At Belovodsk the following day, he undid his trousers and showed YY the bleeding stump and, in the palm of his hand, the blackish testicles mixed with biscuit crumbs, asking him and others who had gathered around whether they would be able to sew them back on at the hospital.

Finally, at the top of the slope, we too came in sight of the village where the fighting was taking place.

Antonini had now managed to get himself dragged along a bit, tied to a mule's tail. I was tired but had no intention of slowing down, since I was afraid that the rear guard, which was completely undefended, might at any moment be attacked by the Russian tanks.

Among the first scatterings of isbas.

Dead Germans on the snow. Burned-out enemy tanks.

A Russian tank deeply entrenched in the snow: only its turret stuck out of the ground. Behind it there was the hole that had hidden the wicked mortar that had fired on the column.

Several isbas were burning, with reddish tongues of fire.

On the roadside, an old Russian with a long pointed beard was desperately flinging buckets of water and snow onto a thatched roof that had been transformed into a pyre.

How minute and alone he was! Didn't he realize how pointless his efforts were? Like as not, though, he was intent on performing any kind action to stave off madness.

Above a bare clump of trees, not far off, the Stukas were keeping up their furious nosedives.

Near the end of the village there were numerous dead Russians. One was wearing an Italian fur-lined greatcoat.

We passed Lieutenant Maestri, who was now completely back in shape, and a small group of officers in the company of Major Y. I suggested joining them, but Antonini wouldn't hear of it.

In that village the horse carrying Lieutenant Zanetti of the Thirtieth Brigade command collapsed. So, after vainly attempting to walk on gangrenous feet, Zanetti got someone to lead him away and abandon him in an isba.

But he didn't stay there. We were some way off when he came out and in the immense silence started following the column, occasionally dragging himself along on his hands and knees. He survived, but lost both legs in the process.

Later I learned that Candela too had to go practically the whole way on foot and had gotten seriously frostbitten. And Lugaresi also, on the arm of Bozza, his orderly. These two followed the column's tracks for hours on end in appalling solitude, leaning against each other, without a voice around them save, occasionally, that of the whistling wind.

*

With the village behind us, we started skirting a very long, shallow *balka* strewn with the bodies of dead Russians. In it the snow seemed to have been scored with the furrows left by passing German tanks.

Suddenly, three extremely fast-flying planes appeared from the right: they headed toward the front of the column, which was hidden from us by the long grass. Were they Russian or German? At the time there wasn't a Stuka in the sky.

They then veered around impetuously and flew over the column at a few dozen meters, riddling it with machine-gun fire from one end to the other.

We flung ourselves to the ground. When the planes had gone, Antonini and I got to our feet again.

Luckily, this time too (I don't know whether things are different now) the Russians proved to be hopeless aviators: in the column in front of us only one man died.

A long halt.

The light was beginning to fade; the wind, which had diminished greatly in the course of the day, now turned south and started blowing insistently, and icily. Every now and then I stamped my feet laboriously.

I decided to take advantage of the halt to eat a bit of biscuit and canned meat. But the meat was reduced to a block of ice, and with my pocket knife all I could do was scratch away at it, tearing off meager scraps.

We then busily set about helping get the column into some kind of order again and reestablishing the subdivision between the Torino and the Pasubio. Eventually I gave up trying.

Standing there beside us now was Second Lieutenant Conti, our fellow tenant in the hut at Chertkovo. Imitating what we saw others doing, Conti, Antonini, and I tried to form into a small knot to protect ourselves from the cold: forming a circle, we put our foreheads together and covered ourselves with my blanket.

We stayed like this for a while.

Not far off, in the unmoving crowd, a soldier was speaking "low" Milanese.

It was hard to believe my ears when I heard that language, in that place: it was the dialect my mother used to sing in to lull us to sleep when we were children. I was strangely and sadly moved.

But no time for that!

Why was the halt lasting so long?

Was the line still a long way off?

And was it true that first we would have to reach and liberate a besieged German garrison?

The cold was increasing.

By now it was becoming nearly impossible to keep still, and our hopes were waning.

When we got going again, the sky was already violet.

The last Stukas swooped down, saluting us as best they could with the no-longer-resounding but drawn-out and singularly melancholy wail of their sirens; then flew off.

We bore right, northward. Why northward? Our route cut through an immense sweep of very tall, dead grass. It was like walking between two walls. Every so often, the odd rifle shot in the distance. The hiss of stray bullets.

In spite of several more brief halts, the column had become regular again. The separation between the Torino Division and the sleigh leading the Pasubio marchers was maintained by an NCO from the *bersaglieri* who shouted incessantly and every so often fired his pistol into the air.

Across a vast snowy, now grassless hollow.

As we walked, we looked westward, on the off-chance of making out some sign of friendly lines.

Instead, we were greeted in that very place by a hail of *katyusha* shells: they smacked down onto the mauve-colored snow, sending up clouds of virulent golden smoke. So enemy troops were there too.

Keep moving. Try not to think.

Eventually, Antonini and I passed the line of demarcation between the Torino and the Pasubio.

Two or three officers and some soldiers I knew; all of them were walking wearily. It was dark by now.

We veered left, westward again.

The column was thinning out and splintering into small, isolated groups. We discovered that between the Germans with the Italians at the head of the column, and the Pasubio and the throng at its rear, there was a sort of vacuum: if the rear was attacked, since it was unarmed, it would be left to fend for itself.

We entered a village, probably Streltsovka.

We were all reduced—the Germans no less than us—to a herd of exhausted wretches.

I asked Antonini to go on slowly with Bellagente. Meanwhile, I would push forward toward the head of the Italian column, where our baggage wagons were, and try to get a clearer idea of the situation. My nerves wouldn't let me walk slowly.

In the darkness I could make out a good number of German squads, immobile—possibly because they'd taken up position—here and there among the isbas.[20]

Antonini exploded: "So you want to leave me? All right, clear off, then!"

I stormed off. I justified this by saying to myself: "If you think I'm prepared to put up with temper tantrums . . . ." But the truth of the matter was that by acting like that I was again spitting in the face of my conscience and every elementary sense of dignity. I was no longer master of my nerves . . .

It wasn't long before I heard Antonini's impassioned voice calling out to me in the darkness: "Corti . . . Corti." I didn't answer. And so I abandoned my friend simply because he had taken me to task.

(When we met outside the pocket a few days later, he didn't say a word; he just embraced me.)

30

I was alone now.

A volley of *katyusha* fire on the village: the Germans were flinging themselves to the ground; the darkness was filled with the myriads of large sparks spraying forth from the flame bursts. Luckily, no one was killed.

Forward.

A few mortar shells came over as well.

Around the last houses.

Later on there was a hill that seemed to have no end in the snow's reflection.

The column had split into two parallel files, which were already reascending it: on one side, to the left, trucks, sleighs, baggage wagons, including Italian ones; on the other side, one or two kilometers to the right, the just-visible restless snake of men.

Before beginning the ascent, I tried to enter an isba to rest a little in the warmth. But didn't succeed. So I sat down on the snow in a row with others, against the wall of a ruined building.

It was frighteningly cold. A short spell of immobility and I had to get up.

I began the ascent in the same column as the wagons.

Here were some Italian sleighs: perhaps Antonini would be able to find a place on one.

I went about looking for him. Every so often I shouted out to him. But, like everything around us, my shouts met with no reply.

In the end I ruthlessly stifled the thought of him: I had to concentrate all my energies on the effort to keep going.

How much longer would I manage to resist?

The German vehicles, emitting thick vapor, were roaring up the slope, their wheels black against the snow.

The mules and horses were plodding up laboriously; on every one of our sleighs, the souls of one or two wounded men literally hung, with mortal anxiety, on the efforts those animals were making.

And the wind wouldn't let up. It explored every part of our bodies, tirelessly intent on wringing the life out of us.

What a joy it would have been to be able to lie down on the floor of a hut for a few hours! Not a heated one—no, that was too much to ask for—but one with walls that at least kept you sheltered from that wind . . .

I thought of our leaders, who had declared war: at this moment they were in Rome in the warmth, living in their habitual luxury; very likely sleeping in soft beds.

And to think that they had sent their soldiers into this climate, with these shoes, equipped like this! "The swines! The sons of bitches!"

For all that, I now had the powerful sense that they themselves were no more than wretches, mere instruments like any others in the hands of Providence.

Each and every one of us, with greater or lesser clarity, according to our powers of intuition, felt this. (And so far more rarely than when things were going well did we speak about our leaders, or inveigh against them.)

It seemed to us impossible that events as terrible as those we were experiencing simply depended on the whims of a few small men.[21]

Those men were nothing other than a castigation for the whole of mankind.

Only God can castigate mankind.[22]

Only this way can war be explained.

Even if we came through this, and found a way of making others, and especially the culprits, understand what war is, there would still be wars in the future, in defiance of all human logic.

In the past too, for that matter, man would never have wanted war, had it been in his power not to want it. To prevent war occurring, therefore, mankind as a whole had to cease making it inevitable by accumulating before God one sin after another—sins that at a certain point become an avalanche, which moves, and strikes, and engulfs.

I saw Trivulzi on an artillery captain's sleigh, poking his head out of a blanket he was huddled under. The moment he saw me he hid himself: he was obviously afraid that I somehow wanted to partake of his good fortune. Incapable of getting the message, I took to following that sleigh like an automaton.

The wagons were jolting along rapidly. As soon as they stopped, I sat down on a corner of the sleigh.

The captain—though still proceeding—started staring at me with hostile eyes: only then did I realize that he wanted me to clear off.

For a moment I grabbed onto the back of what I thought was an Italian cart. It was German. A German saw me and yelled at me to beat it.

On we went.

The track, still going uphill, was immensely wide and white.

When you defied the wind's unspeakable scourge and lifted your eyes to look around you, far off to the right you could still see the swarming column of men between the humps of snow. To the left were sparse, bare woods.

Finally I reached the overhanging plain.

We passed a number of field-artillery pits, with German guns pointing our way.

Behind them, the uneven mounds of earth covering the gunners' shelters were sticking out of the snow.

Did I have any idea what those gun pits meant?

I don't rightly remember.

What I do remember is that in front of those cannon in the snow lay a great number of dead Russians. One, a Mongol, was lying practically across the track; he was wearing a fine, thick balaclava, which covered his whole face apart from his eyes.

I took it off him; I had some difficulty, because the dead man's ears were like ice. I noticed that the balaclava was stained with blood; the dead man's broad face was likewise sullied with frozen blood.

I slipped his balaclava over mine: soon it unfroze a little, and started giving off a mild, strange odor: "The smell of a Siberian," I thought with a smile; but now, though still lacking my service cap, I no longer needed to hold the blanket over my head to keep the wind off me.

Despicable episodes occurred along that slope.

An Italian officer offered the Germans one thousand marks (the equivalent of seventy-six hundred lire) so that they would let him stay on one of their sleighs for ten minutes. The Germans let him on, then after three or four minutes, having pocketed the money, flung him out onto the snow. But he was at death's door and could do nothing to them.

Another gave them a gold watch. Some, dying of fatigue, gave them their pistols, which were much sought-after by the Germans.

We had really come to a sorry pass.

A German NCO, walking along the track with a handful of comrades, told me cordially, in French, that we had crossed friendly lines. I don't remember now whether I was already aware of this.

Finally, its full significance came home to me: we were out of the pocket!

As he walked on, the German told me that about twenty kilometers farther on there was the first town, Belovodsk: from what the radio said, within a few kilometers we would find a fleet of Italian trucks, which would load us all up and take us into the town. There would be German trucks as well.

I thought bitterly that those German trucks would be there all right, but not the Italian ones.

And I was right.

✻

We came off the surface of ice onto a magnificent road.

It was flanked by regulation posts, crowned by small bundles of straw, placed there as road markers in the event of blizzards or snowdrifts.

Both branches of the column converged into the road.

There was now another series of long mounds of earth; poking out of them were stovepipes with sparks coming from them. Our shelters on the banks of the Don came back to my mind.

There was no mistaking it—we were out of the pocket.

Out of the pocket!

I would no longer have to flee like a hunted animal, with death at my heels. And I would be able to see my family, my house, and Italy once again.

I should have shaken, laughed, shouted with joy!

I suppose I should have!

I bowed my head and as fervidly as I could thanked the Madonna for saving my life.

Then, as I walked on, the memory of the others began to come to my mind . . . With violent anguish I thought of how many had been left there along the road of our calvary. All too likely at that very moment some were alive in enemy hands. Thousands and thousands possibly? Or had they all been killed?

Zorzi!

He had last been seen in the attack shouting and laughing: "Blood was gushing like a fountain from one of his feet," Montresor had said. Now Zorzi seemed to be looking at me in silence, with the very same look that he had back in the Valley of Death.

And where, for that matter, were the soldiers of my battalion? The humble, undemanding friends with whom I had lived for so many months! They too had done all they could to save themselves. But they had fallen irremediably behind . . . "We too have our mothers at home, *signor tenente*, but . . ." (and they would shake their heads disconsolately), "but we won't be returning to them."

And all the other dead, not only Italians, but Russians as well, and also Germans? Particularly those who had died opening the road for us.

I began to pray for the dead.

By our calculations, of about thirty thousand Italians from the Thirty-fifth Army Corps who were encircled on the Don, around eight thousand had made it to Chertkovo. On the evening of January 15, counting the troops that we found in the town on our arrival, there were about seven thousand. About five thousand of us left Chertkovo, and not many more than four thousand made it out of the pocket.

Of these four thousand, at least three thousand were afflicted by frostbite or wounded.

Most of the remaining thousand were also in a pitiful state: their nerves in pieces—sick—filthy.

After a month's encirclement, all that remained of the front-line troops of an efficient army corps was a handful of poor wretches who were barely able to stay on their feet. Not so much men as mere semblances of men.

Big wooden signposts saying: "Belovdsk," "Starobelsk".
I was alone again because the German NCO had also left me.

As the night progressed, the cold progressed too; the wind, for its part, continued pounding us from the south relentlessly, stubbornly. Masks of ice gripped our faces more tightly than ever. (Later Bellini told me that a thermometer he had seen displayed outside a house in Belovodsk had read -45 degrees.)[23]

Twenty kilometers more, the German had said . . . After an hour on the road, I doubted whether I would manage to cover that distance. And once again I invoked the Madonna of the Wood: praying for Her aid, so that I might reach Belovodsk.

Here were the German trucks, though not many of them. They were now plying back and forth between Belovodsk and the village where I had left Antonini (Streltsovka?), which remained garrisoned until the morning.

Not one Italian truck.

I was later told that a few days earlier one of our convoys, which had been ready for some time at Belovodsk to run this service, had been diverted elsewhere by the Germans to serve their own needs.

When the Germans had finished transporting their men, that night their trucks started transporting the Italians. But many of our compatriots in difficulty, who couldn't be loaded in time, were left there on the snow, though they had now crossed the lines.

Every so often at the sides of the road there were empty weapon pits consisting only of snow. I tried to figure out what purpose they served, but gave up. My mind was exhausted.

The column now seemed to have thinned out greatly, to be reduced to small, isolated groups. At times I was utterly alone in the dark, on the road of shimmering ice.

A stationary Italian ambulance: I walked around it, sorely tempted to get taken aboard. I would probably have succeeded; then thought of the infinite number of men in worse condition than I was and continued on my way.

At the very end of the road, which now went downhill, there was a pinpoint of light: a red beacon going rhythmically on and off: it must have been Belovodsk. But what a distance away! The farther forward I went, the more I had the feeling that I would never succeed in reaching it.

Clutching the blanket tightly around my shoulders, I was walking, walking, beneath the wind's lash. And the wind assailed me ceaselessly, sucking up the skirts of my blanket and my greatcoat, cold beyond human imagining. This—I stuttered in my mind—is what the dead coldness of the abysses between the stars must be like: a cold from other worlds.

And above us and above the myriad of stars, God reigned over that cold as well!

Two or three German wagons squeaked past me.

I hung onto the last of these, my belly leaning against the side, my legs dangling down. This suddenly brought on a fit of dysentery.

I had to stop.

Then onward again, alone, through the night. I had the feeling that very soon I would no longer be able to put one foot before the other. Was this possible? After those entire nights I had spent walking? And those spent sleeping out on the snow? Why, this time, was I unable to resist?

Three or four kilometers from Belovodsk I had really had it. An Italian sleigh was going by, dragged by an exhausted horse, at whose side a large, equally exhausted mule had been tied, to take over for him.

I waved down that sleigh. It was carrying two men with frostbite, one huddled at the front, the other at the back, with the equipment between them.

I said: "I'm an artillery officer. I'm on my last legs. Make a bit of room for me."

"But the horse is dying; it's just not possible," was the driver's distressed reply.

What did it matter if the horse was dying? So long as we covered those last three or four kilometers.

The driver began grumbling. I promised him a good tip and climbed up in the middle of the cart, onto the load. I wrapped my blanket around me as best I could, against the wind's onslaught.

After a bit I was trembling and my teeth were chattering so furiously that they could undoubtedly be heard meters away.

What a fever I had!

Once or twice we had to stop because part of the load had overturned.

A short way back from the road a first hut, which had been set fire to by soldiers who were warming themselves around it. It was all I could do to stop my new companions from diverting the sleigh.

Finally, the start of the town. An abandoned factory. The driver and the others resolutely brought the sleigh under one of its porticos. They unhitched the animals.

We entered a pretty ghastly, freezing-cold room with a straw-covered floor and no doors or windows, into which the gusts of wind made their occasional entry.

Ah, for a nice, warm little room! There had to be some, not far away.

But this was too much for me to hope for.

I ate the last pieces of biscuit that I had in my pocket and stretched out on the straw under my blanket.

The soldiers generously removed other blankets from the sleigh, laying them over me as well.

After a while a fire was lit in the room too. Shivering with cold and from my high fever, I fell asleep.

That was the night of January 17.

OUT OF THE ENCIRCLEMENT

31

My diary ends here, because our days in the pocket end here.

Our sufferings didn't end. When we got up the following day it was bright: cannon were thundering insistently northwest of us. Beyond us, then.

In the gelid entrance facing that wretched room, a horse was writhing on the ground in agony. (I can't remember whether it was the one that had brought us there or belonged to one of the other sleighs that had arrived during the night.) I finished it off with a shot through the head.

To headquarters on foot.

I now learned why we had been given the desperate order to abandon Chertkovo so suddenly. The Germans of the Nineteenth Armored Division (armored only in name by now, since it had practically no tanks left), who, together with some M Battalions, had been trying for weeks to force their way through to the besieged town, were in no condition any longer to face enemy pressure, and their withdrawal was imminent.

I covered the fifty kilometers or so from Belovodsk to Starobelsk, where the Eighth Army command was stationed, on a truck.

Soon after I had left, some Russian planes flew over Belovodsk. Their bombs took a fairly heavy toll among the survivors from the pocket who were crowded around headquarters.

Belovodsk was suddenly abandoned by the headquarters' staff the afternoon of that same day, January 17, before all of the survivors of the pocket had been transferred by truck to Starobelsk. Many of them withdrew with the Germans. Some, though, undoubtedly remained in Russian hands.

At headquarters in Starobelsk we met a group of survivors from Kantemirovka.

We learned that Kantemirovka[24] and Millerovo had been evacuated at the same time as Chertkovo—the former using planes, which at a certain point had no longer been able to land because the last remaining (German) forces had been routed by the Russians, the latter through a corridor that armored forces had opened up in enemy territory.

Halfway between Starobelsk and Voroshilovgrad, along with others, I was blocked by the snow, for a day and a night, in the village of Novoaydar. We were in danger of being encircled once again: it was enough to drive us out of our wits.

I left Voroshilovgrad and, again using one form of transport or another, reached Yasinovataya in the Donetz, where the remnants of the army corps were assembling.

From there a goods train "equipped as a hospital" took me to Leopol in Poland.

Those days we spent on the train weren't much fun either: we were crammed two men to a bunk on the coaches, constantly tormented by hunger and lice and surrounded by the stench of gangrenous limbs. We stopped continually—for hours on end at times—at the stations and railroad halts. Many men died, including Scotti, whom I had met at the hospital in Chertkovo.

Few retreated from the Donetz in any way other than on the "equipped trains", and several of these died of cold: between Stalino and Grisino, fifteen of the one hundred men belonging to a training battery commanded by Conti froze to death on the flatcar of a train transporting coal.

Others died at the hospital in Leopol, where I spent seven days; even more on the hospital trains (genuine, fine Italian hospital trains) that took us from Poland to Italy.

Of my acquaintances who left Chertkovo with us, I heard that, besides Scotti, the following failed to make it back to Italy: Montresor; my orderly, Reginato; and Bellini's "university sergeants", Pillone and Braida.

Braida, who, though afflicted by frostbite himself, had gone to such trouble on the last evening to procure the horse that had saved Zanetti.

In Italy too (I spent twenty-three days in a military hospital at Merano, with rheumatic pains and fevers) every so often somebody died.

I followed the torment of the letters: innumerable letters from mothers, fathers, relatives, asking for news of those who didn't return.

Some of these letters fairly broke one's heart.

In all those months of imprisonment, only a few compatriots in Russian hands succeeded in letting their families at home know they were alive. You have to have witnessed the anguish of these relations at close quarters to understand the cruel effect of being left in that state of ignorance.

For us survivors it was the predictable consequence of Bolshevik barbarity.

In March, on convalescent leave, I went to Miramare di Rimini to visit Candela, who was at a seaside holiday camp that had been converted into a hospital.

I found him in bed. Both his legs had been amputated below the knee. Part of his nose was missing, and most of his fingers had been amputated. Curiously small now, he lay on his back, barely conscious. The stumps of his two legs were lifted upward, and he moved them rhythmically, insistently, as if he were rocking a baby.

AUTHOR'S NOTES

I began setting these recollections down in about the middle of February 1943, while I was at the military hospital in Merano. I made use of a few scraps of paper (postage-free cards, money-order forms, and so on) on which, during the siege of Chertkovo, I had carefully written down events and episodes in chronological order. I completed the manuscript on May 8, during convalescent leave, less than four months after the last episode referred to.

It came to a small volume of about three hundred sheets, dense with episodes and reflections, which, in its existing form, could only be of use to me, as a means of ensuring that I forgot none of those tragic experiences with the passage of time. When I went back into the army, I left it at home.

On September 8 of the same year, 1943, there was the armistice, and much of Italy fell into German hands. I was serving at Nettunia: with another second lieutenant I managed to reach the German-British front in the mountains; we had an eventful journey getting past it; and faithful to our officers' oath, we reported to the regular army that, in the teeth of difficulties of every kind, was forming up again in Puglia.

I only saw my home again in 1945, after having made my way up most of the peninsular with the *Corpo Italiano di Liberazione* (Italian Liberation Corps) (distressed at finding myself indirectly allied with the Bolsheviks, just as, in Russia, I was distressed about our alliance with the Nazis).

Given the danger of German house searches, my little volume had—on my instructions—been wrapped in waterproof sheeting and buried underground. On being discharged at the end of September, I dug it up; it was in a pitiful condition, much like the state of my spirit. Nevertheless, I managed, with the patient help of one of my sisters, to recopy it without anything, or with hardly anything, being lost in the process.

In the following months—alternating this work with periods of study to get through my university exams (one had, after all, to return to normal living)—I prepared these recollections of our encirclement with a view to publishing them.

My main concern was to respect the whole truth: to the point of being able to swear to the contents not just of the work as a whole, but of every single sentence. And not just this: in my respect for the truth, I went so far as to record details, sensations, reflections, which to many might seem, how can I put it? . . . so much deadwood, fearing that if I omitted them I would not be recounting the situation exactly as I myself had seen it. And, by the same token, I stopped writing when I realized that I couldn't sufficiently clearly remember something, whatever it might be, that I was on the point of writing about, even if this meant damaging the narrative. There is also very little dialogue in the text: I recorded only those dialogues that I remembered with precision.

I may, therefore, be accused of everything, but not of having failed to respect the truth.

Most of these pages undoubtedly represent only my own personal story.

I didn't have the means to be able to write in any other way. I do, however, believe that by writing as I have, I have succeeded in giving an overall idea of things, without ever giving way to generalizations that might well have proved inexact.

✻

When I left for the Russian front, I was convinced that the Italian soldier was "the best of the lot". I am well aware that man was not born to wage war; yet it grieved me to see this conviction of mine belied so harshly by the facts. Nor was it any consolation, during the war in Italy, to observe that militarily the British and their minor allies (I didn't see the Americans put to the test) were, in many respects, no better than us.

While writing I was therefore tempted more than once to stop: I was ashamed at what I would have to recount about us Italians as soldiers.

What made me continue was the thought that ignorance is impermissible: if we wish to correct ourselves we need to know ourselves.

In my own small way I was able with my own eyes, given the circumstances in which I found myself, to see things that most did not see. And I am passing them on to others.

Fortunately, it's my duty to point out that things went very differently for the Alpini than for us. I have reliable testimonies that in the pocket in which they found themselves encircled, they proved to be superior troops to any others, the Germans included. Unlike ours, their retreat was not simply a terrible combination of horror and suffering: it was also a succession of consistent, inexpressible acts of heroism.

⁂

Finally, a word about dates. As I state in the text, a few days after we began the retreat we had lost count of them: opinions varied.

According to the brief plan for the diary that I sketched out in Chertkovo, we reached the town on December 28; if it wasn't for the fact that at those headquarters (where I went repeatedly to check) it seemed for certain that we got there on December 27.

Equally certain is December 19 as the date on which the retreat began.

How can I account for that extra, inexplicable, day? I don't think it can have been one of the days of our march. The error lies rather in those days of stagnation in "the Valley of Death": for, while by my reckonings they come to four, almost everyone else recalls three. However, try as I have both then and now, I am unable to merge two of those days into one. So as not to falsify my memories, I have therefore left the period we spent in the Valley of Death subdivided into four days: I have simply omitted the dates for that period.

This quandary also serves to give an idea of the state in which we found ourselves.

⁂

1. The truth of the matter was that, unbeknownst to us front-line troops—at least the lower-ranking ones—some reorganization had taken place, so that the Thirty-fifth Army Corps consisted, at that date, of only two divisions: the 298th German and the Pasubio. Its command was entirely German; which explains why—as I state a few pages later—the order to fall back was issued to the Pasubio by the Germans.

2. A *pattugliere* or *ufficiale capo pattuglia* OC (or *Osservazione e Collegamento*)† was, as regards "observation", "the advance eye of the artillery" who, posted at the infantry front line, fired from a lookout position overlooking enemy terrain (unlike normal artillery batteries, who cannot see the enemy). In the matter of liaising *(Collegamento)*, the *pattugliere* was the link between any single infantry command and his own artillery unit, to which he transmitted orders to open fire.

The men belonging to the OC patrols—who were normally sent ahead to perform these tasks—were regarded somewhat as the *arditi*, or daredevils, of their battalions. As a *pattugliere* I had always acted as a liaison with my own battalion, which is why in this diary I speak about two distinct groups of friends and acquaintances: one from the artillery group, the other from the infantry.

3. Desertion—as I was subsequently told by officers who had closer contact with command—was extremely common, at times rife, when the enemy put troops who had never been under fire into the line. The Russian command had dealt with this problem by adopting a system of infiltrating the deserters with individuals they trusted who, once beyond the line, became partisans. The German command had duly decreed that all deserters were to be treated as common prisoners—that is, inhumanly, and at times killed—and when news of this got around, it very soon put a stop to desertions.

4. In the Italian text, I used the same script for place-names as appeared on the military topographical maps (which were generally German) or on the road signs. In this edition the orthographical transliterations are those of the American BGN (Board of Geographical Names) and the PCGN (British Permanent Committee on Geographical Names).††

5. In November and early December in the Thirty-fifth Army Corps, the former CSIR, all the troops who had spent the previous winter in Russia had been substituted and repatriated. Of the *vecchi*— or veterans—the only ones remaining were those like myself who had

---

†Tr. note: Chief Observation and Liaison Patrol Officer.

††Tr. note: The translator is indebted to Dr. R. A. French of the Department of Geography, University College, London, for his invaluable help in providing these transliterations.

arrived after December 31, 1941 (in my formation fewer than one-quarter of the full number).

6. I was only able to reconstruct things completely and definitively many years later, in 1977, following the publication by the *Ufficio Storico dello Stato Maggiore* (Historical Office of the General Staff) of detailed (though not, in my view, always accurate) information regarding all the main events. For the purposes of this publication the *Ufficio Storico* made use not only of Italian material to which it had exclusive access but also of Soviet material as it gradually came to be published in the postwar years.

I thus discovered that the enemy forces coming from the breach that had been opened to the west of us were far more numerous than we had imagined: there were two entire Russian armies (the First Armored, with thirteen brigades, and a total of 754 tanks, and the Sixth Infantry, with ten ordinary divisions and four motorized brigades). Their objectives were: Kantemirovka, Millerovo, Tatsinskaya, and Morozovsk, which meant that they were heading south and southeast and not, as we had mistakenly believed, west or southwest. At the same moment another Russian army was advancing on Morozovsk from the east—in order to close the pincer. This was the Third Red Guard, with the same number of forces as the Sixth Infantry.

(As for Stalingrad, the Sixth German Army, with a few units from the Fourth, found itself encircled by no less than seven Russian armies.)

7. One such proposal led to my being awarded the decoration on May 21, 1948.

8. The P.K.W. IV, or "panthers" (P.K.W. V). Certainly not the "tigers" (P.K.W. VI), which had not yet been used at that time.

9. As regards spies, immediately after the retreat I learned that our column had been infiltrated by a great many Italian political exiles serving in the Red Army, with the task of spying and sabotage. In the main text of earlier Italian editions of this book there is a long digression, which appears here, as in the most recent Italian edition, in somewhat reduced form as a note:

This is what I was told about a month later at the military hospital of Leopol by Lieutenant Perelli, adjutant of the Pasubio Divisional Mortar Battalion.

When we were in the Valley of Death, one of his soldiers approached him, claiming to have discovered some traitors at a dressing station. (I don't know which one it was: probably none of those I mention in the text, but—going by Perelli's description—another, which I don't personally recall, consisting of a hut with a haystack leaning against it.)

Here, for one or two evenings in succession, wounded men were transported by truck from other dressing stations, because in the latter many had been found, in the morning, inexplicably killed by a blow to the head.

Perelli's soldier said that in the hut he had noticed four Italian soldiers who, at nightfall, after winning everybody's favor by distributing a little soup obtained "from who knows where", had stayed there to sleep.

The soldier was surprised by the fact that the four of them had an Italian machine gun smuggled under their blankets.

During the night, when some heavy shell exploded nearby, in the growing hubbub and disorder one of them rapidly shot one or two of the wounded men through the head. One of the less seriously wounded, who left the hut to relieve himself, was followed by one of the four, who came back in immediately. While the two men were outside, a machine-gun shot was heard. The following morning the wounded man was lying dead outside the door.

When asked by Perelli, the soldier stated that many of the wounded in the hut had been aware of everything that was going on, but in the horrible confusion no one had listened to them.

Perelli immediately had himself taken along there with two soldiers besides the one who had made this discovery: the latter was so frightened that he had to be threatened with death before he would agree to follow Perelli and identify the traitors. As I remember the story, three of them were detained by the officer. After a brief interrogation the latter did well to send them—escorted by his three soldiers—to General X. The fourth was in a sort of garret above the house, and every so often fired the machine gun wildly at the nearest Italians, since fighting was going on there.

Perelli, who was armed only with a pistol, had waited a bit for the man to lower himself down through the trapdoor so that he could execute him but decided in the end to go and see what had become of the others.

The latter—two of whom, after stubbornly refusing to say a word to Perelli, had practically admitted to being traitors—had already been released on the general's orders.

242

A Milanese exile was also allowed to go on his way. He had been found—again by Perelli—in a uniform that was half Russian officer's and half Italian lieutenant's. On being detained, he insolently declared (seeing that he had been discovered: by the oddest coincidence he had claimed to belong to the same battalion as Perelli's) that the previous evening he had led a Russian attack on one the slopes of the valley.

Perelli was not present at the general's interrogations; otherwise— he told me—he would have executed the traitors with his own hands.

Why did X give those orders?

The reason put forward was: "They're all delirious; they don't know what they're saying."

Frankly, I'm not in a position to express an opinion . . .

I heard another murky tale, possibly of treason, from a regular lieutenant from the Eighty-second Torino Infantry. Finding himself behind the column for a while, he was harried by several Italians (including one of his colleagues, from Palermo like himself) who attempted to kill him. He only just managed to save himself.

This may, however, have been a case of attempted robbery.

10. I was wrong. At the end of 1942 the Russians no longer killed military chaplains who fell into their hands (as they had with those Poles in April 1940—see note 15). At the end of 1942 the only men they systematically killed were German prisoners; as for Italian, Hungarian, and Romanian prisoners—whether or not they were chaplains—they killed those who were unable to walk, while more often than not they sent the others on foot toward assembly points on the other side of the Don.

As regards the systematic killing of those who couldn't walk, see, for example, the report by 2nd Lt. Mario Pedroni of the Eighty-first Infantry, who was captured with the 111th field hospital belonging to the Torino Division (where he was admitted because he was wounded):

> 19th December 1942. For several hours the column of vehicles trans-
> porting the wounded from the 111th Pasubio division field hospital
> had been vainly trying to find a passage westward. Russian armored
> troops had already blocked the main communication roads. In the
> evening, in order to be able to bring some rest and refreshment to the
> wounded, the column halted in a small village. No more than two hours
> later Russian assault divisions backed by tanks burst into the village.
> In the condition we were in it was impossible to think of any kind
> of defense, which would in any case have compromised our position,

since we were under the protection of the Red Cross and International Law; but the Russians were utterly oblivious to the existence of certain laws and conventions. As soon as we were captured we underwent the first body searches; pieces of equipment absolutely necessary for that climate were confiscated. The most seriously wounded, about 150, were then separated from the rest, herded against an old hut and machine gunned. The tracks of the powerful T.34s then completed this misdeed by grinding that poor flesh into the ground. Everything happened so quickly that there and then we remained speechless and hardly able to believe our eyes before such cruelty. Immediately after that, another episode brought home to us into what hands we had fallen. Some thirty officers and soldiers, incapable of standing on their feet, and still lying in an isba, were barbarously butchered, and the isba itself set fire to. The Russian machine guns can't have killed all of them, though, because as soon as the first flames rose we heard cries of desperation which changed into spasmodic screams of agony when the flames started assailing those poor, already wound-racked bodies.

When they had completed this massacre, the Russians put the survivors into columns and we started the march toward the concentration camp. We walked across the steppe for fourteen days, only once receiving a small piece of bread . . . and it took an eight-day train journey to reach the camp. During this long march the men escorting us missed no opportunity to display their cruelty. Dozens and dozens of prisoners who were no longer able to follow the column were machine gunned and their corpses left at the edge of the track to mark the column's sad progress. The train journey was no less harrowing than the march on foot. Packed unbelievably tightly into the wagons, the only ration we received was a slice of bread; no water, and no aid for the frozen who were dying among the atrocious spasms caused by gangrene. The wagon was opened just once a day to unload the dead, who were left regularly along the railroad track. . . .

11. In earlier Italian editions I stated that only ten percent of the Italians who were captured had survived. The reason for this is that—seeing the magnitude of the disaster—for lack of other information, we survivors had also believed the exultant declarations of Radio Moscow, which claimed that more than one hundred thousand Italians had been taken prisoner. Only in 1977, after the publication of the detailed figures by the Historical Office of the General Staff (*Ufficio Storico dello Stato Maggiore*) (see note 6), was it possible to specify 50,000–60,000 as the number of able-bodied Italians who fell into Russian hands. At the end of the war, 10,030 were repatriated. As for the others, all we have are the estimates made

by the prisoners themselves, according to which about 40 percent of those captured must have died of hunger and exhaustion or else been killed because they were no longer able to walk, during the terrible *"davai!"*††† marches toward the assembly points beyond the Don; of the survivors, again about 40 percent (that is, 25 percent of the total number of men captured) must have died on the bitterly cold trains that slowly transported them toward the camps; finally, another 40 percent, once again survivors (that is, 15 percent of those captured) must have died in the camps during the first four months of imprisonment: again of privations but above all of petechial typhoid epidemics.

12. As I was to learn several months later, the only general who, together with X, stayed with us until the end of the encirclement, was Capizzi from the Ravenna Division.

13. Regarding our far from admirable conduct from the military point of view, I wish to point out a later discovery I made. When, years later, I happened to read Thucydides' account of the foundering beneath the walls of Syracuse of incipient Athenian imperialism, I was astonished at the similarity, indeed—how can I put it?—the virtual interchangeability between the behavior of the Athenians and our own. (Surprisingly similar, too, was the behavior of the Athenians as compared with that of the Dorians, the Germans of the Greek world.) I won't dwell on this but recommend anyone who is interested in such things to read Thucydides' description. Not that I'm claiming to have found an excuse here. On the contrary; it was precisely the military inferiority of Athens that led to the decline of the independence of the city and eventually to the waning of Greek civilization—which was of such incalculable damage for the whole of mankind.

14. Just three wounded men remained on board and perished after only a few minutes or a few dozen minutes. It was the same plane in which General Pezzi and Bocchetti, the medical colonel, had made their outward and homebound journey to us.

15. As regards the directions of the enemy advance, see note 6.

†††Tr. note: The Russian word meaning "Forward!" or "Keep moving!" that was yelled at the prisoners by their captors.

A dramatic episode of which we were at the time completely unaware does, however, need mentioning. At Starobelsk—where the command of the ARMIR had been under siege since October—Stalin's police had, some thirty months before, perpetrated a massacre analogous to the one at Katyn. What happened was essentially this: The Polish officers and chaplains captured by the Russians during the invasion of Poland in autumn 1939 had been interred almost down to the last man—together with other groups of lower-ranking troops—in three camps: Kozel'sk, Ostakov, and Starobelsk itself. They totaled about 15,000 men. From spring 1940 every trace of these prisoners was lost. After we had been repatriated, the Germans discovered in the wood of Katyn near Smolensk—and in April 1943, in the presence of representatives of the International Red Cross, exhumed—the bodies of those who had been interred in the nearby concentration camp of Kozel'sk, a total of 4,413: they had their hands tied behind their backs with metal wire, and almost all of them seemed to have been killed with a bullet through the back of the neck. As could be reconstructed on the basis of the scraps of Russian newspapers found in the pockets of their greatcoats, their deaths dated from April 1940. The bodies of those who were interred in the camps of Starobelsk and Ostakov have not as yet been found (see Robert Conquest's *The Great Terror* and numerous other sources).

16. Years later I learned from Magaldi himself that the Russian head of the family kept his promise: not daring to be seen in enemy company, at the crack of dawn he got the young boy from the isba to accompany the captain to the hospital.

17. Some, who looked like peasants, seemed in death to have goodness bewilderingly stamped on their faces—something I had already noted on the faces of others. (At the time I didn't realize just how much those peasants were victims—nay, martyrs—of the Communist system long before the war.)

18. I don't want to give the impression that the Russians are mediocre soldiers—quite the contrary: they are good fighters, endowed with an incredible, even tragic readiness to act. From my experience of others (in the second part of the war), I regard them as the best of the "Allied" soldiers. Nevertheless, when it comes to efficiency, they are decidedly inferior to the Germans, above all in their handling of technical weapons.

19. Following other testimonies, eventually, years later, I realized that I had greatly underestimated the number of Russian attacking tanks (several dozen, almost all of which were destroyed) and, in general, the scale and importance of this battle. Though lasting only a short time, it was extremely violent and arduous. Readers wishing to know more about it are recommended to read the fine memoir written by Mario Bellini (the friend whom I mention several times in this book), who was himself in the German ranks at this battle (*L'aurora a occidente*, Bompiani, 1984 [213–17]. Ibid., 171 and 172); and also the curious encounter that I mention in Chapter 23.

20. If we were really at Streltsovka, very probably those German squads didn't belong to our column but rather to the Nineteenth Armored Division, which had been vainly trying for weeks to open up the road toward Chertkovo. In any case, at Streltsovka we were out of the pocket but were completely unaware of the fact.

21. Since this conclusion seems very important to me, it is, I think, worth citing the opinion of one of the most enlightened military men of this century, Marshal Foch (which I came across later): "When at a historic moment we suddenly acquire a clear vision of the situation, which may produce enormous consequences—as I believe I had at the Marne and the Yser—we are compelled to acknowledge that we have fallen into the hands of a providential force and that we owe our victorious decision to a will which is not our own, to a superior, divine will. It is never we who make the great decisions."

And it was, I think, this "force" that Hitler, who sensed it repeatedly, had in mind when speaking so often (and more often than not so unaccountably) of "providence".

22. A letter to my friend Giorgio Bruno Barresi:

Dear Giorgio,

You've asked me to explain exactly what I mean by the phrase "war as a castigation by God", in order to ensure that "no-one is shocked by it."

In my view, things are like this.

ONE: God (absolute Good) cannot want war (which is evil), because otherwise He would no longer be God, but a self-contradictory being like any other.

Only man can want and—within certain, alas sadly wide limits—accomplish evil.

God's castigation consists precisely in allowing man—who deliberately wishes it—to proceed along the road of evil: in other words, to distance himself increasingly from Him (or, if you like, to set himself increasingly against Him).

Why does He let this happen? Because He is compelled to. Otherwise He would have to denature man, whom he has created free. The most specific freedom man possesses—that which transcends all others, and which is different from the freedom of animals—is this very freedom to choose between good and evil, or to place himself either on God's side or against Him. If God deprived him of this freedom, man would cease to be what he is, and become a sort of semianimal, since then only reason would differentiate him from the other animals.

TWO: At the same time, within providential order ("good may come also of ill") lies an extremely important fact: in experiencing the increasingly terrifying fruits of his distancing from God, man is, with ever greater force, called upon and stimulated to acknowledge his faults (and thus to embrace good).

THREE: In any case, God in His love—though never violating human freedom—intervenes at many decisive moments in both individual and collective history (History with a capital H), for the purpose of helping men, and making history a history of salvation. Men, even the least important individuals, have the opportunity ("knock and it shall be opened") to favor His interventions.

Although He intervenes, God cannot, however (remember my first point), prevent man, or groups of men, when they are really bent on it, from setting themselves against Him, and excluding Him from their lives and their world—in other words, from choosing evil. And so in those years He couldn't prevent them from waging war, and from waging it in that manner.

That being said, it will be clear to you that even while the war was being waged, God continued not to want war—that is, evil.

At this point you may ask me why in my diary I speak of God in such a way as to give the impression that it is He Himself who directly deals out this punishment.

I have no difficulty in replying that in whoever habitually senses God's presence in human life, the space that He is compelled to concede to maleficent freedom (= the worker of evil) on the collective plane does in fact produce that impression. It produced it in me, and not just in me. And in my diary of the retreat I felt it my duty to give a faithful account not only of events, nor only of the thoughts and utterances, logical and nonlogical, of those of us involved in those events, but also our impressions and sensations, rational or irrational.

248

Certainly, even at that time—when I was under fire and in the thick of things—reason told me that it wasn't God who was inflicting those sufferings and those deaths on us by His own hand, like a schoolmaster caning a young scamp. If someone had asked me, I would certainly have replied that He limited himself—in those circumstances—to not intervening, and to leaving men (the Nazis and Communists) a free hand with their barbarous plans and designs.

At the same time, what could I, what could we, have wished for?

Before such unbearable horrors, rather than indulging in disquisitions and reasoned arguments, we would simply have wanted God to intervene, and prevent, in that place and at that moment, man—including me, and all the men who were involved—from continuing to practice evil. Since He didn't do so, all we saw was this—that He didn't do it. (Besides, even from a rational point of view, weren't those horrors made possible precisely by His nonintervention, in other words by His "punishment"?)

Before concluding, I ought here to introduce another vitally important part of the picture (perhaps the most important part of all: point FOUR): how God reclaims the suffering of men, and above all that of innocent men—crucified as innocent Christ was crucified—and how this suffering is thus in no way wasted (and so, those dead men did not die for nothing: do you realize how important that is?).

But this letter is already too long.

I'll develop these concepts more fully in the novel that, as you know, I've been working on, heart and soul, for some time now, and that will probably be titled *I cavalli dell'Apocalisse* (The Horses of the Apocalypse)††††. (By the way, am I wrong in thinking that St. John too, while having his apocalyptic visions, had similar sensations to those we experienced at that time in Russia? It seems to me that there is a clear trace of this in his words . . . Or maybe you don't agree?)

Your friend,

Eugenio

(30th October 1973)

23. This temperature is also recorded by Mario Bellini on page 223 of his book, referred to above. Similar temperatures were registered, not very far from us, at the Third Alpine Julia Artillery Regiment: -42 degrees on Christmas Eve and -46 degrees this night of January 17.

††††Tr. note: Published in 1983 under the title *Il cavallo rosso*.

24. To be precise, it wasn't Kantemirovka, but a smaller village just to the south of it, Gartmishchevka, which had its own railroad station.

❖

In the Italian editions preceding the most recent (Mursia, 1990, reissued in the GUM "Testimonianze" series, 1993), the notes were followed by an appendix that specified which of the people named in the diary survived imprisonment and were repatriated after the war: Corporal Tamburini, infantry Lieutenants Correale and Maccario, Sergeant Pillone, the gunner Catturegli of the Second Battery, Captain Magaldi, and Second Lieutenant Salvador from Trieste.

That appendix also included six letters by repatriated men, with brief accounts of their imprisonment. I had thought it necessary to add them to the book, because at the time of its publication (June 1947) no, or hardly any, testimonies of imprisonment in Russia had appeared, and the Italian public had next to no information about it.

Today, after the publication of numerous memoirs recounting the terrible reality of that imprisonment—including the horrors relating to acts of cannibalism in the camps—those letters seem superfluous. I shall therefore quote no more than two extracts (both written by private C.P.) describing what happened at Chertkovo after our departure.

From the letter dated January 22, 1947:

> You ask me what time the Russians arrived at Cercovo [*sic*], it was seven in the morning on January 16th, when, in the town I heard the first Lugers firing and said to another bloke from the infantry who had come to the hut where you left me, in a bit we'll be in the hands of the Russians, and that's what happened, it was 8 when a partisan with a saber raised and a pistol in his hand turned up, I thought he was going to shoot us, but he searched both of us and took from us all the stuff he liked and then took us to where the other captured Italians were, all the frozen wounded and sick were there, they left us in these houses like that abandoned by everyone with one or two of their guards, the guards though couldn't have cared less, particularly if they were given some Italian object, then about ten of us of those in the best shape left we gave them some objects to the guards and went out we went to the families like beggars and they gave us something to eat, and also a little to take to those poor blighters who couldn't move, after 13 days they gave us something to eat, then got us all to gather

at the schools, you can imagine little to eat without treatment, every day a lot of wounded and frozen men died, there were 2500 of us and after a few days about 250 who were those they'd cut off from your column, after 40 days or rather February 28th orders came to leave and we went over the Urals I went with a Russian to draw provisions and of the 2700 of us at the time we were captured we drew them for 1225, I was one of the lucky ones they chose 42 who still had a bit of strength, and I stayed at Cercovo working for the Russians, and stayed there until April 25th, then we who'd stayed behind also got the same treatment, they took us to the station, loaded all 42 of us into a wagon, and we traveled for 22 days.

From the letter dated February 1, 1947:

You ask me about the Germans who stayed behind at Cercovo how they finished up, badly, they took them just out of the town and shot them without mercy, since immediately after the defeat the Germans killed them all they took all of them then orders came from Stalin that there was no need to kill any prisoner who was taken, and it was like that, after a bit we saw Germans and Romanians arrive who'd been taken prisoner almost on the Nieper, but I tell you this, they no longer killed them as soon as they captured them, but let 80 per cent of them die of hunger during 3 years of imprisonment, so many of our brothers would've suffered less if they'd killed them straight off, but instead they reduced them to an unimaginable state and they had to die in the barbarous Russian lands, how many poor mothers are still waiting anxiously for them, but this waiting will be in vain.

Born in Besana Brianza, Italy, in 1921, **Eugenio Corti** marked his debut as a writer with *Few Returned*. He went on to write works of historical fiction (including *Il cavallo rosso*), drama, and essays.

Peter Edward Levy teaches English at the University of Siena in Italy. He has published translations of contemporary Italian poetry and critical essays about British poets.

Carlo D'Este is a military historian and the author of four books about World War II. His most recent book, *Patton: A Genius for War,* was published in 1995 by HarperCollins and in 1996 by Harper Perennial.